Decadence and Danger:
Writing, History
and the Fin de Siècle

Decadence and Danger:
Writing, History
and the Fin de Siècle

Edited by
Tracey Hill

SULIS PRESS

First published in 1997 by

SULIS PRESS
Newton Park
Bath BA2 9BN, UK

Printed by Antony Rowe Ltd.,
Chippenham, Wilts.

Cover design by Malcolm Herrstein Design

ISBN
0 9526856 1 2
0 9526856 2 0 (pbk)

British Library Cataloguing in Publication Data

A catalogue record of this book
is available from the British Library

Contents

CONTENTS

Acknowledgements

The editor would like to thank all the contributors for their forbearance and helpfulness during the production of this volume. I am also grateful to my colleagues in the Faculty of Humanities at Bath Spa University College for their support and encouragement throughout. Special thanks are due to Margaret Tremeer, who typed the manuscript, to William Hughes and Terence Rodgers for their assistance and expertise, and to Neil Sammells for his comments on the introduction and help in the final stages of production.

1

Introduction:
Decadence and Danger

Tracey Hill

'In my end is my beginning'[1]

I

As the end of the twentieth century approaches, critics and commentators are drawn increasingly to re-evaluate *the* defining fin de siècle, that of the last century.[2] This volume of essays plays its part in that process. It is helpfully characteristic of the 1880s and 1890s that they too had their theorists and their cultural critics. Indeed, as the final years of the nineteenth century progressed, a striking note of self-consciousness was apparent in much writing of the time; so much so that Oscar Wilde was able, at that century's end, to pronounce himself in a typically acute instance of self-definition: 'a man who stood in symbolic relations to the art and culture of [his] age.'[3] Our fin de siècle too has in recent years exhibited a similar kind of introspection: claims of scientific apocalypse, environmental catastrope, urban societal disaster, the New Feudalism, the End of History, and so on, are exemplified by a feature from 1994 in *The Guardian* newspaper entitled 'We're All Doomed: the Dark Ages are coming back'.[4] Journalistic hyperbole aside, it is clear that commentators perceive – or rather, believe they *should* perceive – cultural crisis at the fin de siècle.

What both fins de siècles share is an almost tangible sense of temporality, of the reality of time. When the end of a century looms, it seems, the very fact that one is living in a particular chronological moment takes on a significance entirely lacking in, say, 1837, or 1964. The very progression of time itself becomes an object of scrutiny rather than a backdrop, as historical context moves to the foreground and becomes a subject in its own right. As this increasingly comes to be represented in cultural forms, it becomes artistically visible. The fin de siècle has the status of a fixed point (albeit one that can last for decades) standing as a marker of transition between one time, one whole century, and another. Standing at the end of one period of time, and at the very beginning of another, a dizzying prospect confronts all latter-day Januses.

1

Hence, perhaps, the terminal sense of exhaustion that exudes from so much fin-de-siècle culture. However, if the fin de siècle straddles ends and beginnings, it follows that it is more of a median point than a zenith or nadir. It stands, in fact, as a register of temporal movement, the indicator in the middle of time of how much has changed from the end to the beginning – and from the beginning to the end.

Time can therefore be seen, from the perspective of the fin de siècle, as a continuum. Rather than an erratic business of termini and initiations, it appears now a seamless continuity, a reassuringly constant process. Like a literary text, time is a narrative with a teleological author. We are telling ourselves stories in the guise of history, narrating our time to give it shape and meaning. And, from the vantage-point of the 1990s, we can see that the fin de siècle is one of the more pressing and abiding stories, one that we feel compelled to repeat when the time comes round again. Now that the moment has arrived for us, we create a new version of what it is to live at this crucial moment – but the novelty of what we have to say about the present fin de siècle is tempered by our memory of the last. Our narratives of the nineteenth-century fin de siècle (which is composed, of course, partly of the twentieth century) are inflected by present concerns; we cannot, even if we wanted to, recapture the experience of the original. So contemporary readings of the 1880s and 1890s are as much readings of the 1990s: hence the dual focus of this volume of essays. However, it is not simply a matter of enumerating parallels (they used opium; the drug of choice is now heroin). The more interesting approach, and the one taken by the essays in this book, is to regard the relationship between this current fin de siècle and the last as *dialectic*, not opposed. History, as Marx taught us, is a dialectic process; the case of the fin de siècle demonstrates that no clear separation can be upheld between ends and beginnings.

Culture too takes on dialectical forms. Writing at the fin de siècle is a matter of negotiating pre-existing conceptions of that historical moment: writers, particularly in the 1880s and 1890s, were conscious, perhaps all too conscious, that their work would be regarded in the light of dominant notions of the period. The fin de siècle almost became a quantifiable essence, consisting of a set of characteristics that could be identified and then celebrated or condemned. Pre-occupations of the moment were given fictional form in a variety of cultural media, from the ephemera of popular journalism (opinionated columns in *Punch*, or articles in *The Yellow Book*) to weighty morality tales by the likes of Marie Corelli, such was the public appetite for representations of its own moment. It is significant, then, that the term 'fin de siècle' is contemporary to itself (Lyn Pykett has dated its first appearance at around 1888).[5] The Victorians were, of course, notably interested in describing themselves, and like so much

2

else, this trend became all the more excessive at the end of the century. A telling instance of the late nineteenth century's fascination with itself can be gleaned from the first page of Max Nordau's *Degeneration* (1892), where he states authoritatively: 'The *fin-de-siècle* state of mind is to-day everywhere to be met with.'[6]

That we at the end of the twentieth century can recognise so much of our current plight in accounts of the previous fin de siècle suggests that such a sensibility does not reside exclusively in the 1880s and 1890s. Indeed, it might be seen to be moveable, in a sense, or at least be a feeling that can be rehearsed and re-framed for a different historical context. Peter Nicholls argues convincingly in his essay in this volume that the fin de siècle should be regarded 'more as a mode than an epoch': a set of conceptual parameters, rather than a specific historical moment. Symmetries can be seen to exist between the two fins de siècles, but it is never clear if typically fin-de-siècle phenomena are the inevitable consequence of the end of a century, or whether the imminent arrival of the fin de siècle prompts us to reiterate apparently appropriate behaviours. The latter is more conducive to an historicist interpretation, in that it permits one to take into account *differences* between the two epochs, as well as their similarities. The Victorian fin de siècle persists, even, or perhaps especially, as we get nearer to the twenty-first century largely because we want it to. Those essays in this collection that address both moments strive to keep an eye on their historical realities, and not to be entirely seduced by the myth of the fin de siècle. It clearly is a resonant means for us to understand ourselves, a process which can be undertaken as much by differentiation as by analogy. Equally, not every text produced during the 1880s and 1890s partook to the same degree in the characteristics of fin-de-siècle culture as works by Wilde, Beardsley, Huysmans and other deliberately Decadent stylists.[7] It is revealing that, with one hundred years' worth of hindsight, our perception of this period should be so indebted to what we now regard as typically fin-de-siècle. Crucially, the fin de siècle should be understood as a powerful metaphor, one which certainly has residual valency in even a postmodern historical context, but which should not be used to erase difference.[8]

As the essays in this book demonstrate, the 1880s-90s and the 1990s are made to reflect back and forth on each other: we cannot help but see the late-nineteenth century through the prism of our own anxieties, and must perforce theorise the contemporary in the light of the past that has formed us. Again, it's a *dialectic* process.

II

'Decadence and Danger', the title of this collection, encapsulates two major aspects of the fin-de-siècle phenomenon. The term 'decadence' is derived from 'falling down' or 'falling away'; or, as Peter Nicholls has it in his essay, 'a dying fall'. In the course of the late nineteenth century it came to stand for a complex set of attributes related to decay, dissolution and decline; it also indicated a form of hedonism and self-indulgence which was widely regarded as being tantamount to dancing on the edge of the abyss. Indeed, some of the more intemperate critics of decadence implied that decadent behaviour was of itelf bringing about the end of time towards which they were all inexorably moving. Both decadent behaviours and moralistic commentary shared a sense of running out of time, of incipient disaster – of not being able to see beyond the ending symbolised by the date, 1899.

Decadence is related too to notions of degeneration, as expounded most famously in Nordau's *Degeneration*. It is not for nothing that late-Victorian society evinced so much concern over *purity*: social and racial decline and intermarriage, food adulteration, gender instability – all these contribute to a threatening array of hybrid forms. The dangers so apparent in this kind of adulteration were infringing the integrity of a variety of crucial forms of nineteenth-century identity. The late-nineteenth-century conflation of Englishness and masculinity, which a number of the contributors to this volume explore, exemplifies this tendency to defend hegemonic ideals by yoking them together for mutual strength. However, as the Victorians, as evidenced by the hysteria of their denial clearly knew, and as we (post-Derrida) also know, establishing rigid conceptual boundaries is a business fraught with difficulties; such binaries carry their own undoing within them. Protecting conservative and conventional value systems by punitive means, such as Wilde's trials, or by rhetorical means, like Nordau's attack on foreignness and degeneration, merely reveals the extremity of the dangers posed and the tenuousness of the structures so upheld. The Decadents, for their part, often reified that which their opponents so feared, flagrantly revelling in the excess and perversity that their works (and lives, in most cases) exhibited. Both sides of the debate, though, whether or not they welcomed it, echoed the conviction that these were the last days, that society was teetering on the brink of dissolution.

So what of the future? What of the firm belief in human progress that is commonly held to be characteristic of the Victorian Age? Paradoxically, for all its obsession with decay and endings, the Victorian fin de siècle is as much a mode of the future as of the past, and this is where its relationship with postmodernity really comes into focus. Its interest in novelty is symptomatic:

the New World, the New Woman, were after all features of the time, and decadence was nothing if not avant-garde. The fin de siècle could be seen as an opportunity for revitalisation as much as for post-mortems: looking forward to the beginning of the New, as well as bemoaning the loss of the Old. The past may seem *ennuyé*, but the future might hold new promise.

Culture has the role in society of setting out and testing the limits of the sayable, of creating new worlds: this is as true of the artistically experimental decadence as it is of the self-consciously postmodern cultural vanguard of the late twentieth century. H. G. Wells's Time Traveller can now be seen as a metaphor for the Janus-face of the fin de siècle: a metaphor which has still more currency as we look back one hundred years. Time travel is a means of gaining perspective, of seeing from a distance, and no matter what kinship we feel to the Victorian fin de siècle, we always have to be aware of that temporal distance. The fin de siècle itself, with its relentless and heightened temporality, demands this of us.

III

The essays in this collection fall into two groupings, which, in true fin-de-siècle style, overlap and negotiate each other.

The first essay begins from a similar standpoint as this Introduction. Peter Nicholls addresses the fall-out of late-nineteenth-century decadence from a postmodern perspective. His account sets up and critiques many of the conventional antitheses of literary history in relation to decadence and modernism: feminine sophistication versus masculine rigour, self-indulgence versus self-discipline, for example. In so doing, he recalls Gautier's remarks of 1868, well before the onset of the fin de siècle proper, that decadence was consciously working at the limits of both artistic production and of time, reflecting what Nicholls calls 'an inward turn'. Indeed, decadent writing can be regarded as postmodern *avant la lettre*: sceptical about representation and the transparency of language, experimental in its forms. It is Nicholls's insight that these characteristics, contrary to the clichéd view of literary progression *from* decadence *to* modernism, were in fact present in the former before modernism apparently displaced it. As Nicholls argues, 'the idea of a decisive break with decadent modes may now start to look a little less convincing'. The ostensible displacement of decadence by modernism after the turn of the century was thus more rhetorical than real, and was largely influenced by a desire on the part of modernist innovators like T. S. Eliot and Wyndham Lewis to create a properly masculine literary discourse, rejecting the perceived feminine excesses of

5

preceding forms. Women's writing from within the modernist canon exposes this strategy, by being as deliberately transgressive in linguistic terms as the demonised decadents. Finally, Nicholls makes a claim for decadence, as the 'limit case of modern writing', to be the real precursor of postmodern culture, a theme that is further explored in some of the essays that follow.

Moving away from literary history, Denis Judd's magisterial survey of the British Empire in the late 1890s pivots around Queen Victoria's Diamond Jubilee celebrations of June 1897. The imperial strength and national pride exemplified by this event ostensibly offer up the image of a nation and a society at the height of its economic and political powers. However, Judd exposes just how much of these celebrations was propagandist, and how much was rhetorical excess intended to disguise an increasingly precarious imperial situation. He highlights the parlous economic state of Britain in the 1890s in order to reveal the realities that lay behind the self-mythologising efforts of the Jubilee. Rather than demonstrating secure national (and hence masculine) identity, the Jubilee was, in Judd's words, 'whistling in the dark', a moment of frantically over-enthusiastic triumph existing briefly in a context of national decline and pessimism mirroring the prevalent note of fin-de-siècle culture. Perceived symptoms of this decline – nationalism, socialism, sexual depravity, feminism – are here set against the historical context in order to explore the ways in which the Jubilee was used to gloss over severe problems. Judd makes it clear that national and imperial integrity was predicated on a structure of stable ideologies which were becoming increasingly fragmented and questioned as the end of the century drew nearer. Chief amongst these ideologies were those of race and masculinity, personified by the Empire itself. Two essays that follow Judd's pick up on and further explore this nexus.

Terence Rodgers's chapter on Rider Haggard and the Orient has two major strands: he is interested in Haggard as a writer who is in many ways symptomatic of fin-de-siècle culture, and also in the significance of Haggard's writing about the East to an understanding of late-Victorian imperialism. Rodgers takes up Patrick Brantlinger's notion of 'Imperial Gothic', but orients it towards Haggard's relatively under-explored fictions of Egypt, rather than of Africa. Haggard's Eastern texts, Rodgers asserts, reflect the importance of that region to late-Victorian imperialist policy, and in so doing inadvertently raise many of the other preoccupations of the fin de siècle, specifically those to do with race and sexuality. The East was not only a region for colonial exploitation, but also stood in the culture of the time for a complex relationship between imperialist masculinity and the perceived exoticism and eroticism of the 'feminine' Orient. As such, Haggard's eastern fictions depict problematic representations of sexualised femininity and masculine neurosis. Rodgers traces the presence, all the more powerful for being covert, of 'the queer decadent self' in Haggard's ostensibly manly romances.

Tim Youngs's account of H. G. Wells's *The Time Machine* has a similar focus on other lands and the challenges they presented to late-Victorian ideals. In this case, of course, the foreign place is a whole other world, but it too offered Wells a typically fin-de-siècle opportunity to reflect upon the notions that underpinned his own society and to create a testing-ground for their validity. 'Bourgeois Victorian England' is presented, through the persona of Wells's narrator, with an alternative perspective on itself; this process is continued by Youngs's analysis, where he is able to add a further dimension to an understanding of how this text narrates its own time. *The Time Machine*, according to Youngs, questions a number of current discourses: 'scientific' notions of racial and social make-up, Spencerian theories of savagery and civilisation, and the characteristically Victorian teleological idea of progress. However, Wells's initial interpretation can itself be interpreted; Youngs describes how the character of Weena, a young woman, destabilises the masculinist, pseudo-scientific tenor of the text. Wells's attitudes to his own fin de siècle, like those of today, are more ambivalent and contradictory than certain.

Michael Paris returns us to the question of empire at the fin de siècle. His focus is on juvenile fiction, specifically that written for young boys, from the 1870s through to the Edwardian era. Paris discusses the ways in which juvenile fiction was used to voice anxieties about national security and the threatened existence of the Empire, and identifies a fin-de-siècle 'sense of impending catastrophe' within these popular militaristic texts. Journalistic and popular cultural forms fed the public appetite for fictions of the fin de siècle, and were another means, like the Diamond Jubilee, of holding back the forces of national decay and decadence, whilst at the same time expressing the paranoid fears of a generation under siege.

A sense of danger emerges clearly too from Bridget Bennett's suggestive account of the death of Harold Frederic in 1898. Frederic's death, as Bennett has it, can be read as a kind of text, one which is redolent of fin-de-siècle anxieties. The dangers raised in the events surrounding Frederic's death, Bennett claims, are those presented by religious controversy ('feminised' Christian Science versus traditional 'masculine' Anglicanism) and challenges to social orthodoxy (marriage versus cohabitation and illegitimacy). Unlike the desire for closure which Bennett identifies in contemporary representations of Frederic's demise, her account is more interested in ambiguity and in the impossibility of 'an authoritative narrative of presence'. Just as Frederic's fate

7

was regarded by some of his contemporaries as symptomatic of fin-de-siècle degeneracy, so Bennett believes that his story is illustrative of the contingency and the uncertainty of our fin-de-siècle moment.

Narrative and its discontents come under further scrutiny in Sue Zlosnik's essay on George Meredith, where Meredith's fictions of the 1890s are read for their scepticism towards realism and narrative linearity. Meredith's concern with the authority or otherwise of representation and with the possibility of textual difference and deferral make him, according to Zlosnik, a writer on the verge of modernist, if not postmodernist, innovation. As his interrogation and/or rejection of conventional narrative form suggest, realism imposes ideological limits on what a text can say, and Meredith's use of irony further compounds his subversiveness. Gender too is made provisional by Meredith's experimental approach, and Zlosnik explores the way in which irony and postmodern feminist theory can combine in a reading of Meredith's novels to offer a critique of patriarchal hegemony. Ultimately, Meredith's fictions of the 1890s are 'disruptive and disquieting' in both generic and political terms.

The following two essays concentrate on women writers of the fin de siècle. Sally Ledger discusses the writing of Sarah Grand in the context of fin-de-siècle debates about decadence, feminism, and the Woman Question, and also explores Wilde's attitudes towards gender as revealed in *The Picture of Dorian Gray* and in his editorship of the *Woman's World*. The 'New' Woman, according to Ledger, was categorised in the same kind of negative terms by conservative commentators as all other forms of 'new' thinking, and Wilde's fall was declared equally the fall of such unconventional feminine behaviour. Sarah Grand's novel *The Heavenly Twins* participates in current controversies about sexuality, syphilis and decadence, and Ledger traces within it a latent representation of androgynous cross-dressing which offers up a challenge to conventional morality and gender identity, albeit one which is never realisable.

Deborah Tyler-Bennett's wide-ranging discussion of women poets of the 1880s and 1890s is equally concerned to explore the limits of women's writing of the period. She examines some lesser-known female poets in the light of the stereotypes of femininity utilised by their male counterparts, and describes the innovative tropes and images that the former are able to construct. More specifically, she returns us to the subject of oriental mythology and exoticism which is discussed in earlier essays in this collection, but which Tyler-Bennett reads through feminine rather than masculine literary strategies. Many of the women writers she addresses subvert and sometimes offer alternatives to dominant notions of the feminine and dominant uses of myth, displacing those of male writers. Romance, female passivity, male heroism, the myth of the Sphinx: all come under scrutiny in the context of a feminine tradition of writing, and all are shown to be arbitrary and hence open to revision, suggesting, as Tyler-Bennett remarks, 'new possibilities for the female form'.

William Hughes's essay on *Dracula* takes another revisionist stance, one critiquing dominant readings of Stoker's novel that focus, *pace* Foucault, on questions of sexuality. Hughes is rather more concerned to address the text in the light of the late-Victorian obsession with purity: purity of racial descent and purity of commodities, both medical and culinary. In the process of his analysis, Hughes explores the connections between *Dracula*'s concern for sanguinary purity and some contemporary medical products which were marketed in very similar terms. Medical practice in the text is shown to be implicated in discourses of the time about social and national characteristics. This renders the text open to an interpretation which can accommodate *Dracula* within fin-de-siècle theories of degeneracy: Hughes's interest in what the text has to say about national, racial and even individual integrity thus reveals the ways in which Stoker fictionalises many concerns of his moment. Such concerns can be read, as Hughes explains, as representing in the text 'a microcosm of a ... community fighting for the greater as well as the individual good'.

Oscar Wilde is of course the fin-de-siècle artist *par excellence*, and for that reason a number of chapters in this volume discuss Wilde from various perspectives. Marie Mulvey Roberts's essay puts forward a reading of some of Wilde's stories in the unusual context of Freemasonry. She reads Wilde's initiation rituals into Freemasonry as precursors of his better-known and more public trials at the Old Bailey in 1895, and as a similarly self-defining moment for Wilde himself. Wilde's involvement in Freemasonry and Catholicism can be seen to point up certain aspects of his life-style – gender ambivalence and flamboyant dress, for example – which make ambiguous these ostensibly male-dominated preserves. His fascination with both organisations is also discussed for the light it can shed on certain of his stories, notably 'The Birthday of the Infanta', and for the ways in which the stories can be seen to echo Wilde's personal history. Hence, Wilde is shown not only to exhibit a symbolic relation to his own time, but also perhaps a symbolic relation to his own life.

Wilde's work is revisited by Julian North in relation to other fin-de-siècle writers who revelled in the era's excess and hedonism. Beginning with an account of the late-twentieth-century War on Drugs, she takes issue with the 'paralleling urge' some critics of the fin de siècle reveal and cautions that one should read symmetries between the 1880s-90s and the 1990s more circumspectly. Recreational drug use in the Victorian fin de siècle, she argues, was characterised by its representation in a variety of contemporary texts as a *pleasurable* activity, albeit one that transgressed a number of social norms and values. With this in mind, she then goes on to explore a range of fin-de-siècle texts, from Dr H. Obersteiner's work on opium dens, *via* Arthur Conan Doyle's Sherlock Holmes stories and Henry Havelock Ellis on mescal to Wilde's *The Picture of Dorian Gray*, to trace their negotiations of images of foreignness, decadence and vice. In these she finds a stronger sense of familiarity than estrangement or moral condemnation; the drug-taker is often 'both insider and outsider'. She concludes with the reflection that 'what are often assumed to be typically late-twentieth-century anxieties about the drug user ... were already at work in late-Victorian culture'.

Dual attention to both fin de siècles is also evident in Nickianne Moody's discussion of women's science fiction. She interprets the rise of cyberpunk and feminist science fiction in the 1980s and 1990s in a social context, specifically focussing on their representations of utopias and dystopias. Late-nineteenth-century writers were equally drawn to the utopian form to create alternative and/or critical images of society. It is, she argues, in women's writing in particular that one finds a range of political options explicitly evaluated. Debates about the Victorian 'Woman Question' and discussions of women's role as social citizens are apparent in works from Britain, North America and Australia by authors including Charlotte Perkins Gilman and Mary Ann Moore-Bentley. Moving forward to the contemporary, Moody claims that the novels of Marge Piercy bear out the thinking of Raymond Williams and Donna Haraway that human decisions, not simply technological advances, lie at the heart of political action. 'Concerted communal action' is envisaged in women's utopian writing, unlike the bleak masculine dystopias of cyberpunk.

Another contemporary woman writer is tackled in Antonio Ballasteros González's essay on Anne Rice's 'Vampire Chronicles'. González commences with an account of the role of the vampire, the 'epitome of Victorian decadence', at the last fin de siècle. In contrast, Rice's vampires are, he argues, characteristically postmodern rather than Victorian: they exhibit, for example, 'postmodern attitude[s] of detachment and loss'. In their interest in mass popular culture they deliberately flaunt post-Victorian images of vampirism, and in Rice's texts they perform on a postmodern function, revealing a 'knowingness' and 'playfulness' towards their representational status, unlike in Stoker's *Dracula*, where the vampire is more passively represented. The vampire Lestat, for instance, takes on the role in Rice's texts of a 'dandy-like and elegant serial killer', *au fait* with late-twentieth-century technology and comfortable in modern US cities like Miami and New Orleans. Rice's vampires' decadence is more cosmopolitan, more heterogeneous, than that of the traditional Victorian vampire. Rice's novels are testimony, as González asserts, that the immortal vampire lives on in our culture in one form or another.

10

Postmodern society forms the backdrop to Tim Middleton's critical juxtaposition of Joseph Conrad and Bret Easton Ellis. These writers, he argues, are paradigmatic of certain fin-de-siècle notions of subjectivity, specifically masculine subjectivity. Conrad's *Heart of Darkness* provides a limit case of Victorian imperial masculine identity: the character of Kurtz, Middleton claims, shows the contradictions inherent in this ideological formation. Kurtz's significance, by this account, lies in the way in which he fragments and alienates representation itself, destablising narrative structure; Kurtz is therefore 'incomprehensible', in the widest sense of the word. The ideologies of Englishness, heroism and masculinity have no purchase on him. In a similar fashion, Middleton asserts, Ellis's *American Psycho* 'reworks conventions and concepts from eighties American culture'. Bateman is the postmodern protagonist: amoral, not immoral, stylish yet violent, but, like Kurtz, his identity lies elsewhere and his meaning is excluded from the text. Both are 'hollow men'.

'Stylish amoral violence' defines the films of Quentin Tarantino in the eyes of many of his critics. It is Neil Sammells's view in the final essay in this collection that these epithets have a surprising degree of relevance to the works of Oscar Wilde as well. He sees Wilde as a figure whose resonance extends far beyond the clichés of fin-de-siècle decadence; Wilde anticipates, he claims, 'contemporary cultural theory', and finds 'an unlikely successor' in Tarantino. The link between the two is camp, and, following Sontag, Sammells describes the major characteristics of camp culture. He is then able to draw a number of parallels between Tarantino's fascination with popular, even kitsch, culture, his 'distanced' treatment of morality and his subversion of contemporary conventions, and Wilde's aestheticism, his disdain for moral categories and his deliberately transgressive attitudes. Both writers are deeply theatrical, both are interested in pastiche, and both have been accused at various times of cultural relativism. All these are, of course, the commonplaces of postmodern culture. It is for this reason, Sammells concludes, that Wilde and Tarantino offer us the opportunity to confront *our* fin de siècle with 'laughter, exhilaration and style'.

NOTES

1. T. S. Eliot, 'East Coker', *Four Quartets*, London 1968, 15. This poem in its entirety can be read as a very suggestive meditation on historical change and repetition.

2.   See, for instance, Sally Ledger and Scott McCracken, eds., *Cultural Politics at the Fin de Siècle*, Cambridge 1995; Elaine Showalter, *Sexual Anarchy: Gender and Culture at the Fin de Siècle*, London 1992; Linda Dowling, *Language and Decadence in the Victorian Fin de Siècle*, Princeton 1986; John Stokes, *In the Nineties*, Hemel Hempstead 1989; Mikuláŝ Teich and Roy Porter, eds., *Fin de Siècle and its Legacy*, Cambridge 1990; John Stokes, *Fin de Siècle/Fin du Globe: Fears and Fantasies of the Late Nineteenth Century*, London 1992; Lyn Pykett, ed., *Reading Fin de Siècle Fictions*, Harlow 1996; J. B. Bullen, ed., *Writing and Victorianism*, London 1997; Ian Fletcher, ed., *Decadence and the 1890s*, London and New York 1980; William Greenslade, *Degeneration, Culture and the Novel 1880–1940*, Cambridge 1994 .

3.   Oscar Wilde, *The Complete Works of Oscar Wilde*, London 1966, 1020.

4.   *The Guardian*, 'The Guide', 26th November – 2nd December 1994.

5.   Pykett, op. cit., 1.

6.   Max Nordau, *Degeneration*, London 1898, 1.

7.   See John Stokes, *Fin de Siècle/Fin du Globe*, op. cit., 2–4, where Stokes discusses John Galsworthy as one who 'at heart ... was everthing that Wilde ... and the Decadents were not', but who was still an important writer for an understanding of late-nineteenth-century culture.

8.   Sally Ledger and Scott McCracken provide a useful summary of this problem: they state that 'the parallels between the two fin de siècles are indeed suggestive, but ... an historiography which seems to see the problematics of the present so clearly in an earlier historical period must surely be open to question.' See Ledger and McCracken, op. cit., 2–3.

2

A dying fall?
Nineteenth-century decadence and its legacies

Peter Nicholls

As we approach the end of the century, our critical vocabulary is becoming increasingly preoccupied with ends and beginnings. My own interest in the relation of nineteenth-century decadence to the modernist phase hinges, however, on the idea of middles – on the process of *transition* between these two cultural moments. The story is one we know almost too well, a story whose outcome is predicted in the very names of its principal actors, for who would not rather be 'modern' than 'decadent'? At least this was, until quite recently, the way we had tended to think about the wave of avant-garde activity at the beginning of the century, that somehow it 'saved' us from an aestheticism which had become self-indulgent, anti-social, and effeminate.

This familiar account of modernism has several main features: first, it dramatises the outbreak of avant-garde activity as a moment of rupture with what had gone before, as a radical break with the exhausted forms of decadence; and, second, it makes of that break a pivotal moment in what might be called a narrative of emergence, according to which modernism variously constituted itself as a return to health after the malaise of decadence, or as a growing up and out of a sort of introverted childhood.

It was probably Hugh Kenner who taught us most persuasively to revere the Anglo-American modernists for liberating culture from the dark days of decadence. At least Kenner's *The Pound Era* was once particularly good at convincing me that Pound's 'invention' (as Kenner called it) of a clear, hard language should not only be welcomed but should be seen as a *necessary* move to redeem literature from what had gone before.[1] Exactly what was so unequivocally good about a language that was 'hard' rather than 'soft' was a question rarely directed then at Kenner – perhaps because, without thinking too much, we already knew how those terms had been loaded. Instead, the rediscovery of sculptural 'hardness' in poetic language simply became part of the great narrative of a modernism engaged in (as Pound liked to put it) a sort of literary hygiene, a purging of 'rhetoric' in the name of stability and objectivity.

Kenner, of course, didn't himself invent this narrative; indeed, one of the striking things about modernism is the extent to which some of its key players – Pound, Eliot, Lewis – used their critical essays to construct their own myth of an heroic emergence from decadence. So powerful is the proleptic force of those founding statements – their claim to determine artistic activity *in the future* – that we may miss the extent to which their writers were at the same time busily constructing a history of modernism *as it happened*; a history which subsequent literary critics often believed themselves to be writing for the first time. The 'now' of the manifesto also implies a narrative of deliverance from another time, announcing a ruptural moment which halts the dying fall of a culture in decline. The critical writings of Pound, Eliot and Lewis contain a sort of self-narration which associates formal experiment with a history of successful individuation: the modernist comes of age through his emergence from the 'womanish introspection' which Yeats, for example, discerned in his own early work.[2] Yet such emergence could be hard-won: Pound's own career was exemplary in this respect, since it took him a whole sequence of volumes to cast off – incompletely, one might argue – the burden of decadent influence.

This was one reason for Pound's immense admiration for the early Eliot: 'He has actually trained himself *and* modernized himself *on his own*', marvelled Pound.[3] Eliot had apparently done this partly through his discovery of the French poet Jules Laforgue, whose particular forms of social irony, pastiche, and colloquialism offered one possibility of a distinctively 'modern' idiom. But, characteristically, the implication of Eliot's discovery was actually more far-reaching, since it also encoded a rewriting of recent literary history; elsewhere Pound smoothly concluded that Laforgue 'marks the next phase after Gautier in French poetry'[4]. This is in some ways a remarkable judgement, reminding us that the enormously influential reading of nineteenth-century French poetry jointly proposed by Pound and Eliot was one which largely omitted Baudelaire, Rimbaud, and Mallarmé! The assumption, of course, was that modernism could come into being only by ostensibly cancelling or bracketing the decadent legacy of solipsism and hermeticism; Eliot had modernised *himself* because he had apparently been able from the first to grasp the line of continuity running from the hard, 'plastic' qualities of Gautier to the supple ironies of Laforgue and Corbière. This was modernism at a stroke, then, one not requiring Pound's awkward detour through late romanticism.

Needless to say, Pound's account of Eliot's punctual self-modernisation was rather different from Eliot's more measured sense of his own poetic development. In *The Use of Poetry*, for example, Eliot has this to say about his early encounter with romantic verse:

14

I took the usual adolescent course with Byron, Shelley, Keats, Rossetti, Swinburne.... At this period, the poem, or the poetry of a single poet, invades the youthful consciousness and assumes complete possession for a time. We do not really see it as something with an existence outside ourselves; much as in our youthful experiences of love, we do not so much see the person as infer the existence of some outside object which sets in motion these new and delightful feelings in which we are absorbed....[5]

The process of self-modernisation is more gradual here, running parallel to a move from adolescence to emotional maturity – a move in which the self acquires a degree of independence from the objects with which it is first fascinated. Once again, the snippet of autobiography provides a figure for the more momentous history of modernism, recapitulating the fear of 'possession' by a decadent other (be it the past or Woman), and stressing the need for clear boundaries to be drawn around the self. Yet the magisterial tone of the passage, its way of speaking from a position of assured maturity, almost conceals its residual anxiety about the power of decadent feeling to 'invade' or 'possess' consciousness. If the modernists frequently tended to think of artistic style as a sort of *defence* against the excesses of a decadent tradition, it was because decadence, far from being a dead letter, was actually still a pervasive force within early modernism.

But what, precisely, was the decadent legacy left to modernism? We can discount the more spectacular fin-de-siècle obsessions with sexual inversion, satanism, amoralism, and so on, most of which had already been present in Gothic fiction anyway. Much more important was a set of attitudes toward language and style which developed from Mallarmé's work, and were then given extreme expression in the eighties and nineties. It was at this moment that certain connections between a decadent language and a particular conception of the self emerged; these connections would be fundamental to subsequent forms of modernism, either as bonds to be broken, or as fictions to be developed further.

Let us go back for a moment to one of the most influential nineteenth-century accounts of decadence, Gautier's preface to the 1868 edition of Baudelaire's *Fleurs du Mal*. This edition would remain the only popular one in circulation until 1917, so Gautier's essay quickly took on the status of a manifesto of decadent writing. Decadence, Gautier suggests, expresses the inner logic of a modernity which has reached the terminal point in a trajectory already traced by the ancient civilisations. Like them, the modern period has exhausted itself in the search for ever greater sophistication and intensity of experience. The new artistic styles which have appeared therefore aim, like their decadent precursors, at impossible horizons and are condemned to endless disappointment:

> This decadent style [says Gautier] is the final expression of the Word which is called upon to express everything, and which is worked for all it is worth. In connection with this style may be recalled the speech of the Lower Empire, that was already veined with the greenish streaking of decomposition, and the complex refinement of the Byzantine school, the ultimate form of decadent Greek art. Such, however, is the necessary, the inevitable speech [*idiome*] of nations and civilisations when fictitious life has taken the place of natural life and developed in man wants till then unknown.[6]

According to Gautier, 'Refinement' is not only complex but excessive, and speech itself starts to become strained and corrupt as man's desires exceed the norms of nature. Significantly, Gautier understands the decadent style not as just one style among many, but as the expression of a deeper logic in all cultural production: for in so far as the arts seem to develop toward ever greater formal complexity, so style is at once supplementary – it adds nuance and detail to its object – and destructive – it 'decomposes' the matter upon which it 'works'. In a decadent period, Gautier suggests, death and corruption will find their true home in the domain of such an aesthetic.

This art denigrates life and the body but at the same time, vampire-like, it seems to appropriate human energies for itself, becoming monumental in just the proportion that its protagonists are drained of energy and life.[7] Style is now associated with an inward turn which signifies both aristocratic renunciation and a desperate sense of exile to a claustrophobic and interiorised world. The motif of the hot-house which is everywhere in the writing of this period (for example, in Zola's *The Kill* (1872), Joris-Karl Huysmans's *Against Nature* (1884) and Maurice Maeterlinck's collection of poems called *Hot-houses* (1889)) combines artifice and luxuriance with this sense of suffocating richness.

And the hot-house is not simply the place of languorous sensuality: in decadent writing, artifice is increasingly wedded to cruelty, and the dandy's cultivation of tropical plants 'like hospital patients inside the glass walls of their conservatory wards',[8] provides a 'sickly' reminder of the corruptness of sensual existence, along with a notion of the 'perverse' intelligence which nourishes itself upon them. In *Against Nature*, the unnaturalness of these blooms hints at a corruption of the flesh which Huysmans persistently links to the virus of syphilis which infects his hero, Des Esseintes. This artificial garden is a scene of pain and degeneracy, a symbolic site which will receive consummately horrific treatment in Octave Mirbeau's *The Torture Garden* (1898).

We can trace this particular way of associating art with violence to Baudelaire's concept of the dandy, where it was already clear that cruelty displayed towards nature and the (social) body also entails cruelty toward the self and the 'aesthetic' mutilation of what it shares with others. As art becomes more self-consciously anti-social, so it is driven to adopt ever more extreme forms of artifice to secure its own autonomy. Literature becomes a form of morbid machination, mesmerised by the idea of a 'pure' intelligence freed from the bondage of bodily desire. In Gabriele D'Annunzio's *The Triumph of Death* (1894), for example, the hero Giorgio is obsessed with the possibility of 'detaching the individual will which confined him within the narrow prison of his personality, and kept him in perpetual subjection to the base elements of his fleshly substance.'[9] The intelligence in such works is characterised by its 'cruel lucidity',[10] by its truly Sadean way of making instrumental rationality the foundation of the aesthetic enterprise, so that the hero of Huysmans's *Against Nature*, Des Esseintes, is forever 'experimenting' on other people, testing their susceptibility to corruption, while D'Annunzio's Giorgio undertakes the 'transformation, so intoxicating to a lover of intellect – the metamorphosis of the woman he loves to his own image'.[11]

Yet this preying upon another person represents only one facet of decadent psychology. In D'Annunzio's novel, Giorgio finally leaps to his death from the hill-top. He has been in love with death all along, and his suicide discloses another aspect of the decadents' 'cruel' aesthetic: namely that its sadistic drive always in the end recoils upon the self. Just as Huysmans's Des Esseintes cannot finally escape the 'weight' of his body, which continues to affirm his likeness to others, so the turning back of cruelty upon its instigator constantly undermines the fantasy of the disembodied intelligence.

In a sense this aspect of decadent desire prefigures Freud's view of sadism as rooted in a masochistic identification with its object.[12] Even more important, the tendency to self-destruction which is the privileged trope of decadent writing is one which also destroys language as the medium of self-expression. For as the cruel intelligence inflicts its aesthetic violence on the world, forcing its elements into new, inorganic forms of order, so its sadistic energy is also turned back on to the language of artifice which constitutes its medium of expression. One cannot help also thinking here of Freud's account of the death drive as the desire for a return to the inanimate,[13] for the decadent aesthetic projects a desire for death and dismemberment into the style itself, producing a peculiar petrifaction of language. Words are no longer connected to a world of objects which can be dominated, but tend to become things in themselves, opaque and material.

Contemporary accounts of the style thus stress its likeness to jewelled ornamentation, brilliantly hard yet reified and atomistic. Oscar Wilde's Dorian Gray, for example, describes decadent writing as a 'curious jewelled style, vivid and obscure at once, full of *argot* and archaisms, of technical expressions and of elaborate paraphrases'.[14] The decadent style is, above all, excessive, always obsessed with local effect at the expense of overall sense. It is, in Gautier's memorable phrase, 'worked for all it is worth',[15] but the refinement of effect also produces a deliberate impurity of tone. This is already in evidence in some of Mallarmé's poems where we find a deliberately recondite vocabulary (*ptyx, nixe, lamphadore*, and so on) combining with a use of words which suddenly shifts or lowers the tone (as in, say, 'The Jinx' and 'Alms').

The full-blown decadent style would go far beyond this, however, as Huysmans notes in his description of Barbey d'Aurevilly's writing as 'full of twisted expressions, outlandish turns of phrase, and far-fetched similes, [he] whipped up his sentences as they galloped across the page, farting and jangling their bells'.[16] This sounds boisterously carnivalesque, but the deliberate *over*-working of the style also testifies to the return upon the expressive self of that sadistic energy which had originally been exerted to ensure its transcendent superiority. The decadent style is gamey (*faisandé*, in a favourite epithet of the time) partly because its dispersive tendencies register the corruption of the self's relation to others.

This is especially clear in the decadent cult of the so-called 'rare word'. Such words have a closed opacity which makes the habitual comparisons to jewels particularly apt. The tremendous power of the foreign or 'alien' word is frequently invoked in this style so as to create the effect of a language partially dead and not in any practical sense for use. This is the extreme reach of Mallarmé's linguistics and we can discern analogues everywhere in the period: in Stefan George's arcane vocabulary and eccentric coinages,[17] for example, and in the purple prose of Walter Pater. It was precisely this aspect of the new aesthetic which Paul Bourget focused on in a famous contemporary critique which Nietzsche would later draw upon for his own account of decadence.[18] Bourget called attention to the decadent preoccupation with forms of decomposition, noting how its habitual intellectualism worked upon sensations with, he said, 'the precision of a prism breaking down light'.[19] This tendency toward fragmentation led to a breakdown of the unity of expression which ran parallel to an increasing atomisation of the social order: 'A decadent style is one where the unity of the book is broken down in favour of the independence of the page, where the page is broken down to allow the independence of the phrase, and [similarly] the phrase in favor of the word.'[20]

A decadent literature sequesters the reader from a shared reality, and the high artifice of the style deepens that divide between spoken and written language which Mallarmé had opened. Decadence spells the end of the 'classical' ideal, and Bourget observed of the Goncourts' style that 'it delights in witticisms and couplings of terms which make the reader jump, while classical prose tries [to ensure] that no word of the phrase comes loose from the securely woven web of the style as a whole'.[21] The relational economy of classical prose has broken down, and in place of the intersubjective 'web' of a social language we now have neologisms and eccentricities which bespeak the loss of any shared horizon. Bourget's point, put another way, is that we are now talking not about *discourse* but about language as an agglomeration of only loosely related words.

It is worth pausing for a moment to consider the implications of this critique. For Bourget's account of the decadent disruption of 'classical' style may remind us of nothing so much as Roland Barthes's description of how 'modern poetry destroyed relationships in language and reduced discourse to words as static things.' And Barthes's definition of 'the economy of classical language' also sounds remarkably like Bourget's: it is, says Barthes, 'relational, which means that in it words are abstracted as much as possible in the interest of relationships. In it no word has a density by itself...'.[22] For Barthes, then, as for Bourget before him, 'modern' writing perpetrates a kind of violence on language and on the forms of social cohesion it should promote.

This comparison reminds us that if the principal features of decadent style – its sceptical view of representation and linguistic transparency, its mixed registers and tendency toward fragmentation, its analytic intelligence and problematic materiality – if these seem somehow familiar, it is because they are all qualities we are accustomed to discover first in *modernist* style. The idea of a decisive break with decadent modes may now start to look a little less convincing. For it is not so much a matter of 'inventing' a new language, in Kenner's sense, as of *reconfiguring* decadent style, of dissolving the tie between art and masochistic desire while remaining within its clearly experimental format. In this sense it was no accident that Eliot should pinpoint Swinburne's poetic language as an example of a decadent failure of objectification, for Swinburne's own notorious masochism was coupled, in Eliot's view, with a failure to present the object world. In his work, says Eliot, 'the object has ceased to exist', meaning is 'uprooted' and 'has adapted itself to an independent life of atmospheric nourishment.'[23]

Much turns on this idea of the false autonomy of decadent style, its 'independent life', as Eliot puts it. Modernism would seek to reverse the masochistic tendency of decadent art and to reopen the social horizon which fin-de-siècle aestheticism had closed, but in doing so it would perpetuate the decadent connection between art and cruelty. Nowhere is this clearer than in Italian Futurism, from which the Anglo-American modernists learnt the basic lessons of avant-gardism. Marinetti's key polemical move was to invent modernism by directing violence *outwards*, away from the self and toward other people. Writers like Pound and Eliot had no time for the resulting aesthetics of war, but their whole way of formulating a definitively modernist aesthetic would hinge on the radical dissociation of self and other; only in that way could the artist recover that measure of critical distance which, it was felt, the unstable, death-desiring subject of decadence had eroded.

This is why so much of the early polemic of Anglo-American modernism turns on the question of objectification, with all that that word implies for a correlative sense of social relations. And we can see too why this break with decadence asserts itself so deliberately as a kind of sexual politics, for the failure of objectification is constantly referred to what Eliot calls in Virginia Woolf's case a 'feminine type' of writing, which makes 'its art by feeling and by contemplating the feeling, rather than the object which has excited it or the object into which the feeling might be made'.[24] Eliot's suspicion of forms of writing which make the word somehow self-sufficient, ('feminine' or narcissistic forms because language has not there become a register of differentiation of self and other), are shared in various ways by Pound and Lewis. Pound, for example, always understands historical decline in terms of a loss of clarity, a descent into the 'brown meat' of Rembrandt, the 'thickening line', and the increasing opacity of the word,[25] and Lewis, with his commitment to the 'external method' of satire and the values of the visual imagination, derides the 'heavy, sticky, opaque mass' of Gertrude Stein's writing and the 'stupendous outpouring of matter, or stuff' which is Joyce's *Ulysses*.[26] The 'true' modernist aesthetic is thus supported by a mechanism of reference and metaphor, and a related concern with outlines and borders which protect against the 'chaos' of subjectivity. As Eliot famously puts it, poetry offers the much-needed 'escape from personality', an escape from emotions which are immediate and shared by 'working them up into poetry'.[27]

The key terms of this modernism, then – 'image', 'form', 'energy', 'objectivity' – define the agonistics of this avant-garde, with an emphasis placed on technique as a kind of mastery. In contrast to the decadent writers, these modernists seek the ideal unity of 'tradition' as a bulwark against the centrifugal tendencies of an impressionistic 'subjectivity'. 'Form' must be seen to be won through what Pound, in a discussion of Lewis's painting, calls the 'combat of arrangement',[28] a combat only marginally less dramatic than his description elsewhere of the artist as 'the phallus or spermatozoide charging, head-on, the female chaos'. The connection exceeds simple analogy, reminding us that this privileging of intellect above emotion, along with its related activities of 'seeing' and 'knowing', leads not to forms of rigorous *self*-scrutiny but rather to an often aggressive objectification of the other. Yet this objectification is generally presented as a purely technical matter and, by implication, as an act of singular *self-discipline*, as an ascetic refusal to follow the decadents in conflating art and life. The 'clean', 'hard', 'non-human' values of imagism and vorticism thus appear as the only ones capable of sustaining an 'intelligence' which works by reduction, denying itself the immediate pleasures of what Pound terms the 'caressable' and mimetic. In this way, the 'inorganic' style of decadent writing is not so much jettisoned as reworked, so as to produce an ideal of psychic authority and coherence where the fin-de-siècle writers had discerned the very extinction of the self.

The break with decadence, then, was much less clear-cut than canonical modernism would have us believe; and this becomes even more complicated when we acknowledge that that version of modernism is only one of several different tendencies within the Anglo-American tradition. Indeed, when we look to the work of writers like H.D. and Gertrude Stein, it is as if the very decadent legacy which Eliot and Pound reject is reformulated to provide an alternative kind of modernism which is *not* tied to what they regarded as emancipatory forms of objectification. H.D.'s early poems are particularly interesting in this respect, since on the face of it they seem to accord quite closely with Pound's prescriptions for imagism. The poems are compressed, hard-edged, and shorn of sentiment and rhetoric. At the same time, though, they turn out to be marked less by cool detachment and balance than by forms of psychic violence which keep the poetic 'I' in the foreground. And where Pound's imagism is all about modes of differentiation, H.D.'s is much preoccupied with what seems other but turns out to be the same. This doubleness unsettles that autonomy of the closed self which is so much prized by Pound and the other 'Men of 1914', H.D. developing instead the decadent fantasy of engulfment, as in the famous 'Oread', so as to *open* the self to what is outside it. Quite deliberately, H.D. appropriates Swinburne's sadomasochistic figuring of desire, though she does so in order to interrogate the act of writing in relation to problems of sexual identity.

This set of possibilities is pursued definitively in the work of Gertrude Stein. Stein shares with H.D. the desire to move beyond an object-based poetics which derives its force from a repudiation of the feminine, and to discover in its place a form of writing which reveals continuities between self and world. If the entry into (modernist) language no longer presupposes a break with the feminine and maternal, then the various fantasies of mastery and objectification lose their hold

21

and are no longer assumed to be part of the purpose of writing. Language begins to assume a new opacity, blocking any easy passage between words and Eliot's 'world of objects'.[29] Stein, we might say, invents another version of modernism by circumventing the image altogether and by exploring precisely that self-sufficiency of language which had seemed to Eliot so damagingly decadent in Swinburne's work. The words Stein particularly likes using – verbs and adverbs – have, she says, 'one very nice quality and that is that they can be so mistaken'.[30] Error, errancy, drift, sensual 'wandering' (as in *Three Lives*): these are qualities quite opposed to those of what Stein later calls 'Patriarchal Poetry' (1927), with its obsession with 'origin and history', as she puts it. In Stein's own world of lesbian desire, however: 'I double you, of course you do. You double me, very likely to be.' As in H.D.'s novel *Her*, this 'twin-self' abolishes any notion of 'male firstness' (to use an apt phrase of Derrida), and opens the way to a continuous relation between self and other which does not depend upon the 'right' word (the *mot juste*) to bring a world into being.

For the 'Men of 1914', of course, such continuity spells the end of any properly *critical* relation to modernity. Yet this second main form of modernism – H.D.'s and Stein's – also managed to avoid the temptation of totalitarian politics as a public forum in which to play out the tensions between subject and object, and it did so partly because it turned the critical function of writing back on the self. Once again, the relation to fin-de-siècle forms is central: while the 'Men of 1914' version of modernism repudiated a masochistic aesthetic in the name of a coherent and masterful self, seeking to overcome the decadent death drive by reintegrating the aesthetic within valued forms of cultural authority, the other version *appropriated* the linguistic opacity and psychic disunity of a decadent aesthetics, not with a view to self-destruction but as a means by which to reject an imaginary coherence of the self which these writers understood as purely conventional or ideological.

The work of Mina Loy is a particularly interesting example of this move. Her writing has a deliberately rebarbative quality, with its contorted, often verbless constructions and its recondite and latinate vocabulary. The decadent 'rare' word returns, but this time with a compressed and epigrammatic cadence which gives the poems a calculated sense of posturing. The high artifice of the writing complements Loy's satirical sense of the ego as construction, but not as some kind of defence or stability within a world of flux, rather as the self-aggrandising disguises adopted in that 'masquerade sex', as she calls it, which is the outward form of an ideology of romantic love. In Loy's *Love Songs*, for example, modernist irony is fundamentally reformulated, as the reflexivity of her style turns the force of critique back upon the self instead of directing it outwards, against other people. It is not, of course, that her satire lacks an object, but rather that the impulse of negation works also to reduce self to style. Where Pound's Hugh Selwyn Mauberley finds in aesthetic style a kind of 'armour', as he calls it, for the self, Loy discovers in the self's very fictionality a release from the ideological 'truths' of gender.

Here the frame of what we normally think of as Anglo-American modernism is turned inside out, as style is grasped not as the privileged vehicle of avant-garde authority but rather as witness to its metaphysical pretensions. In this respect, Loy's work prefigures the playful transgressions of Virginia Woolf's *Orlando*, and the more darkly baroque underworld of Djuna Barnes's *Nightwood*, both works which also play knowingly with the tropes of decadence.

It is a curious reflection, perhaps, on our present cultural moment that this second version of modernism, which is able to construct a sexual politics from the aestheticism of the decadents, is in some ways more accessible to us than the agonistic postures of the first version. At least it is perhaps testimony to our own scepticism about the truth-telling capacity of art that the great myths of canonical modernism – myths of identity, origin, nature and tradition – now seem, if anything, more artificial than the most elaborate fin-de-siècle fictions. And if we look beyond the modernists' own narrative of emergence from decadence and acknowledge instead the persistence of decadent elements within the new aesthetic, these myths seem increasingly problematic and unstable.

One is reminded of more recent arguments about myth by the French philosopher Jean-Luc Nancy. In a book called *The Inoperative Community*, Nancy characterises myth as a desire for communion, 'fusion in a shared, immanent Being', as he puts it, in the community that becomes '*a single* thing (body, mind, fatherland, Leader)'. By way of contrast, Nancy proposes an idea of community based on 'being *in* common' in which there is no single social identity, but rather an experience of 'singularity' through which Being is understood as divided and shared.[31] It is through this notion of singularity that Nancy arrives at his key formulation, namely that we can understand writing as constituting in some sense an 'interruption' of myth: 'once myth is interrupted,' he says, 'writing recounts our history to us once again'.[32] It is a simple proposition on one level, drawing on a familiar poststructuralist notion of linguistic temporality: deferral, difference, the failure of language as an expression of Being and its resulting 'withdrawal into the singularity of the word'.[33] But perhaps this opposition of myth to writing offers one way of understanding the tense relation between decadence and the modernism of Pound and Eliot. For, as I suggested earlier, the fin de siècle had effectively discovered what might be called the excessively 'writerly' text, in Roland Barthes's sense. No wonder, then, that one group of modernists tried to cancel altogether the decadent legacy, for their wedding of politics to myth could not confront the decadent sense of an ungrounded language. No wonder, also, that for another group of modernists, the opaque and fragmented forms of decadent writing offered a means of undermining ideologically-loaded notions of subjectivity.

The decadent legacy in that sense has been a far-reaching one: not just in that its particular forms of scepticism resonate with our own fin-de-siècle mood, nor that our own time has become preoccupied with the same sadomasochistic activities that fascinated the decadents. Arguably more important is the obsession we share with *writing*, an obsession which has issued in a similar move away from an object-based poetics toward one of diminished reference. The legacy of the decadents thus has a surprising reach, extending from the Steinian form of modernism all the way through to the so-called Language poetry of our own time.[34] We shall always have problems with this word 'decadence', with its implied sense of falling and ending; yet its persistent ghosting of modernism (and, it might be argued, of our own *post*modernism) perhaps suggests that we should think of it more as a mode than an epoch,[35] more as a sort of limit-case of modern writing, than as the terminal point of an exhausted tradition.

NOTES

Parts of this essay are drawn from my *Modernisms: A Literary Guide* (London: Macmillan, 1995) which contains a fuller account of relations between modernism and decadence.

1. Hugh Kenner, *The Pound Era*, Berkeley 1971.
2. W. B. Yeats, ed. Allen Wade, *The Letters*, New York 1955, 434.
3. Ezra Pound, ed. D. D. Paige, *Selected Letters 1907–1941*, London 1971, 40 [Pound's emphases].
4. *Literary Essays of Ezra Pound*, ed. T. S. Eliot, London 1968, 282.
5. T. S. Eliot, *The Use of Poetry and the Use of Criticism*, London 1964, 33–4. Cf. *Selected Prose*, 108, where Eliot speaks similarly of 'an invasion of the adolescent self by Shelley'. See also Cassandra Laity, 'H.D. and A. C. Swinburne: decadence and modernist women's writing', *Feminist Studies*, 15:3 (Autumn 1989), 467–70.
6. Théophile Gautier, trans. and ed. S. C. De Sumichrast, 'Charles Baudelaire', in *Complete Works*, London n.d., Vol. XII, 40.
7. Compare Walter Benjamin's discussion of baroque allegory in *The Origin of German Tragic Drama*, London 1977.

8. Joris-Karl Huysmans, trans. Robert Baldick, *Against Nature*, Harmondsworth 1959, 98.
9. Gabriele D'Annunzio, trans. Georgina Harding, *The Triumph of Death*, Sawtry 1990, 253–4.
10. ibid., 289.
11. Huysmans, op. cit., 141.
12. See Sigmund Freud, 'Instincts and their vicissitudes' (1915), *Pelican Freud Library*, 11, Harmondsworth 1984, 126. See also the discussion in Leo Bersani and Ulysse Dutoit, *The Forms of Violence: Narrative in Assyrian Art and Modern Culture*, New York 1985, 24–39.
13. See Freud, 'Beyond the pleasure principle' (1920), ibid., 310.
14. Oscar Wilde, *Plays, Prose Writings and Poems*, London 1961, 173.
15. Gautier, op. cit., 40.
16. Huysmans, op. cit., 164.
17. See Enid L. Duthie, *L'Influence du symbolisme français dans le renouveau poétique de l'Allemagne. Les Blätter für die Kunst de 1892 à 1900*, Paris 1933, 169–71.
18. Nietzsche draws on Bourget's two volume *Essai de psychologie contemporaine* ([1883-5] Paris 1924) in *The Case of Wagner* (1888).
19. Paul Bourget, *Essai de psychologie contemporaine* (1883-5), Paris 1924, I, 7.
20. ibid., 20.
21. ibid., II, 173.
22. Roland Barthes, trans. Annette Lavers and Colin Smith, *Writing Degree Zero*, New York 1968, 49, 44.
23. T. S. Eliot, 'Swinburne as poet' (1920), in *Selected Essays*, London 1972, 327.
24. T. S. Eliot, 'London Letter', *Dial*, 71 (August 1921), 216–17.
25. See Pound's Cantos LXXX and XLV, for example.
26. Wyndham Lewis, ed. Paul Edwards, *Time and Western Man* (1927), Santa Rosa 1993, 59, 89.
27. Eliot, *Selected Essays*, op. cit., 21.
28. Pound, 'Affirmations' (1915), *Gaudier Brzeska: A Memoir* (1916), Hessle 1960, 121.
29. Eliot, *Selected Essays*, op. cit., 327: 'The bad poet dwells partly in a world of objects and partly in a world of words, and he never can get them to fit.'
30. Jean-Luc Nancy, trans. Peter Connor *et al*, *The Inoperative Community*, Minneapolis and Oxford 1991, xxiii, xxxix.
31. ibid., xviii.

32. ibid., 69.
33. Herman Rapaport, *Heidegger and Derrida: Reflections on Time and Language*, Lincoln and London 1989, 149.
34. See my 'Difference spreading: from Gertrude Stein to L=A=N=G-=U=A=G=E poetry', in Antony Easthope and John O. Thompson, eds., *Contemporary Poetry Meets Modern Theory*, New York and London 1991, 123-4.
35. Cf. Jean-François Lyotard's characterisation of the postmodern in *The Postmodern Condition: A Report on Knowledge*, trans. Geoff Bennington and Brian Massumi, Manchester 1984.

3

Queen Victoria's Diamond Jubilee of 1897: unashamed triumphalism or whistling in the dark?

Denis Judd

Between 19th and 24th June 1897, Britain and the British Empire celebrated the sixtieth anniversary of Queen Victoria's accession to the throne. During these days the public was able to gorge on a rich diet of ceremonial and display, speech-making and official processions. Among the events held to mark the Jubilee were a military tattoo at Windsor, a Special Service at St George's Chapel, Windsor, where Madam Albani sang Mendelssohn's 'Hymn of Praise', the Countess of Jersey's Garden Party at Osterley Park, the great royal procession to St Paul's Cathedral for the Thanksgiving Service on 22nd June, and countless street parties, speeches, receptions, balls, shows and even the Princess of Wales's Feast in benefit of the Outcast Poor.

Tribute, much of it material, was paid to the monarch. Among the presents sent to the Queen-Empress was a diamond, valued at £300,000, from the Nizam of Hyderabad, which was unfortunately stolen before it reached its destination. Throughout Britain and the Empire, statues were unveiled, free food distributed to impoverished families, prayers and incantations raised, Royal Navy warships dressed overall, toasts drunk and vast quantities of food consumed. The Princess of Wales's Jubilee Feast for the Outcast Poor, aimed at feeding 400,000 people throughout London, needed 700 tons of food, nearly 10,000 waiters, and the support of the retail millionaire Sir Thomas Lipton, who sent a sensibly priced menu and a cheque for £25,000.[1]

Reactions from many other nations, especially those which had cause to feel jealous of Britain's imperial supremacy, were generally charitable, as if hostilities had been temporarily suspended. The French newspaper *Le Figaro* pronounced that Rome itself had been 'equalled, if not surpassed, by the Power which in Canada, Australia, India, in the China Seas, in Egypt, Central and Southern Africa, in the Atlantic and in the Mediterranean rules the peoples and governs their interests'. The *New York Times* even went so far as to assert 'We are a part, and a great part, of the Greater Britain which seems so plainly destined to dominate this planet'. The Berlin *Kreuz Zeitung* described the Empire, perhaps with some regret, as 'practically unassailable', and in Vienna the Emperor Franz Josef called at the British Embassy wearing the uniform of his British regiment and the insignia of the Garter.[2]

For the populace as a whole, both rich and poor, the climax of the Jubilee celebrations was the great royal procession to and from St Paul's cathedral on 22nd June. Before she left Buckingham Palace at 11.15 am, Queen Victoria pressed a button sending by telegraph her personal message to every corner of the Empire: 'From my heart I thank my beloved people. May God bless them.' Within two minutes this bland and predictable greeting had passed through Teheran and was speeding on its way to India and all the eastern possessions of the Crown. Then, with the national hero, Field Marshall Lord Roberts, V.C. – known affectionately as 'Bobs' – at its head, the whole procession set off. Over 50,000 troops in wave after glittering wave made up the procession: Hussars from Canada, the Royal Nigerian Constabulary, the Cape Mounted Rifles, the Trinidad Light Horse, Zaptiehs from Cyprus (whose fezzes caused some in the crowd to hiss them as Turkish interlopers), head-hunters from the dyak police of Borneo, 'upstanding Sikhs, tiny little Malays, Chinese with the white basin turned upside down on their heads', Hausas from northern Nigeria, Jamaicans in white gaiters, and turbanned and bearded Lancers of the Indian Empire 'terrible and beautiful to behold'.[3]

As the writer Mark Twain so shrewdly observed, however, the Queen herself was the real procession and 'all the rest was embroidery'. Wearing a bonnet with ostrich feathers and sheltering beneath a white silk parasol, Queen Victoria gravely acknowledged the tumultuous acclamation of her people.

The Diamond Jubilee celebrations were, at one level, a self-indulgent affirmation of the achievements of the British people and of the glory of the British Empire. It was marked by over-wrought sentiment, financial extravagance, brash and patriotic tunes thumped out by brass bands, and by flags and bunting and glittering illumination. The *Daily Mail*'s brilliant young correspondent G. W. Steevens wrote that it was 'a pageant which for splendour of appearance and especially for splendour of suggestion has never been paralleled in the history of the world'. *The Times* believed that 'History may be searched, and searched in vain, to discover so wonderful an exhibition of allegiance and brotherhood among so many myriads of men.... The mightiest and most beneficial Empire ever known in the annals of mankind'.[4] The Jubilee Hymn, composed by Sir Arthur Sullivan, was to be used in all churches and chapels on Sunday 20th June. The Poet Laureate, Alfred Austin, composed a celebratory poem, which provoked some sharp contemporary criticism, and included the verse:

From steel-capped promontories stern and strong,
And lone islands mounting guard upon the main,
Hither her subjects wend to hail her long
Resplendent Reign.

When the celebrations were over, *The Daily Graphic* delivered a self-contented summing up:

> To us the survey of the Sixty Years Reign and of the microcosm of Empire with which we have filled our streets has been a source of subjective complacency. It has told us nothing we did not know before; it has been prized for no ulterior purpose. To the foreigner, however, it has been a revelation. He has been enabled to realise for the first time the stability of English institutions, the immensity of the British Empire, and, finally, the strength of the bonds by which the family of nations owing allegiance to the British Crown is united.... He now finds that England has sources of strength in her internal social peace and in the enthusiastic loyalty of her Colonies by the side of which the alliances of a Continental Power, or even of a group of Continent Powers, is of small consequence. In a word he has realised that Splendid Isolation is not an empty British boast.[5]

The Diamond Jubilee was staged for a variety of reasons, some idealistic, some cynical, some confused – even contradictory. It was not, of course, the first such celebration during Queen Victoria's reign. The Golden Jubilee of 1887 had both provided a dress rehearsal for the larger-scale event in 1897 and also indicated the potential benefits that could accrue from such a national and imperial extravaganza.

It was no coincidence that Joseph Chamberlain, appointed Colonial Secretary in 1895 and profoundly committed to the expansion and consolidation of the Empire, was one of the chief instigators of the celebrations. Chamberlain was the foremost example of a new breed of politicians who were skilled in public relations: of relatively humble social origin, but with considerable personal experience of industry and commerce, he was a brilliantly effective communicator able to utilise the press, particularly the newly established popular press, to outstanding propaganda effect.

In the hands of such astute organisers, the Diamond Jubilee was meant to make the vast majority of British citizens feel proud of their country and Empire and as a consequence to be content with their lot. During the hectic few days of the Jubilee celebrations, there is no doubt that the mass of the population were sufficiently intoxicated, often quite literally intoxicated, to participate with gusto. The historian G. M. Young believed that the Jubilee represented 'the concentrated emotion of a generation', and the future Fabian and socialist luminary, Beatrice Webb, recorded in her diary: 'imperialism in the air, all classes drunk with the sightseeing and hysterical loyalty.'

On this analysis, therefore, the monarchy, the political establishment, the aristocracy and gentry, the wealthy manufacturing classes, the established church, most of the 'haves' and even a vast majority of the 'have-nots' could share in both the immediate splendour and in the warm after-glow of the Jubilee, and as a consequence feel, at least for a time, strengthened and fulfilled by it.

Imperial propagandists hastened to cash in on the imagery and symbolism of the Diamond Jubilee. Even the use of the description 'Diamond' was unusual, part of the invention of imperial tradition, and also a reminder that the Empire contained the diamond fields of South Africa and, as a result, had put the wearing of such jewellery within the grasp of millions of British females, including newly-engaged young women from relatively humble backgrounds. Imperialists also took pleasure in the representation of so many subjects of the Empire in the spectacular procession of 22nd June. A great deal of irrational pride was taken in the physical size of many of the participants, and Captain Ames, at six feet and eight inches the tallest man in the British army, was put at the front of the Jubilee Day procession, proof positive that British was not only best, but biggest. One image that was processed and reprocessed, in numerous speeches, but more especially through the columns of a variety of newspapers, was the concept of the Empire as a great international organisation, essentially a family firm, in which the British and their white colonial cousins were the natural leaders, instructors and bringers of civilisation. No journalist encapsulated these sentiments more vividly or more movingly than G. W. Steevens:

> Up they came, more and more, new types, new realms at every couple of yards, an anthropological museum – a living gazetteer of the British Empire. With them came their English officers, who they obey and follow like children. And you began to understand, as never before, what the Empire amounts to. Not only that we possess all these remote outlandish places … but also that all these people are working, not simply under us, but with us – that we send out a boy here and a boy there, and a boy takes hold of the savages of the part he comes to, and teaches them to march and shoot as he tells them, to obey him and believe in him and die for him and the Queen.… A plain, stupid, uninspired people, they call us, and yet we are doing this with every kind of savage man there is. And each one of us – you and I,

and that man in his shirt-sleeves at the corner – is a working part of this world-shaping force. How small you must feel in face of this stupendous whole, and yet how great to be a unit in it![6]

There were, however, some dissenting voices. The Labour politician, Keir Hardie, wrote a trenchant piece several days before the beginning of the Jubilee:

From the uttermost ends of the earth statesmen and soldiers will ride in princely possession in the train of Queen Victoria, the titular head of the British Empire. East, West, North and South would be lost to view for the moment – absorbed in the world-embracing Empire.... To the visitor from Mars, two things might seem incontrovertible – first, that the world was at peace; second, that the thrones of the world were firmly embedded in the hearts of a loyal and grateful people.... And yet the Martian visitor would be totally mistaken. The cheering millions would be there and cheer just as lustily if the occasion were the installation of the first President of the British Republic; the soldiers are there because they are paid for coming, and nine out of every ten of them will heartily curse the whole affair as a disagreeable and irksome additional duty; the statesmen are there because Empire means trade, trade means profit, and profit means power over the common people.... Millions will go out on Tuesday next to see the Queen. What they will see will be an old lady of very commonplace aspect. That of itself will set some a-thinking. Royalty to be a success should keep off the streets.... The consolidation of the Empire is a good thing in itself. It is bringing nearer the reign of democracy and breaking down the barriers which keep nations apart. But this has no connection with royalty. The workers can have but one feeling in the matter – contempt for thrones and for all who bolster them up, but nonetheless a genuine desire to bring the nations of the earth closer together in unity – not on the basis of a royal alliance nor on a commercial union, but on that of a desire to live in concord. King and diplomat and trade are each, all unwittingly, preparing the way for this consummation so devoutly to be desired.[7]

Even Rudyard Kipling, unashamed patriot and poet of the Empire, sounded a cautionary note in his poem 'Recessional', published to mark the Diamond Jubilee:

God of our fathers, known of old,
Lord of our far-flung battle-line,
Beneath whose awful Hand we hold

31

Dominion over palm and pine –
Lord God of Hosts, be with us yet,
Lest we forget – lest we forget!

The tumult and the shouting die;
The Captains and the Kings depart;
Still stands thine ancient sacrifice,
An humble and a contrite heart.
Lord God of Hosts, be with us yet,
Lest we forget – lest we forget!

Far-called, our navies melt away;
On June and headland sinks the fire:
Lo, all our pomp of yesterday
Is one within Nineveh and Tyre!
Judge of the Nations, spare us yet,
Lest we forget – lest we forget!

If, drunk with sight of power, we loose
Wild tongues that have not Thee in awe,
Such boastings as the Gentiles use,
Or lesser breeds without the Law –
Lord God of Hosts, be with us yet,
Lest we forget – lest we forget![8]

Kipling's stirring yet disturbing verses were at odds with the over-enthusiastic contemporary reaction to the Diamond Jubilee. Not merely did they contain a sober warning against patriotic and imperial excesses, but they also clearly identified one of the deep, but barely acknowledged, explanations of the Jubilee extravaganza.

Tennyson, also a convinced although less ostentatious imperialist, wrote some equally cautionary, even ominous verses, asking: 'Are there thunders moaning in the distance?/ Are there spectres moving in the shadows?' Quite simply, pessimism, not joyous triumphalism, was the prevailing mood among Britain's leaders and opinion-makers as the century neared its end. The re-emergence of France as a heavy-weight and expansionist European imperial rival, and the eruption on the scene of *parvenu* colonising nations like Germany and Italy, disturbed the old order and put Britain under unwelcome new pressure. The falling order books of British exporters, the fact that Britain's annual balance of trade was only carried into credit on the backs of 'invisible earnings – banking, insurance, dues from merchant shipping and the like – as well as the obvious threat posed to British manufacturing and commercial supremacy by the rapidly expanding capacities of both Germany and the United States, were further, unsettling challenges.

Many late Victorians were also increasingly worried over a variety of perceived problems. These included the 'new', more militant, trade unionism, the 'new' man as well as the 'new' woman, the adulteration and processing of food-stuffs, the dilution of beer, the persistence of Irish nationalism, the perils posed by European and domestic socialism – even anarchism – and the growing anxiety, especially after the conviction of Oscar Wilde in 1895 for homosexual activities, that the nation, the 'race', was on the slippery, downward slope of decadence and decline.

Even Britain's global naval supremacy was under threat. 'Far-called, our navies melt away', Kipling had written in 'Recessional'. The rise of the United States as a great naval power, and Germany's intention, finally made explicit in the 1898 Navy Law, of building a modern fleet, gave substance to this nightmare – a nightmare soon given menacing fictional form in Erskine Childers' best-selling novel *The Riddle of the Sands*, published in 1903. The world, it seemed to many, was being rapidly divided up among a few vigorous and single-minded nations. It was this fear of losing out in the division of the spoils that prompted Britain to take so active a part in the 'Scramble for Africa'. Suddenly it appeared, to Western eyes at least, that the world was running out of space. Time did not appear to be on Britain's side.

As the end of the century approached, the impression of running out of time was heightened. The nineteenth century, which many British people associated with imperial expansion, naval supremacy, commercial and industrial success, rising living standards and a host of comforting manifestations of international supremacy and domestic success was dying. It was also evident that three of the leading totemic national figureheads were nearing the ends of their lives. For as long as most people could remember Queen Victoria had reigned over them; since 1880 – save for the two years of Lord Rosebery's premiership from 1894–5 – two major statesmen had alternated as Prime Minister, W. E. Gladstone for the Liberals and Lord Salisbury for the Conservatives. In 1897 Gladstone was stricken with cancer of the throat, and neither the Queen or Salisbury could expect to live much longer. In the event, Gladstone died in 1898, the Queen three years later and Salisbury two years after that.

There was, admittedly, enough to destabilise the most resilient of British observers at the end of the nineteenth century. Both the external challenge, and the crowding in of a host of internal problems and anxieties, provoked sufficient clamour and strident sentiment to convince both critics and supporters of

Empire that unprecedented forces were in operation. The term 'New Imperialism' was coined to describe an apparently powerful phenomenon. Although British imperial expansion continued at much the same rate as at previous periods in the nation's history, the perception of a 'New Imperialism' lent a fresh and vivid urgency to the proceedings.

The jingoism of the music halls, and the literary and journalistic excesses of imperial devotees, became more assertive and apparently self-confident as a number of confrontations with European imperial rivals, as well as successful military campaigns fought against generally backward and 'uncivilised' indigenous peoples, seemed to confirm British supremacy. The competition for colonies in Africa and the deepening crisis in the Transvaal lent an untypical excitement to routine diplomatic and political manoeuvring. It was now, moreover, easier than ever before to put vivid and accessible accounts of these great affairs before the late-Victorian public.

The Daily Mail had been launched in 1896, an event which, despite the Prime Minister, Lord Salisbury's, contemptuous dismissal of the paper as being 'written by office boys for office boys', led to the rapid development of a cheap popular press that could present great events for the digestion and titillation of a barely literate readership and fired countless starved imaginations – after all, the office boys needed information and entertainment as much as aristocrats; moreover, many of them now had votes, while the peers did not. Industrialisation had herded Victorian working men and women into factories and workshops, subjected them to industrial regulation and control, while at the same time the constitution had denied them full political freedom; it should be remembered, after all, that until 1918 no British women had the vote and neither did approximately forty per cent of British men. It was thus understandable that many contemporaries took a personal pleasure at the far-flung victories of the British Army or of the Royal Navy. A sense of national pride therefore became commingled with revived imperialist sentiment.

Feelings of national insecurity, however, were at least partly at the root of much jingoistic exaltation and triumphalism. For all Britain's imperial pomp and splendour, the country was, during the 1890s, without allies and openly – indeed passionately – disliked by many in Europe and the United States. 'Splendid Isolation', so accurately and pessimistically diagnosed by Lord Salisbury, was in truth uncomfortable and increasingly costly: a rationalisation of a predicament, not a calculated and self-confident policy. The over-reaction of the public to military triumphs such as the slaughtering of the dervishes by western military technology at the Battle of Omdurman in 1898, or to the over-due relief of the besieged town of Mafeking during the Boer War two years later, can be interpreted as the responses of an insecure and uncertain people.

In this sense, the Diamond Jubilee celebrations of 1897 were a fundamental part of the process of 'inventing tradition': of using the purely fortuitous longevity of Queen Victoria, and the nearing of the end of the century, as means of focusing unprecedented attention upon the British imperial achievement and, in the process, preaching a revamped, more coherent, version of the gospel of Britain's imperial mission. At the same time, the faltering sense of national purpose could be refurbished and revitalised for the undoubted challenges of the imminent new century.

On this analysis, the extravagant celebration of Empire in 1897 was both a means of focusing attention on British achievements and of boosting flagging national morale. It was a further manifestation of the imperative to use Empire as a means of diverting attention from fundamental failures and chronic uncertainty. The Jubilee thus provided a gaudy and brightly-lit shop front while, inside, the shops' owners faced bankruptcy and ruin amid their increasingly outmoded stock. Britain's faltering great power status could thus be underwritten by magnificent displays like the Diamond Jubilee, and her position of global supremacy therefore preserved. In short, it amounted to a gigantic confidence trick.

The potency of the Empire's appeal as the key to the nation's future was difficult to ignore. An active, expansionist and consolidationist imperialism was seen as a remedy to an unspecified number of national ills; both the 'gorgeous East' as well as the freshly opened-up 'Dark' continent of Africa would be sources of incalculable profit. Best of all, the New World, chiefly in the shape of the white-dominated self-governing colonies, could come to the rescue of Old World Britain.

By the end of the nineteenth century, the dependent empire was a jumble of possessions. There were crown colonies, like Ceylon, Jamaica or Trinidad, ruled by the Colonial Office through a Governor, who was sometimes assisted by Executive and Legislative Councils. There were also protectorates, such as Uganda, Nyasaland or Aden, mostly ruled by the Foreign Office, and frequently maintaining local institutions. Protected states within the empire were one stage removed from protectorates, in that indigenous rulers remained in office but were subject to the advice of powerful British Residents. This meant that the protected states, from friendly Tonga to strategically vital Egypt, were also a Foreign Office responsibility. There were, in addition, the chartered territories, like the Rhodesias and North Borneo, which were governed by chartered companies allowed virtually a free hand by Westminster. The Empire also contained two condominiums, the Sudan and the New Hebrides, which were ruled jointly with Egypt and France respectively.

The quest to find and to consolidate links binding this global, and potentially ramshackle, imperial structure together was lent a new urgency by the fresh challenges that Britain faced at the end of the nineteenth century. One central link was, of course, the British crown. The monarch was Queen not only of the United Kingdom, but also of all the self-governing colonies. She was Empress of India, and elsewhere a focal point of allegiance and respect, if not always of love. At the time of the Diamond Jubilee, it was discovered that even very large numbers of British citizens were surprisingly ignorant about the Empire whose scope and splendour so many of them were passionately celebrating. It should not be supposed, therefore that a dyak in Borneo or a Hausa in northern Nigeria had an especially clear picture of the distant British monarch. Citizens of Vancouver or Adelaide were undoubtedly better informed, but even in their case, the British royal family was very far removed from their daily experiences and impacted very marginally upon their everyday lives. All the same, the authority bestowed by the crown was evident throughout the Empire in the deportment of its representatives, from the Viceroy of India to the most isolated district officer.

Apart from the monarchy, the only realistic and historically validated imperial link was the experience of British rule. The dependant territories were controlled, either directly or indirectly, by Britain. The self-governing colonies, however, were free of such subordination. In general, they need only co-operate with the mother country when, and how, they saw fit. They could not be brow-beaten into obedience, although they might, on the other hand, be wooed. It was inevitable, therefore, that talk of imperial unity concentrated almost exclusively upon the relationship between Britain and the self-governing colonies. These were not only the most advanced components of the Empire, in terms of their economies and their political institutions, but they were also the territories which displayed the most independence.

While the 1897 celebration of Empire was an attempt to gloss over the disunity and confusion within the imperial system, a wide range of political and academic propagandists had, for some time, recognised the problems. Earlier, Sir John Seeley's *Expansion of England*, J. A. Froude's *Oceana*, and Charles Dilke's *Greater Britain* had powerfully put the case for greater imperial unity, and were read by tens of thousands of people in many editions. In 1884 the Imperial Federation league had been founded to propagate the theme of imperial co-operation through constitutional reform. The English-speaking Union was another body dedicated to the cause of Anglo-Saxon global solidarity. By the end of the century the Round Table group had also emerged as eloquent advocates of imperial consolidation, preaching their message chiefly through the regular publication of a journal of that name. In 1895 the cause of Empire had received a dramatic political boost when the most dynamic and persuasive advocate of greater imperial unity, Joseph Chamberlain, became Colonial Secretary; Chamberlain held the office for eight years, ostentatiously playing the part of an imperial knight errant in relentless pursuit of the elusive grail of imperial co-operation.

What remedies lay at hand for those who wished to consolidate and unify the Empire, and at the same time to protect Britain from the unwelcome impact of increasing international competition? The attempt to hoist imperial issues to the top of the national political agenda was essentially a failure. The public's attention could occasionally be concentrated, and then only by an effort, upon matters of great imperial portent, such as the African partition, the Boer War, or the need to replace free trade with imperial preference. For the most part, however, the late-Victorian population stuck to what they perceived as bread and butter issues, literally so in the case of food prices, but also conditions of housing, the threat of unemployment, the reform of education, and so forth.

Exasperated by this domestic taste for navel-gazing, imperial reformers and expansionists pressed on with their programme of regeneration and revivalism. One means of attracting the public's attention was to advertise the virtues of the English-speaking people. With Chamberlain as its chief apostle, but strongly supported by men like Cecil Rhodes and Alfred Milner, and by a number of newly-founded organisations, the movement to glorify and to promote the Anglo-Saxon race did not pull its punches. As well as attempting to foster closer relations with the English-speaking populations of the self-governing colonies, the activities of Pan Anglo-Saxonists concentrated on improving relationships between the United States and Britain.

Facing up to the prospects of its own inevitable decline, Britain thus made a calculated attempt to encourage a global partnership with the United States. This was made possible for a number of reasons. One was that, overwhelmingly, Britain's global interests were not seriously in conflict with those of the United States. Where clashes did occur, over the Venezuelan boundary with British Guyana, over the Hay-Pauncefote Panama Canal Treaty, and over the Alaska border with Canada, Britain sold out on each occasion to the demands of the United States. Appeasement of the United States, not a genuine partnership, characterised the relationship. Another factor was the substantial level of social interaction between leading British and American families. This manifested itself most strikingly in marriages between British statesmen and American women, most of them of considerable financial means. Among those Britons who married American women were Rudyard Kipling, the Liberal statesman Lewis Harcourt (Colonial Secretary in the years prior to the First World War), the Duke of Manchester, Lord Randolph Churchill, Lord

Curzon and Joseph Chamberlain. During the 1880s and 1890s, it was commonplace to find British statesmen and opinion-makers emphasising Anglo-American links rather than differences. A shared cultural, political and legal inheritance also played its part in smoothing the way toward *rapprochement*.

On this analysis, the Americans stood shoulder-to-shoulder with the British people as upholders of Anglo-Saxon civilisation. Speaking in 1887, Chamberlain said: 'I refuse to think or to speak of the USA as a foreign nation. We are all of the same race and blood. I refuse to make any distinction between the interests of Englishmen in England, in Canada and in the United States.... Our past is theirs – their future is ours ... I urge upon you our common origin, our relationship.... We are branches of one family.'[9] He was to return often to this theme, announcing, for example, 'I have been called the apostle of the Anglo-Saxon race, and I am proud of that title.... I think the Anglo-Saxon race is as fine as any on earth.' Kipling's much-quoted poem, 'Take up the White Man's Burden', was an exhortation addressed, not, as is commonly supposed, to British imperialists, but to the United States during its war with Spain in 1899. In a host of histories, novels and, most perniciously, school textbooks, Anglo-Saxon racial superiority was not merely taken for granted, but vehemently asserted.

Britain's resolve to use the United States as a means of lightening the burdens which she bore, 'staggering like a mighty Titan beneath the too vast orb of its fate', was carried into the early years of the twentieth century. The Fisher naval reforms of the Edwardian era depended at least partly for their success upon withdrawing Royal Navy warships from Caribbean and North American waters, and, as a consequence, handing over the protection of British and imperial interests to the United States. The myth of the 'Special Relationship' between Britain and the United States, which was to last for nearly a century, was not much more than the rationalisation of this necessary accommodation.

Imperial defence seemed to offer one of the most promising areas for promoting greater unity and co-operation within the Empire. The defence of Britain and her colonies was not a matter to be taken lightly, and some of the issues involved could be presented as matters for practical and urgent decision. To a large extent, the diversity and confusion which the British government faced in the late 1890s in the field of imperial defence was the result of earlier administrations' determination to pass over as much of the cost as they could to component parts of the Empire. India not only paid for its own defence, but also maintained an army which was often used to support the activities of British forces in a variety of world trouble-spots. As internal self-governing status had been bestowed upon the majority of the colonies of European settlement from mid-century onwards, the burden of shouldering local defence costs had also been devolved upon these emergent communities. By the early 1870s local military defence was clearly the responsibility of the self-governing colonies. During exceptional emergencies like the Second Maori War or the conflict with the Boers in South Africa, however, the intervention of British regular troops was considered to be essential. These divided responsibilities underlined the case for a more efficient approach to inter-imperial defence planning and co-operation, particularly as regards the land forces of the Empire.

Naval defence, however, was still overwhelmingly the responsibility of the British government. Although by the beginning of the twentieth century self-governing colonies of some standing like Canada, or the newly-federated Commonwealth of Australia, were seriously addressing the task of building up their own naval forces, it seemed impossible to contemplate an era when the Royal Navy did not provide the whole imperial system with its main bulwark of defence against foreign aggression and interference.

It might have been innocently imagined that the issue of imperial defence would have been of such importance as to have miraculously concentrated the minds of statesmen and of military and naval leaders. This would be, however, to misunderstand the competing and often contradictory factors at work. The self-governing colonies, constantly treading the devolutionary path, and confident that in an emergency the British army would come to their defence, were in general extremely reluctant to commit themselves to any military arrangement that might prove embarrassing and inappropriate. Within Britain, those politicians, like Arthur James Balfour, who were beginning in the latter years of the nineteenth century to coordinate the activities and responsibilities of the British army and navy, were encountering serious obstacles.

The main obstacle was that the British army and the Royal Navy were not necessarily willing or co-operative partners in the matter of defence planning. Both services had to compete ferociously for the relatively scarce resources which went toward the annual defence estimates passed through the House of Commons, and as a result tended to see themselves as rivals rather than allies. A surprisingly large numbers of senior staff in both services tended to view their opposite numbers with suspicion, even occasionally with hostility and contempt. Before the end of the nineteenth century, neither service was anxious to let the other know details of its strategic planning.

At the time of Queen Victoria's Diamond Jubilee, progress towards a greater degree of inter-imperial defence planning seemed to have been made in only one area. The breakthrough had come as a result of discussions between the British government and colonial Prime Ministers who had assembled in London for the Golden Jubilee celebrations ten years earlier. At this time, the Australian colonies and New Zealand had accepted the British case that the maintenance

39

of squadrons of the Royal Navy in Australasian waters was a costly business. From 1887, therefore, the Australian colonies and New Zealand agreed to make annual payments for the upkeep of the Royal Navy. In the first year, £850,000 was appropriated, a substantial amount in contemporary terms.

It was possible to see this apparent breakthrough, however, in terms of self-interest rather than of imperial patriotism. The Australasian colonies were sparsely populated European settlements on the fringe of the Asian land mass, and conscious of their isolation. The rising power of Japan, and the heavy, if demonstrably inefficient, presence of Russia in the Far East, heightened the sense of isolation and insecurity. There is no doubt that the colonies were buying a measure of security with their annual payments to the Royal Navy's upkeep. At the Diamond Jubilee of 1897, which once more provided the opportunity for the British government to enter into formal conference with the leaders of the self-governing colonies, the Cape also agreed to contribute to the navy's upkeep. The gesture was timely in view of the growing crisis in South Africa. By the time the next Colonial Conference met in 1902, Natal, too, had joined the list of subscribers, although this decision could be seen primarily as a vote of thanks to Britain for her role in recently subduing the Boer Republics.

Other attempts to improve imperial defence co-operation bore little fruit until the early years of the twentieth century. Until 1878 the final responsibility for the defence planning for the Empire was borne by the Cabinet, a body frequently ill-equipped to give sufficient time or consideration to such problems. The creation of a Colonial Defence Committee in 1878 was largely an *ad hoc* response to the Russian war scare of that year. It was, however, a feeble body and expired within a year. The incoming Salisbury government of 1885 revived it, and it continued to collect and circulate information in a rather lackadaisical fashion. In 1890 a Joint Naval and Military Defence Committee was established, but it was bedeviled by inter-service disputes, and its work generally lacked clarity or distinction.

The Conservative and Unionist general election victory in 1895 led to the establishment of the Cabinet Defence Committee. The self-evident growth of the external threat to Britain's military and naval integrity was a powerful boost to the establishment of this committee, as was the development of an influential and articulate services lobby in the Houses of Commons, and the skilful and persistent advocacy of Arthur Balfour, Lord Salisbury's nephew and ultimate successor as Prime Minister. The Cabinet Defence Committee, however, was not particularly successful. It lacked real authority, and the Prime Minister of the day, as well as the Foreign and Colonial Secretaries, and even the professional heads of the armed services, did not attend its deliberations. No minutes were kept of its meetings, and its work was fundamentally ill-defined and ineffective.

The accession of Balfour to the premiership in 1902, coming hard on the heels of the embarrassing military fiascos of the Boer War, paved the way for a more effective initiative. By 1904 the Cabinet Defence Committee had been reconstituted as the Committee of Imperial Defence. It had a permanent secretariat, in itself a revolutionary step, was chaired by the Prime Minister, and included the Secretary for War, the First Lord of the Admiralty, as well as the First Sea Lord, the Commander-in-Chief, and the heads of Naval and Military Intelligence. It was also able to invite any minister, service expert or colonial statesman to its meetings. Although essentially an advisory body, it was a powerful one because of its membership. At least now an appropriate mechanism had been established for better co-operation between Britain and the self-governing colonies in matters of defence. Not all of Balfour's aspirations for the Committee of Imperial Defence were fulfilled, but at least a precedent had been established and it was capable of healthy and sustained growth.

Imperial trade seemed to offer another promising area for improved co-operation. By the end of the nineteenth century the proportion of Britain's trade with the Empire was a little less than one third of the whole, and actually declined from 28.5 per cent during the 1880s to 27.5 per cent by 1900. The European and United States markets were still vitally important to Britain, but here the British balance of trade was ominously and regularly running into deficit. Nor was Britain able to keep as far ahead of her main trading rivals as hitherto; the gap was steadily closing. Although in absolute terms British foreign trade increased by a healthy 25 per cent between 1880 and 1900, in relative terms it was falling as compared with some of its chief competitors – Germany's foreign trade, for instance, grew by 80 per cent during the same period.

Since the principles of free trade still dominated British economic theory, and commanded bi-partisan support in Parliament, the opportunities for restructuring imperial trading relationships on the model, say, of Imperial Germany's *zollverein* (or customs union), were severely limited. In the case of the British Empire, imperial loyalties, such as they were, were less significant than commercial realities.

From the 1870s, however, the mid-Victorian economic boom began to fade, chiefly due to the competition of other manufacturing and industrial countries. During the 1890s there were a number of economic depressions, culminating in the Great Depression of 1896. British exports suffered alarming fluctuations and there were severe bouts of commercial dislocation and unemployment. Not merely were other nations, notably Germany and the United States, expanding their industrial activities on a scale which threatened eventually to overtake Britain's early lead in a comprehensive fashion, but, by the 1890s, most of the major manufacturing countries had adopted some measure of fiscal protection. Britain alone clung to free trade. As a result of this, the 1880s and 1890s saw the rise of a protectionist lobby in Britain, its views most clearly articulated by the Fair Trade League.

The accession of Joseph Chamberlain to the Colonial Office in 1895, with his political power-base in the industrial West Midlands, his experience of Birmingham manufacturing, and his self-declared mission to promote a greater degree of imperial unity, put a potentially deadly enemy of free trade in a position of considerable influence. By 1902, Chamberlain, frustrated in his plans for imperial councils and for precise schemes of imperial defence, sought to amalgamate economic self-interest with the cause of imperial unity in a crusade for tariff reform, expressed through a system of imperial trade preferences.

An imperial common market, however, was still way beyond reach. Self-interest dominated colonial economic policies, not imperial idealism. Colonial statesmen still wanted to protect their infant industries, and British politicians feared the electoral consequences of taking in foreign food made dearer by the imposition of protective tariffs. In the end the best that could reasonably be achieved was the construction of a system of tariff barriers, both in Britain and in the self-governing colonies, which would in effect impose taxes on foreign goods entering those countries. Imperial preference could then be introduced by the lowering of these tariff barriers against goods produced in the Empire. At the time of Victoria's Diamond Jubilee, this potential programme of fiscal reform was fundamentally unpopular within both major political parties, and needed passionate and inspired advocacy to sell it to a confused, unconvinced and generally uninterested public.

If the push for imperial preference, or tariff reform, had not yet properly developed, plans for imperial federation also remained unfulfilled. Although there were enthusiastic exponents of federation in Britain and the self-governing colonies, including the Imperial Federation League, the practical difficulties facing such a proposal were enormous. Any rational plan for imperial federation begged the question of the composition and power of a centrally situated Imperial Assembly. What subjects were to be reserved for this legislative body? How was it possible to avoid clashes and a chronic collision of interests over sovereignty between any central body and the parliaments of the self-governing colonies? Who would sit in any prospective Imperial Federal Parliament? If delegates were to be elected on the basis of proportional representation, then the

British members would swamp those from the self-governing colonies, with their much smaller populations.

Although proposals for imperial federation were not finally to be disposed of until just before the First World War, the surface show of unity and cohesion which marked the Diamond Jubilee encouraged federationists to believe that their hour had come. Such perceptions, however, were illusory. Political expediency and the already well-established realities of colonial devolution proved insuperable obstacles. The upshot, as was so often the case, was a typically pragmatic British compromise. The result was uncontroversial, reasonable, economical and, by choice rather than by accident, not particularly efficient. Since it was impossible to agree on the form and structure of an Imperial Federal Parliament, the empire determined to make the best use it could of the Colonial Conference system. The first Colonial Conference had met at the time of Victoria's Golden Jubilee celebrations in 1887, and this precedent was repeated at the Queen's Diamond Jubilee in 1897. The establishment of this precedent probably constitutes Victoria's most valuable contribution to the evolution of her Empire. It was an achievement that owed nearly everything to her longevity rather than to her innate abilities. By attaining a ripe old age, Queen Victoria provided a substantial measure of practical assistance to the better organisation of the imperial family.

At the Jubilee of 1897 it was agreed to hold Colonial Conferences at five-yearly intervals. The system thus established, with suitable adaptations, led directly to today's regular meetings of the heads of Commonwealth governments. The conferences that met in the late nineteenth and early twentieth centuries were never occasions for dynamic and fateful decision-making. Hefty agendas were presented to the delegates, who ranged freely over many topics of common interest, but any policies agreed at the conference had then to be vetted by the local colonial legislatures. The principle of colonial autonomy was thus retained intact. In a word, the Colonial Conferences could only be as useful as the delegates wanted them to be. They did, of course, have some symbolic significance, and their participants frequently felt that the free exchange of opinions helped to clear the diplomatic air.

In the final analysis, the Diamond Jubilee of 1897 achieved very little of any practical significance. It allowed an outpouring of emotion from those who wished thus to liberate themselves, but it did not change the imperial structure to any significant degree. As the captains and the kings departed, or, more accurately, as the colonial statesmen and the huge crowds of metropolitan onlookers departed, long-standing political imperatives silently reasserted themselves, and the vast bulk of active celebrants among the public returned to the mundanities of daily living.

A realistic assessment of imperial weaknesses and strengths had ultimately prevailed. It was generally accepted that the most realistic course of action was to fasten onto those links that already existed between the component countries of the Empire, rather than to forge new and potentially troublesome ones. The existing bonds of Empire, though unrestrictive, were not without intrinsic strengths of their own. These included the monarchy, a shared history, a common law and civil institutions, and, at least for the great majority of white citizens, a sense of cultural identity. These, if anything, were the bones that held the imperial body together. Imperfect though any of these links and bonds undeniably were, they were essentially organic growths rather than the result of hasty grafting and abrupt surgery. Thus, loyalty to the Mother Country, no matter how vaguely and fitfully expressed, was better than a formal alliance; a set of common interests was more reliable than a formal set of bi-lateral treaties. Thus constructed, and acknowledged, the relationship between Britain and the self-governing colonies that dominated the British Empire at the end of the nineteenth century, was to prove capable of the most remarkable endurance.

As it turned out, the Empire as a whole was to demonstrate considerable resilience, as pragmatism triumphed over fits of ideology, during the first half of the twentieth century. Although it had essentially disintegrated by the mid-1960s, both the Sterling Area and Imperial Preference took a little longer to collapse, and the new, non-directive Commonwealth positively flourished amid the ruins.

In the light of all of this, had the Diamond Jubilee of 1897 been worth it? If it failed to realise the highest hopes invested in it, neither did it descend to the futile and sterile depths that some anti-imperialists had anticipated.

Above all, it had happened. Tennyson perhaps got to the essence of this when he wrote: 'A song which serves a nation's heart,/ Is in itself a deed.' The 'deed' of the 1897 Jubilee was, in truth, chiefly an act of defiance in the face of decline, a truculent assertion of national greatness amid fears of decay and failure. The answer to Tennyson's unsettling questions, mentioned earlier, was a resounding affirmative. There were indeed 'thunders moaning in the distance' and 'spectres moving in the darkness', as the years between 1897 and 1914 were so terrifyingly and unambiguously to demonstrate.

A century later, we shall be fortunate if fate deals more kindly with us.

NOTES

Some of the material in this chapter appeared earlier in the author's book *Empire: the British Imperial Experience from 1795 to the Present*, and is reproduced here by kind permission of HarperCollins.

1. C. Chapman and P. Roben, eds., *Debrett's Queen Victoria's Jubilees, 1887 & 1897*, London 1977.
2. J. Morris, *Pax Britannica: The Climax of an Empire*, London 1979, 28.
3. ibid., 34.
4. ibid., 31.
5. *Daily Graphic*, 25th June 1897.
6. *Daily Mail*, 23rd June 1897.
7. *Labour Leader*, 19th June 1897.
8. Rudyard Kipling, *The Definitive Edition of Rudyard Kipling's Verse*, London 1940, 328.
9. C. W. Boyd, ed., *Mr Chamberlain's Speeches*, Vol. 1, London 1914, 321.

4

Queer fascinations:
Rider Haggard, imperial Gothic and the Orient

Terence Rodgers

Reading I admit I like ... I study the Bible, especially the Old Testament, both because of its secret lessons and the majesty of the language of its inspired creators.... For the rest I peruse anything to do with ancient Egypt that I happen to come across, because this land and its history have a queer fascination for me, that perhaps has its roots in occurrences or dreams of which this is not the place to speak.[1]

I

Rider Haggard occupies a distinctive place in the late Victorian period. For long either ignored or dismissed by modern critics as an above-average practitioner of adventure stories, Haggard's writing, and notably his core fiction of the 1880s, has in recent years been subjected to a major process of scrutiny and re-evaluation. This new interest, as well as assisting in the reclamation of his novels for present-day readers, has shifted Haggard's work towards the centre of two important and sometimes overlapping regions of debate in literary and historical studies. First, in the growing field of postcolonial criticism, Haggard's texts have become co-ordinates for the detailed exploration of late-Victorian and Edwardian narratives and ideologies of empire, and those related and intersecting discourses of knowledge, commodification and difference which helped to condition the apparatus of colonialism and control.[2] Second, both Haggard's fictional and non-fictional writing have been recovered and positioned as a major reference point in analyses of the socio-cultural politics of the fin de siècle and some of the preoccupations, anxieties and expectations of the period.[3]

Haggard's best-known work, both during his lifetime and after, were his imperial romances and, in particular, his three sensational novels of the 1880s: *King Solomon's Mines* (1885), *She: A History of Adventure* (January 1887) and *Allan ' Quartermain* (July 1887). Located in and moving between rural England and black Africa, the 'Dark Continent' of the Victorian imagination, these books were more than just adventure stories. Rather, they comprised a loose imperial trilogy in which familiar strategies of romance and high adventure were blended with identifiable gothic elements to create what Patrick Brantlinger has called an 'imperial Gothic'. As he has argued in a wide-ranging discussion of some of its practitioners, imperial Gothic combined 'the seemingly scientific, progressive, often Darwinian ideology of imperialism with an antithetical interest in the occult'.[4] According to Brantlinger's account, the connection between this type of imperial fiction and the occult was especially symptomatic of the anxieties which attended the climax of the British Empire. In part, he suggests, imperial Gothic testified to a fin-de-siècle search for new faiths to replace a declining confidence in Christian theology and observance, but it also signalled a moment of wider cultural significance. For beyond a veneer of scientific and technological superiorism, which was characteristic of some of these narratives, imperial Gothic expressed fears about the weakening of British imperial hegemony and accelerating social entropy; producing images of the invasion of imperial borders by the agents of barbarism, the subversion of the imperial centre by liberal and socialist cosmopolitanism, and perhaps even more seriously, collective and individual degeneration. 'No form of cultural expression', Brantlinger concludes, 'reveals more clearly the contradictions within that climax [of empire] than imperial Gothic'.[5]

As a recognisable genre, imperial Gothic flourished between the 1880s and the First World War, and as some literary historians have proposed, may be viewed as having prepared the ground for the emergence of the modern science fiction novel.[6] At its height around the turn of the century, the form was sustained by a variety of writers, including Flora Annie Steel, Rudyard Kipling and Joseph Conrad. However, Rider Haggard was certainly one of the central figures in its invention and a notable voice in its exposition. In that regard, his celebrated association with Africa was as vital as it was to be prolonged. As one of Haggard's publishers noted, Africa was 'the land of his greatest triumphs' to which he turned 'again and again for inspiration in projecting his famous romances'.[7] In Haggard's extensive canon of fiction, some fifty-six works in all, black Africa was a new continent where imagination merged with ostensible fact and where entry was gained through obscure maps, parchments and curious artifacts; a continent which carried both the promise of utopia and the threat of dystopia, generating expectations of ideals fulfilled and material reward, but also suspense and terror. Here, in 'the heart of the darkness', Haggard's quest stories depicted a dialectic where intrepid agents of order and progress were pitted against backwardness and the 'primitive', post-Darwinian and Spencerian presumptions about western civilisation were displayed, and where social pathologies of the unknown were cashed out and resolved.[8] This also was the landscape where Haggard introduced his two most memorable characters, each defining important polarities of imperial identity and gender power in his imperial narratives: Allan Quartermain, imperial subject and masculine hero, and Ayesha, the eternal queen figure in *She*, and object of male desire and fear.

As critics such as Laura Chrisman and Anne McClintock have recently shown, Haggard's African romances offer valuable insights into the nature of colonial discourse and its energising myths, western notions of African place and identity, and the irrepressible urge to name, classify and catalogue the 'Dark Continent'.[9] Yet equally, these texts give us a view into the cultural tensions which marked imperial Britain at the fin de siècle. Specifically, they exemplify some of the ways in which imperial Gothic as a genre functioned as a vehicle for externalising the fears of a society which, for all its formalised self-confidence, saw its global reach as precarious and its internal as well as its imperial frontiers as vulnerable. In this essay, however, I want to open up and direct critical attention towards another landscape and preoccupation which was an important part of Rider Haggard's contribution to the language of colonialist fiction and to imperial Gothic and which, surprisingly, has received little detailed or sustained attention. This was his lifelong imaginative and practical obsession, his 'strange fascination', or more interestingly in Quartermain's words, his 'queer fascination' with the Orient and in particular with ancient Egypt.[10] While allusions to the Near and Middle East can be found in Haggard's early domestic novels and are conspicuous in some of his African romances, the author's interest in the East found its fullest and most challenging expression in his numerous but now largely ignored oriental romances. Completed and published at a gathering pace up to and after the turn of the century, Haggard's oriental fictions constituted a parallel but different gothic territory to that delineated in his African texts. The latter was essentially a contemporary, geopolitical and racial topos. In contrast, his eastern fictions invited the reader into an epistemological space that was framed in terms of distant imperial epochs; an historical world of ancient and early modern Mediterranean civilisations, but also of occult practices, the supernatural and exotic fantasies.

II

Between his arrival as a writer of popular fiction in the 1880s and the intervention of the Great War, Haggard wrote six novels about the Near and Middle East and a number of short stories. Subsequently, he produced another five eastern novels, the final one published eleven years after his death.[11] His first and undoubtedly most successful eastern novel was *Cleopatra*, published in June 1889. Of the others published before the War, two were likewise concerned with ancient Egyptian and Mediterranean civilisation, one with

Roman Palestine, one with the Byzantine Empire, together with a novel of the Crusades, and a contemporary story set in colonial Egypt. Taken together, and excluding his later eastern fictions, which covered some of the same ground, these novels enclosed coherent and powerful images of the Orient during different periods of a history which had long been inscribed into West's idea of itself and its origins, as well as the idea of its exotic Other. More immediately, this body of work reflected the renewed importance of the Near Orient in the late-Victorian imperial mind and policy. *Cleopatra,* written during the celebrations of Queen Victoria's first imperial jubilee, was published a few years after the British occupation of Egypt and at a time when British political interest in the area was considerable. Other novels, such as *The Brethren,* (1904) and *The Wanderer's Necklace* (1914), articulated through their very subject matter a consciousness of the so-called 'Eastern Question', the long-standing conundrum of declining but still significant Ottoman and Islamic power in the eastern Mediterranean. But, most evidently, Haggard's eastern novels of the fin de siècle coincided with and complemented a renewed explosion of popular and academic interest in the Orient and especially in Egyptology; an interest which, as Edward Said and others have observed, expressed itself forcibly in the literature, art, design, and architecture of the period, as well as influencing the developing imperial sciences of philology, archaeology and anthropology.[12]

In his noted writings on the subject, Said has characterised Orientalism as an imperial and *sui generis* totalising project; a figurative and textual master-narrative which stressed the contrasts and differences between the West and the Orient and which, through its many and various expressions, facilitated the Western appropriation and control of colonial and other cultures in the nineteenth century and beyond. While acknowledging the theoretical and practical utility of Said's approach, some critics have nevertheless questioned its monolithic and all-embracing character. Instead, they have posited and described the existence of different 'orientalist situations' which functioned at different times and places, and have argued for a fuller historicisation of Orientalism, as well as for a deeper appreciation of its linguistic and cultural complexity. Thus, for example, in rejecting Said's monolithic and binary definitions between the Occident and the Orient, the historian John MacKenzie has recently highlighted the ways in which nineteenth-century Orientalism, although dominating in its intent and appropriative in its nature, nevertheless could and often did involve a degree of cultural intercourse and exchange. As he puts it succinctly, 'in reality, Orientalism was endlessly protean, as often consumed by admiration and reverence, as by denigration and depreciation'.[13] However, what needs to be underlined for the purposes of this study is the way in which from about the mid-1880s onwards the Orient became a recognised discursive construct for the interrogation of modernity and for the negotiation of contested social and cultural meanings; an inherited but nevertheless fresh text upon which decadents and counter-decadents alike, as well as professional orientalists like Sir Richard Burton, were able to inscribe their own and society's preoccupations with the boundaries of convention, explore 'new' socio-cultural phenomena and articulate territories of different linguistic, psychological and moral behaviour.[14]

As with his association with Africa, Haggard's literary dialogue with the Orient rested upon and was informed by a deep personal interest and regard for the region. In January 1887, shortly after the publication of *She*, he travelled to Egypt for the first time. There he was spellbound by the great sites of its ancient civilisations at Luxor and Thebes and by the archaeological work being undertaken. 'It is impossible to begin to tell you the impression that all this has made upon me', he wrote to his wife.[15] In 1900 Haggard embarked upon an extensive tour of Palestine and Syria, and later made two further visits to Egypt. During these years he immersed himself in the literature of Orientalism and Egyptology, became engrossed in the history of eastern texts, religions and occultism, and established close links with some of the leading figures in the field, such as Lord Amherst and Ernest Wallis Budge.[16] When *Morning Star* (his fourth Egyptian story) was published in 1910, Haggard had already acquired a reputation as a lay authority on the region and as a respected voice in eastern antiquarianism.[17] By then, too, the Orient had become more than just a fascination becoming rather, it would seem, the main force behind his continuing desire to write. 'Personally I prefer to write fiction about old Egypt or historical subjects', he told a correspondent. 'But what happens?', he added defensively:

> my name ... is connected in the public idea with a certain stamp of African story and especially with one famous character.... If I write other things I am told they "are not so good", though I well know them to be much better. At the bottom of all this are the fashion-following critics themselves who absolutely resent any new departure....[18]

Although few of Haggard's eastern novels attracted the same degree of critical acclaim as his African tales, their commercial success, particularly that of his Egyptian romances, was considerable. Much of this attention was undoubtedly due to the retroperative and archival character of these books. In part, Haggard's eastern world was a mixture of reconstructed knowledge, recovered artifacts, and historical imagination; stories in which the historical

Orient is narrated, described and classified as an act of cultural authority and power. As such, his novels were distinguished by strategies of reconstruction, antiquarian scholarship and authentication which mimicked the project of academic Orientalism, then approaching its height.[19] For example, in *Cleopatra*, Haggard devoted 'Book I' to an expansive and informed discussion of society and culture in Ptolemaic Egypt, advising those readers who might have little interest in the history of Egyptian civilisation, to 'exercise the art of skipping'.[20] His next novel, *The World's Desire* (1890), written in collaboration with Andrew Lang, is a text frequently disrupted by explanatory footnotes to scholarly and classical sources, while in *Morning Star* he extolled his friendship with Wallis Budge, invoking his name with the deliberate purpose of validating the integrity of the narrative. All three texts, nevertheless, exhibited symptoms of the ambivalent and unstable nature of nineteenth-century orientalist discourse, wherein the eastern Other could invite denigration and depreciation, yet simultaneously inspire and question the conventional. Thus in *Cleopatra* Haggard recounted in semi-biblical language a tale of moral turpitude, sexual decadence and violence, but also paid fulsome homage to ancient Egypt as the 'Mother of Religion and Civilisation' and as a source of wisdom which could still be tapped (viii).[21] Similarly, in *The World's Desire*, a story which moves between Greece and Egypt, the ancient Orient was depicted as a place of unfathomable evil and cruelty, but also as the location of some of the great wonders of civilisation and the source of eternal human, religious and spiritual 'truths'.

Yet, as this indicates, Haggard's eastern fictions of the fin de siècle were concerned with more than simply contributing to an ever-expanding imperial archive of information. Rather, most of them (in some cases first and foremost) were sites for quasi-philosophical speculations by the author about knowledge, ontology and the uncanny. So, for example, in *Cleopatra* and *The World's Desire*, no clear dividing line exists between the physical 'reality' of ancient Egypt and its parallel spiritual world of ghosts and gods, across which characters move with relative ease, although with fear. Likewise, in this 'twilight age' where 'fancy has free play', things are rarely what they appear to be and may be the instruments or objects of magic.[22] In some of these novels, the Orient is explicitly labelled as a realm of psychological difference and psychical activity, and a place where the unconscious or hidden Self can be revealed and recovered. In several cases the main protagonists experience altered states of consciousness or dreamlike trances which bring them into contact with the after world of spirits and ghosts, or enable them to chart the layers of their personality and make contact with a earlier Self and a previous world. In *The Wanderer's Necklace*, the story is recounted by the 'Editor' as

51

a series of self-imposed, semi-hypnotic recollections of his previous existence as a nomadic warrior in the Byzantine Empire of the ninth century, while in a later novel, *The Ancient Allan* (1920), Quatermain embarks on a drug-induced journey through the gates of consciousness and memory into pharaoic Egypt, with the reader enjoined in the act and in the decoding of Quatermain's visions and perceptions. 'What did I see? What did I see?', Quatermain addresses the reader, 'Let me try to recall and record'.[23]

In projecting such philosophical and psychological notions, which imply a number of influences on the author, Haggard's eastern fictions addressed a span of recurring and intersecting cultural archetypes, one of which was the Victorian ideal of romantic heterosexual love. In two popular and well-received stories, *Pearl Maiden* (1903) and *Morning Star*, Haggard's approach consisted of seemingly uncomplicated explorations of the triumph of true love over great dangers and difficulties in ancient times, where Love assumed the role of a metonym for masculine and feminine nobility and the victory of good over evil. But viewed from another angle, these romantic tales can also be read as deliberate attempts to re-valorise the Victorian ideal of Love itself in the form of a distant exotic Other, and to expose the limitations of modern materialism and 'scientism'. As Haggard mused in *Morning Star*, 'it is pleasant to dream that the Gods are on the side of lovers and deign for their sakes to work the miracles in which for thousands of years mankind has believed, although the scientists tell us that they do not happen'.[24] Elsewhere in his eastern fiction, however, Haggard's love stories more usually framed, not as alternatives to a disenchantment with modernity, but rather as discourses and signs of contemporary personal crisis and collective doom. Generally pessimistic, at times apocalyptic and truly gothic in their textual characteristics, the most striking and persistent of these frequently linked discourses concerned women, sexuality and sexual identity.

The whole of Haggard's romance fiction – domestic, African and Oriental – was preoccupied with women and sexuality, and with defining a 'problem' of female generative power for its largely male Victorian readership. Throughout his work, where dominant female characters proliferated, women were represented as icons of beauty and sexual being, and as the timeless objects of 'the great war of the world' between 'pure love' and physical desire.[25] Both at the time and since, Haggard's representation of women has attracted sustained examination, the weight of it focusing almost exclusively upon Ayesha as she first appeared in *She*. Some critics, notably Sandra Gilbert and Susan Gubar, have argued that Ayesha embodies fin-de-siècle male anxieties about the 'Woman Question', the challenge of female political and social emancipation, and more directly, about the 'New Woman', the threat of female sexual dominance. In contrast, Rebecca Stott sees her as the specific product of Victorian attitudes and fears regarding Africa. 'Haggard's novels exploit the notion of a dark Otherness', she writes, 'which is invariably woman as Other, as temptress, as foreign territory ... but above all as a matrix of horror and fear: an all-encompassing and fearful darkness – the black widow.'[26] Nevertheless, although persuasive, what these approaches have neither underlined nor explored sufficiently is the essentially oriental origins and character of Haggard's famous *femme fatale*. Ayesha, 'the lovely, the mystic, the changeful, the imperious', does indeed represent foreign territory and a sexual otherness, but it is an eastern territory and otherness. Ayesha is an immortal and white Egyptian priestess, not a black African queen, and the ruined city over which she presides in central Africa is, as Haggard painstakingly explains, the ruins of an Egyptian city which, he suggests, must have been built by ancient colonists of the Pharaohs. Indeed, not only in *She,* but in Haggard's imperial fiction generally, the real paradigm of the sexualised woman is the (usually semi-naked) female body of the Orient.[27]

The invention in *She* of an eastern presence at the heart of black Africa was a important cultural statement and a signifying device to which Haggard returned in subsequent imperial romances.[28] In part this made reference to contemporary and active ethnographical and anthropological debates about the origins and evolution of human society and its early great civilisations, in which black Africa was usually downgraded and defined as primitive. However, what it also played upon and reinforced was the nineteenth-century identification of the Orient and the 'oriental' with the metaphysical; even more so, with transcendent eroticism and desire, sexual opportunity and sexual experimentation. In Haggard's eastern fiction this asymmetry between history, place and erotic mythology (what Burton in *The Arabian Nights* called the 'Sotadic Zone') was made obvious and exploited more freely and fully.[29] In these texts the ancient East is reconstructed, explicitly gendered as female, and its differences objectified through a variety of stratagems, including the reassembling of archaic styles of speech and the depiction of female sexual hunger and power. As a result, and to an extent which was not possible in his racially-conditioned African fiction, Haggard's Orients were shaped into landscapes of male sexual fantasy, neurosis and gothic terror. This is most clearly witnessed in *Cleopatra*, Haggard's earliest oriental romance and one of his major works of fiction.

III

Haggard started to write *Cleopatra* soon after his first visit to Egypt, and the story initially appeared in serialised form in the *Illustrated London News* between January and June 1889. Haggard, fresh from a string of literary successes, was optimistic about its reception: 'I think and hope it will make the British Public sit up!', he wrote. He also described the book as an 'ambitious project', and for a time considered it the best that he had written and was likely to write.[30] Although these thoughts were not entirely shared by his friends or by reviewers, it was a compelling novel on a subject which reworked a classical story, indeed one which was part of the English literary canon, in an unusual and potentially subversive way. Taking the established tale of Cleopatra, the temptress and undoer of Antony, Haggard repositioned the story as an historical narrative of ancient tyranny and national re-awakening.[31] By this account, Queen Cleopatra's death is brought about by Egyptian patriots intent on overthrowing the foreign Ptolemaic dynasty and restoring 'Harmachis', the last true descendent of the old Pharaohs.[32] However, the restoration fails because Cleopatra, a sexual vampire, seduces the young and pure Harmachis, turning him into a slave for her love, and bringing down the wrath of the watching Gods upon the Queen, Harmachis and Egypt. In this narrative of symbolic seduction, revenge and divine retribution, the figures of Woman and Orient are equated with the corruption of the spirit and the flesh. Thus, for example, before setting out to fulfil his destiny by overthrowing Cleopatra, Harmachis is warned by his father of the dangers ahead: 'but hear this, there is danger in thy path, and it comes in the form of Woman. I have known it long.... Beware, then, of those witches of Alexandria, lest, like a worm, some of them creep into thy heart and eat its secret out' (83).

The allegorical core and the central problematic of the novel is contained in a scene, carefully crafted, where Harmachis is taken to meet Queen Cleopatra and finds her asleep, vulnerable but dangerous. Harmachis enters a room flanked by eunuchs with drawn swords and passes through heavy curtains into an inner chamber where Cleopatra lies. The picture that confronts Harmachis is 'beautiful beyond imagining', the air 'sweet with perfume'. At the further end of the bedchamber, on a veiled couch, rests the sleeping Queen:

There she lay ... fairer than a dream, and the web of her dark hair flowed all about her. One white, rounded arm made a pillow for her head, and one hung down towards the ground. Her rich lips were parted in a smile, showing the ivory lines of teeth; and her rosy limbs were draped in so thin a robe of the silk of Cos, held about her by a jewelled girdle, that the white gleam of flesh shone through it. I stood astonished, and though my thoughts had little bent that way, the sight of her beauty struck me like a blow, so that for a moment I lost myself as it were in the vision of its power, and was grieved at heart because I must slay so fair a thing (106–7).

This depiction of the orientalist/male gaze is typically two-sided, both self-empowering and self-endangering. The scene, as voyeuristic as any orientalist painting of eastern femininity, contained many familiar Victorian signifiers of sexual arousal and danger: the armed eunuchs, the heavy curtains, the veiled couch, and, last but not least, the rich parted lips of Cleopatra, showing her white teeth. The prospect of the loss of male self-control, penetration and rape, is countered by the evident threat of female sexual aggression. In both cases, the mediating sign is the veil. The figure of a veiled female or female form was a recurrent one in Haggard's fiction, but especially in his eastern fictions, and of course in much of the literary and visual arts of the time. However, as Elaine Showalter points out, the veiled woman had many nuances and meanings at the fin de siècle, some of them contradictory. Most commonly, the veiled female form was linked with concealed female sexuality and the veil of the hymen, but at the same time with the erotic invitation of the Orient, sexual potential, sexual otherness, and the lure of the Harem. Equally, however, the veiled female represented a sexual threat. In *Cleopatra* that threat speaks of invasion, entrapment and emasculation; the destruction of masculinity. As Showalter puts it: 'behind the veil is the spectre of female sexuality, a silent but terrible mouth that may wound or devour the spectator'.[33]

Haggard closed this depiction of sexual danger with a vivid metaphorical scene which portends the fate of Harmachis, but which also deceptively invites the reader to share in a fantasy of male phallic display and male/female delight that verges on orgasm. When Cleopatra awakes, she instructs Harmachis (who is masquerading as a magician and seer), to amuse her: 'Come show us thy magic, Egyptian.... What canst thou do? Hast thou no new trick?' Harmachis responds by making his ceremonial staff perform a phallic dance in front of the Queen, where it writhes and bends and stands on end, and then turns into a scaled serpent. Next the serpent turns into a seething sea of snakes, that 'crawled, hissed, and knotted themselves in knots'. Harmachis makes a sign and the snakes entwine themselves around his body, so that only his face is visible. 'Is the Queen content with my poor art?', he asks. 'Ay, that am I, Egyptian', she replies. 'Never did I see its like' (110–11).

However, such textual/sexual moments in Haggard's 'male' eastern romances are open to a different but not incompatible line of interrogation which, drawing on the insights offered by Sinfield, Cohen and others, acknowledges the visible heterosexual eroticism of the narrative, but at the same time stresses the homoerotic and homophobic contents which lie, less obviously, in its faultlines and silences.[34] In the gothic novel, the veil necessarily shrouds grotesque evidence of sin, guilt and future trials. To pass through the veil, or to witness its parting, as Harmachis does in *Cleopatra*, could also be seen as a metaphorical act of male self-revelation, no more so when it is enacted in a historical and contemporary location which was commonly associated with same-sex passion, as well as heterosexual love. Notwithstanding its special female significance, the veil (or what Haggard also described as 'the web'), is a permeable boundary, an symbol of confinement and secrecy that is also very penetrable: 'even when opaque it is highly impermanent, while transparency transforms it into a possible entrance or exit.'[35] In this sense, what the metaphor of the veil also allows for is the possibility of 'doubleness', of access to an alternative space, a different sexuality and another self, the queer decadent self. As Showalter puts it, 'there is always a veiled man hiding in fin-de-siècle stories about the veiled woman. She/he reflects the ambiguity and transparency of sexual difference and the sense of guilt, decadence, transgression and sexual anarchy'.[36] In *Cleopatra* the ambiguity of sexual identity is also marked in the many references which are made to the 'youthful beauty' of Harmachis, to his studied disinterest in women, and to his virginity: 'Never to have loved – 'tis strange!' (151). Significantly, perhaps, the unstable boundaries of masculinity in the story are also encoded in the bi-textual nature of the book itself, that is, in the dialogic relationship between its written and visual texts. Here we find that narrative signs of male effeminacy, ambiguous gender and androgyny are translated into, and 'quoted' in, the exotic illustrations which were carried in the early editions.[37]

The possibilities of sexual transgression, including the threat of male 'sexual inversion', I would suggest, were the barely speakable tensions, the 'strange' or 'queer fascinations' which were located at the heart of Haggard's eastern romances. In the case of *Cleopatra*, these discourses of sexuality, both heterosexual and more obliquely perhaps, homosexual, are given extra resonance through their proximity to more easily and directly acknowledged late-Victorian subjects of attraction and repression. The intertwined fates of Harmachis and Cleopatra are played out in an ancient Egypt scarred by war and strife, but more importantly in a land which, within the contemporary imagination, was synonymous with the mysteries of death, religion and the afterlife. Herein also lie the deeper gothic narratives of the text, for the figure of Cleopatra, traditionally an object of literary eroticism, in Haggard's hands becomes not just the object for sexual curiosity and transgressive fantasy, but the subject for an extended essay on necromancy, spirits and terror.

The novel opens in the present with the excavation of an Egyptian tomb and the unrolling of a mummy by an amateur English archaeologist. In fact, this is Harmachis, the author of the story which is about to be told, and which has been preserved on three rolls of ancient papyri. The manner of Harmachis' death, no ordinary one, is made clear from the outset. He has been embalmed, buried alive and cursed. As the body of this ancient man of royal blood is uncovered, it disintegrates into dust. 'Even the Arabs recoiled from it in horror and began to mutter prayers', the 'Editor' notes (7). This opening and defining moment in the text is echoed later in a second unrolling. But in this case we become the witnesses, not of a modern archaeological discovery, but of an act of sacrilege, performed thousands of years ago and with it, the origins of the curse which has struck the perpetrators down. Cleopatra, in search of gold to finance an army against Rome, persuades Harmachis to join her in desecrating the tomb of an old pharaoh. The finding and opening of this tomb, together with the rough stripping of the mummy, gives Haggard the opportunity to revel in the gothic counterpointing of gathering hysteria with scenes of human decay and to dwell at length, along with his readers, on the Egyptian way of death: 'It was naught – naught but the mind that, in such a house of Horror, bodies forth those shadowy forms of fear it dreads to see.' The two, having made their way into the depths of the tomb, find the mummy, ignore the curse on its sarcophagus and unroll the wrappings of the corpse:

We could in no wise loosen this linen, it held so firm on to the body. Therefore, faint with the great heat, choked with mummy dust and the odour of spices, and trembling with fear of our unholy task, wrought in that most lonesome and holy place, we laid the body down, and ripped away the last covering with the knife (186–7).

The terror which accompanies defilement and death in the novel is joined throughout by the fear of the supernatural and the ever-constant threat of divine retribution. Before embarking on his task, the murder and overthrow of the alien Queen, Harmachis is put through an elaborate induction ceremony by the priests of Isis, which also involves his entry into the world of the dead and an audience with the ancient spirits of Egypt:

Nay, I was dying fast, and oh, the horror of it!.... One struggle and the stillness crept into my brain. The terror passed; an unfathomable weight of sleep pressed me down. I was dying, I was dying, and then – nothingness! I was dead! (63).

Throughout the novel, the Gods and ghosts of ancient Egypt observe events and eventually intervene to confront Cleopatra with her treachery and wicked deeds of the past. Finally, in a Faustian-like scene, she is dragged into hell by the spirits of the dead, separated from her *Ka* (or spirit double), screaming in terror, 'passing with that dread company, to her appointed place' (323).[38]

In *Cleopatra*, then, sexuality and death become fixing metonymies for the Orient, for various forms of physical and moral transgression and for oriental Otherness. However, as well as shaping the gothic interiors of the novel, these metonymies also condition an important historicist parable of imperial decline and nemesis which is evident throughout the narrative and which was echoed elsewhere in Haggard's writing. While Haggard's romance fictions, notably his African tales, have often been read and characterised as confidently imperialist, much of it was nevertheless shot through with a deep vein of pessimism and a fear of regression into disorder. 'Out of the soil of barbarism', he wrote, civilisation had 'grown like a tree'. Sooner or later, it would 'fall again, as the Egyptian civilisation fell, as the Hellenic civilisation fell, and as the Roman civilisation and maybe others of which the world has now lost count, fell also'.[39]

In *Cleopatra,* however, and in Haggard's eastern fiction as a whole, this familiar late-nineteenth-century historicism was modified by the expressed conviction that, as one of the seed-beds of civilisation, the ancient Orient contained valuable philosphical and spiritual 'truths' from which modern society with its obsession with crude materialism and progress could and must learn. In a passage which highlights again the internal complexity of Haggard's oriental narratives, he mused on 'the dear land of Khem', bemoaned its fate after the reign of the Ptolomies: 'I see thy mysteries a mockery to the unlearned, and thy wisdom wasted like waters on the desert sands!' All the same, he foresaw an Egyptian renaissance: 'I see Thee once more great, once more free, and having once more a knowledge of thy Gods – ay, thy Gods with a changed countenance, and called by other names, by still thy Gods!' (335). Two decades later, in dedicating the novel *Morning Star* to Wallis Budge, Haggard described the latter as 'one of the world's masters of the language and lore of the great people who in these latter days arise from their holy tombs to instruct us in the secrets of history and faith'.[40] Finally, amidst the reality of imperial conflict and collapse in 1918, Haggard turned his novel *Moon of Israel,* a tale about the Jewish Exodus, into an clarion call for spiritual faith and regeneration. As he instructed his readers:

Behold! Is it not written in this roll? Read, ye who shall find in the days unborn, if your gods have given you skill. Read, O children of the future, and learn the secrets of that past which to you is so far away and yet in truth so near.[41]

IV

Rider Haggard's oriental fictions constitute a distinct but still relatively unexplored dimension of his voluminous work. Yet, as this essay has argued, it was Haggard's interest in the Orient and his 'queer fascination' with the subject, rather than Africa, which was perhaps the most consistent and powerful force behind his writing from the late 1880s onwards. This centrality suggests that, at the very least, we need to make space for Haggard's oriental romances in the revised canon of colonialist writing which is currently being delineated in literary studies. But it also alerts us Haggard's wider cultural importance. In his oriental fictions, which constructed an eastern, other place of history and the imagination, Haggard brought together fin-de-siècle discourses of the Orient and its histories with a tried and tested gothic aesthetic. In so doing, at least in some of these novels, and notably in *Cleopatra*, he took the genre of imperial Gothic into another realm of difference and the unexpected, where fantasies of sexual transgression and and male sexual transformation, images of the supernatural and allegories of individual and collective destiny could be explored, blended and translated back to the late-Victorian imperial centre. Furthermore, Haggard succeeded in producing a form of popular fiction of the Orient which, although like his African tales was recognisably situated with established traditions of historical romance and adventure narratives, nevertheless served to widen the literary franchise of discourses about fin-de-siècle modernity, as well as directly engaging with it. To borrow a phrase from his most distinguished interpreters, Haggard's oriental fiction was the pivot on which 'the ideas and anxieties of the Victorians began to swivel into what came to be called "the modern"'.[42] More particularly, the concern with the self, sexual identity and the pervading psychologism of so many of Haggard's oriental fictions point to the conclusion that they should be viewed as part of, rather than apart from or antithetical to, the extensive endeavour in the arts between the 1880s and 1914 to redefine the vocabulary and territory of the 'New'. All of this, as well as reinforcing Haggard's now widely acknowledged stature and importance as a writer, also underscores the interrogative and ground-breaking potential of late-Victorian imperial Gothic before it assumed different forms in the early twentieth century. Rider Haggard did not move with that transition, but his imperial Gothic narratives of the Orient functioned as a signpost and surely helped to make it possible.

NOTES

1. H. Rider Haggard, *She and Allan*, London 1921, ix.
2. See, for example, Anne McClintock, *Imperial Leather: Race, Gender and Sexuality in the Colonial Context*, London 1995; Elleke Boehmer, *Colonial and Postcolonial Literature: Migrant Metaphors*, Oxford 1995; Laura Chrisman, 'The imperial unconscious? Representations of imperial discourse', in Patrick Williams and Laura Chrisman, eds., *Colonial Discourse and Post-Colonial Theory: A Reader*, Hemel Hempstead 1993, 498–516; Andrea White, 'The shift towards subversion: the case of Rider Haggard', in Andrea White, *Joseph Conrad and the Adventure Tradition*, Cambridge 1993, 82–99; and Terence Rodgers, 'Empires of the imagination: Rider Haggard, popular fiction and Africa', in Mpalive Msiska and Paul Hyland, eds., *Writing and Africa*, London 1997, 103–21.
3. See, for example, Patrick Brantlinger, *Rule of Darkness: British Literature and Imperialism, 1833-1914*, Ithaca 1988; Sandra M. Gilbert and Susan Gubar, *No Man's Land. Vol. 2 • Sexchanges*, New Haven 1989; Mikuláš Teich and Roy Porter, eds., *Fin de Siècle and its Legacy*, Cambridge 1990; Rebecca Stott, *The Fabrication of the Late-Victorian Femme Fatale*, London 1992; Elaine Showalter, *Sexual Anarchy: Gender and Culture at the Fin de Siècle*, London 1992; and Sally Ledger and Scott McCracken, eds., *Cultural Politics at the Fin de Siècle*, Cambridge 1995.
4. Brantlinger, op. cit., 227.
5. ibid., 228. See also Thomas Richards, *The Imperial Archive: Knowledge and the Fantasy of Empire*, London 1993.
6. See Judith Wilt, 'The imperial mouth: imperialism, the Gothic and science fiction', *Journal of Popular Culture*, 14 (Spring 1981), 618–28, and Edward James, *Science Fiction in the Twentieth Century*, Oxford 1994.
7. H. Rider Haggard, *King Solomon's Mines*, London 1907, 'Editor's Note'.
8. See H. Rider Haggard, *She*, Oxford 1991, 273.
9. See Chrisman, op. cit., and McClintock, op. cit.
10. H. Rider Haggard, *She and Allan*, op. cit., ix. Haggard's preoccupation with Egypt and its origins are discussed in detail in his autobiography, written during 1911–12, *The Days of My Life: An Autobiography*, C. J. Longman, ed., London 1926. See also Peter Berresford Ellis, *H. Rider*

Haggard: A Voice from the Infinite, London 1978, and Tom Pocock, *Rider Haggard and the Lost Empire: A Biography*, London 1993.

11. Haggard's pre-war oriental novels comprised: *Cleopatra* (1889), *The World's Desire* (1890), *Pearl Maiden* (1903), *The Brethren* (1904), *The Way of the Spirit* (1906), *Morning Star* (1910), *The Wanderer's Necklace* (1914). Some of his eastern short stories can be found in Peter Haining, ed., *The Best Short Stories of Rider Haggard*, London 1981. For a comprehensive survey, see D. E. Whatmore, *Rider Haggard: A Bibliography*, London 1987.

12. Edward W. Said, *Orientalism: Western Conceptions of the Orient*, London 1991, and *Culture and Imperialism*, London 1994.

13. John M. MacKenzie, *Orientalism: History, Theory and the Arts*, Manchester 1995. See also Nicholas Thomas, *Colonialism's Culture: Anthropology, Travel and Government*, Cambridge 1994.

14. Sir Richard Burton (1821–90) stands out as a significant figure in this orientalist situation. His translation and publication of *The Arabian Nights* in sixteen volumes between 1885–8 was a runaway bestseller, acquiring notoriety for its explicit discussion of Islamic sexual practices, including homosexuality, pederasty and bestiality. The volumes were almost certainly known to Haggard. See Gilbert and Gubar, op. cit., 39, and Frank McLynn, *Burton: Snow Upon the Desert*, London 1990.

15. Quoted in Berresford Ellis, op. cit., 121.

16. Lord Amherst (1835–1909), collector and antiquarian, and Ernest Wallis Budge (1857–1934), Keeper of Egyptian Antiquities at the British Museum and author of *The Mummy* (1894). Other close acquaintances were Sir Gaston Maspero (1846–1916), Director of Antiquities in Cairo, and Howard Carter (1874–1939), Inspector General of Monuments of Upper Egypt.

17. In 1904, for example, during his second visit to Egypt, Haggard wrote a series of special reports on 'Egypt Today' for the *Daily Mail*. For his growing involvement in antiquarian politics, see D. S. Higgins, *Rider Haggard: The Great Storyteller*, London 1981.

18. Quoted in Higgins, ibid., 222.

19. See MacKenzie, op. cit. On Egypt, the fulcrum of fin-de-siècle orientalism, see Peter France, *The Rape of Egypt*, London 1991, and Christopher Frayling, *The Face of Tutankhamun*, London 1992.

20. H. Rider Haggard, *Cleopatra [Being an Account of the Fall and Vengeance of Harmachis, The Royal Egyptian, As Set Forth By His Own Hand]*, London 1889, 'Author's Note', viii. All further references are to this edition and are given in the text.

21. Contrary to much of late-Victorian scholarly opinion, Haggard championed ancient Egypt, rather than Greece, as the true source of classical civilisation. On this important debate, in which Haggard's oriental fiction was deeply implicated, see Martin Bernal, *Black Athena: The Afroasiatic Roots of Classical Civilisation*, London 1991.

22. H. Rider Haggard and Andrew Lang, *The World's Desire*, London 1924, 'Preface to the New Edition', ix.

23. H. Rider Haggard, *The Ancient Allan*, London 1928, 58.

24. H. Rider Haggard, *Morning Star*, London 1912, 'Author's Note', ix.

25. H. Rider Haggard and Andrew Lang, op. cit., 287.

26. Gilbert and Gubar, op. cit., 7; Stott, op. cit., 125.

27. Gilbert and Gubar are reluctant overly to emphasise Haggard's link with the Orient, but some account of this connection is taken in Norman Etherington, ed., *The Annotated She: A Critical Edition of H. Rider Haggard's Victorian Romance*, Bloomington 1991. The oriental nature of Ayesha was underlined in three subsequent novels: *Ayesha: The Return of She, She and Allan* (1921), and *Wisdom's Daughter* (1923).

28. Notably in *Allan Quartermain*, but other striking examples can be found in *Queen Sheba's Ring* (1910), *The Ivory Child* (1916) and *Elissa; Or, The Doom of Zimbabwe* (1917).

29. See Showalter, op. cit., 81-2.

30. Morton Cohen, *Rider Haggard: His Life and Works*, London 1960, 121, and H. Rider Haggard, *The Days of My Life*, Vol. 1, 271. Here Haggard noted sourly that although the novel 'found many friends ... it was a good deal attacked by critics who were angry that, after Shakespeare's play, I should dare to write of Cleopatra' (272).

31. The literary and figurative historiography of Cleopatra is discussed in Lucy Hughes-Hallett, *Cleopatra: Histories, Dreams and Distortions*, London 1990.

32. Harmachis was the Greek name for Horus, god of the rising sun and a symbol of filial responsibility. His best known monument is the famous Sphinx, near the pyramids of Gizeh.

33. Showalter, op. cit., 146.

34. See, for example, Alan Sinfield, *The Wilde Century: Effeminacy, Oscar Wilde and the Queer Movement*, London 1994, and Ed Cohen, *Talk on the Wilde Side: Towards a Genealogy of a Discourse on Male Sexualities*, London 1993.

35. Showalter, op. cit., 148. Haggard echoed this view when he wrote in *The World's Desire*: 'the web was torn, the veil was rent, the labour was lost, the pictured story of loves and wars all undone' (168).

36. Showalter, op. cit., 149.
37. The illustrations, twenty-nine in all, were by Richard Caton Woodville (1856–1927) and Maurice Greiffenhagen (1862–1931), two notable book artists of the day. For a discussion of bi-textuality and Haggard, see Lorraine Janzen Kooistra, *The Artist as Critic: Bi-texuality in Fin-de-Siècle Illustrated Books*, Aldershot 1995.
38. In Egyptian religion, the *Ka* was the life force or 'genius' of the body, the *Cha*.
39. H. Rider Haggard, *Allan Quartermain*, op. cit., 5.
40. H. Rider Haggard, *Morning Star*, op. cit., 'Dedication'.
41. H. Rider Haggard, *Moon of Israel*, London 1918, 2.
42. Gilbert and Gubar, op. cit., 21. Here the comment is used with reference to *She*, but it is even more apposite in relation to Haggard's oriental fiction.

5

Wells's fifth dimension:
The Time Machine at the fin de siècle

Tim Youngs

Like travel writing, science fiction tells us more about the society that produced it than about the world it purports to portray.[1] It is worth pointing out straight away, then, that *The Time Machine* is a sort of travel narrative. 'Time is only a kind of Space',[2] says the traveller, and just as travellers abroad are in effect commenting on their home society, so travellers to the future are in fact reporting on their present-day world. Many critics have acknowledged this. John Huntington, for example, writes of *The Time Machine* that: 'if the novella imagines a future, it does so not as a forecast but as a way of contemplating the structures of our present civilization,'[3] though we should treat Huntington's possessive pronoun circumspectly and not elide the distance between Wells's age and that of the late twentieth century. But Wells was aware of how a more-or-less straightforwardly allegorical use of other domains made narrative journeys illusory ones in the sense that no ideological or cognitive shift may actually have occurred. By contrast, Wells makes his departure from existing shows of narrative certainty quite clear. This he does partly by complicating the framework of the tale and partly by making interpretation doubtful. An examination of how he does so must involve a consideration of how Wells negotiates what one philosopher has described as the 'intimate relation ... between narrative time and physical time',[4] and of Wells's exploitation of the fact that 'any analysis of "other time" is a simultaneous commentary on "our time"'.[5]

First published in 1895,[6] and reflecting many concerns of the fin de siècle, *The Time Machine* is a story which, in its presentation, bears similarities to Conrad's later *Heart of Darkness*: it has a framing narrator and an audience of professional gentlemen,[7] a psychologist, a medical man, a provincial mayor, a doctor, a journalist, and an editor, all of whom, like the narrator, try to make sense of the tale.[8] This structure is, as Darko Suvin has shrewdly noted, common to many of Wells's early science fiction tales, with their outer and inner framework: the stasis of bourgeois Victorian England is threatened by a dangerous novelty, communicated by the protagonist who also moves in the inner narrative, and which the representatives of the well-to-do are reluctant to take seriously.[9] It is significant that these tales of Wells's occur at around the fin de siècle, a period which encourages introspective attempts at comprehension and self-conscious attention to modes of expression.

Wells has the Time Traveller speak about the problems of comprehending and communicating what one has seen (or not seen) on one's journey:

> Conceive the tale of London which a negro, fresh from Central Africa, would take back to his tribe! What would he know of railway companies, of social movements, of telephone and telegraph wires, of the Parcels Delivery Company, and postal orders and the like? Yet we, at least, should be willing enough to explain these things to him! And even of what he knew, how much could he make his untravelled friend either apprehend or believe? Then, think how narrow the gap between a negro and a white man of our own times, and how wide the interval between myself and these of the Golden Age! I was sensible of much which was unseen, and which contributed to my comfort; but save for a general impression of automatic organization, I fear I can convey very little of the difference to your mind (40).

It is evident from this that Wells's mind is on cultural as much as temporal difference. Post-Darwinian thought intertwined the two, so that the 'primitive' state of 'savage' societies was seen as marking the original condition from which the 'civilised' West had progressed. The Time Traveller's remarks disrupt established ideas about this linear progression in two ways, however. First, the image of a bemused African visiting a strange London reverses the direction of movement common in travel writing of the time (implying also the recognition of a different perspective). Second, the statement that there is little difference between an African and a white person at that point in time challenges the predominant scientific views then current. The effect of the comparison is to suggest the transience of the readers' material existence (a common motif of fin-de-siècle literature). The technological accomplishments and social organisation they take for granted are suddenly seen from another perspective, one which destabilises them.

The Time Traveller's demeanour reflects his difficulty in expressing his experiences. The narrator speaks of him 'as it were feeling his way among his words' (17), a suitable image for the cautious linguistic exploration that is a feature of *The Time Machine*. It is almost as if the effort invested in understanding and articulation becomes a safety-valve for the enervating struggle against the environment. The description also makes a connection between spatial and verbal voyaging. Since the verbal must here involve the textual too, then the metaphor of travel requires us to analyse the narrative structures by which the various juxtapositions are achieved: that is to say, the means by which temporal and physical movements are established. For this, we might turn to Bakhtin's idea of the 'chronotope', which he uses to refer to the artistic expression of the inherent connectedness of temporal and spatial relationships, with time thickening and becoming artistically visible, and space responding to the movements of time, plot and history.[10]

The Traveller's account of the process of time travel may be compared with the act of writing. His description of what he sees oscillates between natural and social markers of time:

> I saw trees growing and changing like puffs of vapour, now brown, now green; they grew, spread, shivered, and passed away. I saw huge buildings rise up faint and fair, and pass like dreams. The whole surface of the earth seemed changed – melting and flowing under my eyes. The little hands upon the dials that registered my speed raced round faster and faster. Presently I noted that the sun belt swayed up and down, from solstice to solstice, in a minute or less, and that consequently my pace was over a year a minute; and minute by minute the white snow flashed across the world, and vanished, and was followed by the bright, brief green of spring (21).

Within this passage we have three kinds of time: that of the natural world, that of the social world, and that of the traveller; besides which, there is the time scale of the narrative itself. We are told by the Traveller near the beginning of the tale that 'I've lived eight days … such days as no human being ever lived before!' (19). The Traveller's observations introduce the theme of a dialectic between natural and social time. With his ability to slip in and out of 'our' own time (though even this term is complicated once Wells's story survives its contemporary context and is read by audiences from later and other societies), and with his observation of time as process as the earth's surface melts and flows, he tries to achieve a synthesis.

Wells has the Traveller tell his audience that 'there is no difference between Time and any of the three dimensions of Space except that our consciousness moves along it' (8). The use of narrative method to demonstrate the problems of distinction and relativity has affinities with what the sociologist Norbert Elias writes of as the fifth dimension. Elias ascribes to this the standpoint of the observer who not only looks on at the four dimensions but who is able to perceive:

the symbolic character of the four dimensions as means of orientation for human beings – human beings who are capable of synthesis and so are in a position to have present at the same time in their imagination what takes place successively and so never exists simultaneously.[11]

For Elias, this idea of synthesis remedies also the false distinction made between the natural and the social. Elias has in mind here the fact that time has both a visible aspect in the natural, physical world (the passing of the seasons, for example) and a symbolic aspect in society, of greater diversity and extensiveness in more complex societies (as he so terms them). Suggesting a model of 'people who can observe and investigate from different storeys and so from different perspectives' (i.e. who can appreciate the symbolic character of the four dimensions), he declares that:

time, which on the preceding step was recognizable only as a dimension of nature, becomes recognizable, now that society is included in the field of view as a subject of knowledge, as a human-made symbol and, moreover, a symbol with high object-adequacy.[12]

Elias's analysis may not satisfactorily resolve the matter of whether or how exactly one can clamber up the extra storeys, akin to the difficulty of stepping outside a particular ideology in order to critique it, but that is beside the point, for what is important here is the effort to discern the symbolic nature of the four dimensions. Surprisingly, Elias makes hardly any reference to literature, and so I shall wilfully take 'storey' to be a typographical error (which, unfortunately, it isn't) and assume instead that he meant to write 'story', for it seems to me that his model of such a vantage point is better applied this way. We can thus say that the Time Traveller's movement through the fourth dimension is observed and investigated by Wells, who uses his story to inspect, from this fifth dimension, the symbolic construction of time in relation to physical, 'natural' time. Wells demonstrates the impossibility of achieving an easy synthesis: much of the latter part of his text is taken up with a kind of dialectic between nature and society, and he deliberately avoids a neat closure of the tale.

Wells, using his traveller's voyages through time, takes existing conditions and tendencies in the city and projects them forward within Darwinist and quasi-Marxist terms and framed in fin-de-siècle mood and imagery. As with many 1890s texts, confidence in domestic society and imperial activity is undermined. Discourses on the primitive and the savage have a vital role in performing this function. When the traveller first arrives in the future, he objectifies himself in a way that recalls contemporary discourses on race. Wondering what changes may have happened to humanity, he asks himself:

> What if in this interval the race had lost its manliness, and had developed into something inhuman, unsympathetic, and overwhelmingly powerful? I might seem some old-world savage animal, only the more dreadful and disgusting for our common likeness – a foul creature to be incontinently slain (23).

Here, the Traveller finds himself potentially in the position of the 'savage', a possible reversal that underlines the fragile basis of any current boasts of superiority. But it is noteworthy that, while assumptions of racial hierarchies are unsettled, gender values are not. 'Manliness' is associated with vigour and is proposed as the vital quality of humankind. The effete Eloi, the 'pretty little people' with their 'child-like ease', their lack of facial hair and their 'Dresden-china type of prettiness' (25), may be superficially attractive,[13] but when the Traveller realises they think he had come from the sun in a thunderstorm (betraying a level of ignorance and superstition commonly attributed to 'primitives'), then the situation becomes more disturbing as they appear to be 'on the intellectual level of one of our five-year-old children' (26). The cause of the shock is the reversal of linear time, in the sense of progress, which it seems to mark. In the Traveller's attempts to account for this situation Wells reflects on the problems of interpretation, and it is in this respect that the narrative is written from, so to speak, the fifth dimension.

The Traveller describes how, 'in costume, and in all the differences of texture and bearing that now mark off the sexes from each other, these people of the future were alike. And the children seemed to my eyes to be but the miniatures of their parents' (30). He notices the apparent absence of 'the single house, and possibly even the household' (29), and deduces that he is witnessing a communistic, more easeful, balanced and secure society. But Wells has the Traveller throw us off balance immediately afterwards by having him admit that he has since had to revise this speculation as he realised 'how far it fell short of the reality' (30). A kind of temporal dialectic is thus set up. We have to absorb the Traveller's 'present' words, knowing that they will be modified by events to which we have to look forward.

Furthermore, what the Traveller describes would indicate, to many of Wells's readers, not progress but regression. It would have been widely known that to many social theorists, notably Herbert Spencer, the specialisation of function whose loss the Traveller celebrates actually constituted the very fact of progress. Spencer had asserted in an essay first published in the *Westminster*

Review in April 1857 that progress in humanity was marked not only by increased differentiation of the 'civilised' races from the 'savage', but by greater heterogeneity within the 'civilised': 'the transformation of the homogeneous into the heterogeneous, is that in which Progress essentially consists', he wrote.[14] There is bound to be some confusion in most readers' minds, then, as there is in the Traveller's, as to whether society has moved backward or forward. This uncertainty is created not just by the Elois' physical features but by their language, of which the Traveller has this to say: 'Either I missed some subtle point, or their language was excessively simple – almost exclusively composed of concrete substantives and verbs. There seemed to be few, if any, abstract terms, or little use of figurative language. Their sentences were usually simple and of two words' (39). From this bare description it would be obvious, even to those who knew nothing of evolutionary theory, that such linguistic simplicity hardly heralds a great advance in cultural development, but for those acquainted with evolutionary ideas, the connotations would be clearer still. This is what Spencer wrote of the identification of language with racial development:

> that language can be traced down to a form in which nouns and verbs are its only elements, is an established fact. In the gradual multiplication of parts of speech out of these primary ones – in the differentiation of verbs into active and passive, of nouns into abstract and concrete – in the rise of distinctions of mood, tense, person, of number and case – in the formation of auxiliary verbs, of adjectives, adverbs, pronouns, prepositions, articles – in the divergence of those orders, genera, species, and varieties of parts of speech by which civilised races express minute modifications of meaning – we see a change from the homogeneous to the heterogeneous. And it may be remarked ... that ... in virtue of having carried this subdivision of function to a greater extent and completeness, that the English language is superior to all others.[15]

Evidently, Spencer's robust confidence in this route of progress is challenged by the condition of the Eloi as Wells forces his readers to confront the possibility of degeneration.[16] The Traveller's fluent relation of his narrative encloses the apparent linguistic deficiencies of the Eloi just as other travellers' narratives contained the so-called primitive utterances of 'savages'. The cultural and temporal confusion in Wells's text is caused by the fact that these inarticulate simpletons, rather than being the readers' forebears, are their descendants.

Through the Traveller's successive modifications of interpretation, as he veers between biological and sociological explanations of what he sees, Wells rejects any one fixed line. Indeed, he frequently exhibits a romantic belief in individuality that cuts against his emphasis on science, for the former involves a rejection of classification and compartmentalisation. For Wells, that which cannot be pinned down is as crucial as that which can:

> Every species is vague, every term goes cloudy at its edges; and so, in my way of thinking, relentless logic is only another name for stupidity – for a sort of intellectual pigheadedness.... Every species waggles about in its definition, every tool is a little loose in its handle, every scale has its individual error.[17]

It is no coincidence, given Wells's domestic circumstances at the time he composed *The Time Machine*,[18] that for his male protagonist the waggling should be performed by Weena, a young woman. The emotional affirmation brought to the tale by Weena is clearly meant to transcend the material changes that occur to her world and to ours, so that, against the Traveller's sight of the desolate beach devoid of humanity later in the future, she comes to symbolise the human against non-human nature.

When the Traveller saves Weena from drowning he is rewarded by her gift of a garland of flowers. As he recalls this episode and its aftermath, the Traveller interrupts himself to declare: 'But my story slips away from me as I speak of her' (43), a statement which interestingly, if unconsciously, attests to the destabilising effects of gender. Furthermore, when he later recounts another episode and remembers that Weena had placed some flowers in his pocket, not only does he break off his narrative but the framing narrator actually comes back into the story for a rare moment: 'The Time Traveller paused, put his hand into his pocket, and silently placed two withered flowers, not unlike very large white mallows, upon the little table. Then he resumed his narrative' (56). The female presence introduces an emotional quality which, although sought after by the narrator as a sign of humanity, is nonetheless dismissed at will as a disruption to rationality and purpose. The Traveller's intention of bringing back Weena to his present world (59) is thwarted by her disappearance and probable death, though we must doubt whether his intention would have been realised in any case.

When the Traveller later catches sight of a Morlock, one of the creatures that have probably caused Weena's death, and which seem like white apes or human spiders (45),[19] he has to modify his social Darwinist reading to account for them:

gradually, the truth dawned on me: that Man had not remained one species, but had differentiated into two distinct animals: that my graceful children of the Upper-world were not the sole descendants of our generation, but that this bleached, obscene, nocturnal Thing, which had flashed before me, was also heir to all the ages (45).

This new interpretation has the Traveller thinking too of the economic environment which can have led to this development, as he considers both the physical and social factors that may have resulted in the emergence of this second, subterranean species; however, he prefaces this reading by warning that 'I very soon felt that it fell far short of the truth' (46). The Traveller posits that the Morlocks toil underground for the benefit of the Eloi. He bases his interpretation on a projection from the current state of things: 'proceeding from the problems of our own age, it seemed as clear as daylight to me that the gradual widening of the present merely temporary and social difference between the Capitalist and the Labourer was the key to the whole position' (46–7). He has in mind the present 'tendency to utilize underground space for the less ornamental purposes of civilization' (47). He lists as examples the Metropolitan Railway in London, the new electric railways, subways, and underground workrooms and restaurants, which 'increase and multiply' (ibid.), almost as if they were a species themselves. And we might add (while we still have a memory of them) the miners who toiled underground to supply society's energy needs.[20] But despite asserting of his explanation that 'I still think it is the most plausible one' (48), it is not long before he recants and feels 'pretty sure now that my second hypothesis was all wrong' (54).

After voyaging much further into the future and witnessing what seems to be the dying of the planet in scenes which (as in *Heart of Darkness*) displace all the social concerns of the text into an ultimately physical end, the Traveller returns to the present. The guests are all sceptical. The only person who seems to have an open mind on what he has heard is the anonymous narrator, who, in the Epilogue, speculates on whether the Traveller has ventured into the future or into the past and wonders what he has found there. The two men had different views on the future for humanity, and the narrator says: 'I, for my part, cannot think that these latter days of weak experiment, fragmentary theory, and mutual discord are indeed man's culminating time!' (83), while he knows the Traveller to have 'thought but cheerlessly of the Advancement of Mankind', and to have seen 'in the growing pile of civilization only a foolish heaping that must inevitably fall back upon and destroy its makers in the end' (ibid.). The narrator is comforted by the fact that Weena's flowers are proof that 'even when mind and strength had gone, gratitude and a mutual tenderness still lived in the heart of man' (ibid.), but some may feel that this instinctive, almost mindless gesture is small consolation for all that has been lost.

We see the competing strains in the genre of the scientific romance as the Traveller has set off armed with a camera (he wished earlier that he had taken a Kodak) and determined to collect and bring back some specimens as proof of his tale. His promised half-hour trip has so far taken three years. The narrator tells us of his inability to reach a conclusion, a failure that is due not just to the Traveller's relation of his experiences, but more broadly to the interpretative uncertainties of the fin de siècle. Suvin rightly suggests that Wells often shifts in his science fiction from economic analyses to a reactionary and fatalistic acceptance of biological determinism, transferring the social-Darwinist model from society to biology.[21] There is no doubt either, as Bernard Bergonzi has noted, that the 'Traveller's gradual identification with the beautiful and aristocratic – if decadent Eloi – against the brutish Morlocks is indicative of Wells's own attitudes'.[22] The contradictions and ambivalence in these alignments should not be seen simply as Wells's own, but as thoroughly symptomatic of the fin de siècle, a time at which one looks both forward and backward and tries to construct a conceptual system and form of expression that will allow both vantage points. It is incumbent upon us at our own fin de siècle, with our continued neglect of the so-called underclass and our own evasion of social determinism in favour of genetic predisposition, to rewrite the economic factor into our criticism of *The Time Machine* and of other texts, the better to appreciate the embeddedness of the material in cultural forms.

NOTES

1.   For more on this view of travel writing see, for example, the introduction and conclusion to Tim Youngs, *Travellers in Africa: British Travelogues, 1850–1900*, Manchester 1994.

2.   H. G. Wells, 'The Time Machine', in *Selected Short Stories*, Harmondsworth 1958, 9. Further page references are to this edition and will be given in the text.

3.   John Huntington, *The Logic of Fantasy: H. G. Wells and Science Fiction*, New York 1982, 41.

4.   Bastiaan C. van Fraassen, 'Time in physical and narrative structure', in John Bender and David E. Wellbery, eds., *Chronotypes: The Construction of Time*, Stanford 1991, 24.

5.   Barbara Adam, *Timewatch: The Social Analysis of Time*, Cambridge 1995, 31.

6.   The story was first serialised in *The New Review* in five instalments between January and May 1895, and was published in book form by Heinemann in May of that year. The blueprint for *The Time Machine* was 'The Chronic Argonauts', a tale by Wells which appeared in three parts in the *Science Schools Journal* in 1888. The version of *The Time Machine* serialised in *The New Review* was itself a rewrite of the 'Time Traveller' articles which had appeared in the *National Observer* and which were in turn based on *The Chronic Argonauts*. In all, the latter tale was rewritten six times and printed in different forms four times. See, for example, Lovat Dickson, *H. G. Wells: His Turbulent Life and Times*, London 1971, 62-3, and David Lake, 'The current texts of Wells's early SF novels: situation unsatisfactory', *The Wellsian*, 11 (1988), 3-12 (esp. 3-6). Lake finds the Penguin *Selected Short Stories* printing of *The Time Machine* to include several misprints, but none of those he lists affects my argument in this essay.

7.   Elaine Showalter has described quest romances such as *The Time Machine* as allegorised journeys into the male self. Elaine Showalter, 'The apocalyptic fables of H. G. Wells', in John Stokes, ed., *Fin de Siècle/Fin du Globe: Fears and Fantasies of the Late Nineteenth Century*, Basingstoke 1992, 73. Of all the texts I have taught, *The Time Machine* is the one that women students have found most alienating.

8.   Chris Baldick speculates that it 'seems quite possible' that Conrad, who had read *The Time Machine* in the mid-1890s, 'lifted' the narrative frame of *Heart of Darkness* from Wells's story. Chris Baldick, *In Frankenstein's Shadow: Myth, Monstrosity, and Nineteenth-Century Writing*, Oxford 1987, 163.

9.   See Darko Suvin, 'Wells as the turning point of the SF tradition', in Bernard Waites, Tony Bennett, and Graham Martin, eds., *Popular Culture: Past and Present*, Kent 1982, 122-32. The essay is taken from Suvin's *Metamorphoses of Science Fiction*, New Haven 1979.

10.   M. M. Bakhtin, trans. M. Holquist and C. Emerson, 'Forms of time and of the chronotope in the novel', in Michael Holquist, ed., *The Dialogic Imagination: Four Essays by Mikhail Bakhtin*, Austin 1981, 84.

11.   Norbert Elias, trans. E. Jephcott, *Time: An Essay*, Oxford 1993, 36.

12.   ibid.

13.   Showalter observes that the Eloi seem 'hyperfeminised' and the Morlocks 'hypermasculinised': Showalter, op. cit., 75-6.

14.   Herbert Spencer, 'Progress: Its Law and Cause', in *Essays on Education and Kindred Subjects*, London 1911, 154.

15.   ibid., 164-5.

16. A number of critics have dwelt on the influence upon Wells of T. H. Huxley's 1893 Romanes lecture, 'Evolution and Ethics'. Claiming that 'the central tenets of Wells's philosophy are contained in this lecture', Krishan Kumar points to Huxley's insistence that the 'evolutionary process was blind, arbitrary and frequently hideously cruel. There was no discernible purpose in evolution, and nothing to justify a belief in progress': Krishan Kumar, *Utopia and Anti-Utopia in Modern Times*, Oxford 1987, 176-7. Wells studied under Huxley at the Normal School of Science from 1884-5.

17. H. G. Wells, *First and Last Things: A Confession of Faith and Rule of Life*, London 1929, 16. This work was first published in 1908.

18. In 1892 he had become attracted to one of his students, Amy Catherine Robbins ('Jane'), for whom he left his wife, his cousin Isabel, in Spring 1894. He divorced Isabel in January 1895 and married 'Jane' in October of the same year. See (among many other accounts) the chronology of Wells's life in John Batchelor, *H. G. Wells*, Cambridge 1985, 164-5. Elaine Showalter also notes the significance of these dates but seems to look for a more direct expression of Wells's break with his first wife. See Showalter, op. cit., 72.

19. For more on this type of imagery, see my essay 'White apes at the fin de siècle', in Tim Youngs, ed., *Writing and Race*, Longman 1997, forthcoming.

20. In the minds of some at least of Wells's readers would have been the bloody events at Featherstone in the summer of 1893, when the Riot Act was read against striking miners. Two innocent bystanders were killed and sixteen injured by shots fired by soldiers. The Government appointed a commission of inquiry after the coroner's jury had returned a verdict which implied censure of local magistrates. See B. Lewis, *Coal Mining in the Eighteenth and Nineteenth Centuries*, London 1971, 116-17.

21. Suvin, op. cit., 129.

22. Bernard Bergonzi, *The Early H. G. Wells: A Study of the Scientific Romances*, Manchester 1961, 56. One might say that this anticipates Tony Blair's 'New Labour' by a century.

6

'Kaiser or King?' Edwardian defence paranoia and juvenile literature, 1897–1914

Michael Paris

By the end of the nineteenth century the British were obsessed with what they saw as the problem of national and imperial security. Periodic concern about national defence had first become evident in the mid-1850s, when French developments in naval technology were believed to pose a major challenge to the supremacy of the Royal Navy. The threat of steel and steam, combined with the perceived imperial ambitions of another Napoleon, were sufficient to create widespread fear that disaster was imminent. Not since the invasion scares of the early years of the century had the British people been so obsessed with the defence of the realm. On this occasion, however, the French menace soon passed, but over the next twenty years a number of other developments ensured that national defence remained a vital issue. The rapid growth of the British Empire in the last quarter of the century inevitably created strategic problems and, in particular, focused attention on the question of how a small, professional army could defend not only the homeland against the threat of invasion, but also the vast new territories against the possibility of insurrection, or the ambitions of the other imperial Powers. The creation of the German Empire in 1871 was initially welcomed by the British as a counter to French domination of mainland Europe, but the very rapid and decisive success of Prussian arms in the wars of unification forced the British to re-consider their own military capabilities and to initiate limited reforms. However, as German expansionist aims became evident, and the Reich subsequently embarked on the construction of a high seas battle fleet, the British perceived yet another major challenge to their national security.[1] Anxiety over defence issues reached a climax during the Anglo-Boer War of 1899–1902, when British military failure combined with almost universal hostility from the other Powers and produced a deep sense of public unease. If the combined military might of Britain and the white dominions was incapable of subduing a handful of untrained farmers, how would the nation fare in a real war against a well-equipped and highly-trained European army? It was a frightening prospect. By the turn of the century, then, the British had become obsessed with national security: a dark paranoid fear that nation and empire were dangerously at risk.

These anxieties were not restricted to polite discussions by the political and military elites about military reform, the possibility of invasion or the size and quality of the Royal Navy, but become a matter of general public concern. What amounted to paranoia was manifested in a variety of ways: in the increasing body of public opinion that favoured some form of compulsory military service, in a demand for an official investigation into the possibility of a foreign invasion, through the formation of pressure groups campaigning for ever greater military expenditure, in the hysterical reactions of the press to the diplomatic doings of the Great Powers, and in an extensive body of popular fiction which attempted to show just how the nation was at risk, and the potentially disastrous consequences of turning a blind eye to such dangers. I. F. Clarke, in his pioneering study, *Voices Prophesying War*, has clearly demonstrated how such fictions emerged with Sir George Chesney's story 'The Battle of Dorking' (published in 1871), and how these tales of future war became an established and popular sub-genre in the years before 1914.[2] But such dire prophecies did more than simply excite and entertain the reader, for they both reflected public concern and further fuelled the sense of impending catastrophe. The anxiety and vicarious excitement generated by these fictions was so powerful that during the first decade of the new century the same ideas were even being reflected in the popular stories and novels aimed at young Britons aged between ten and eighteen years: the future defenders of the nation.

From the early 1880s, war had become both an acceptable and popular subject for the writers of juvenile fiction. By the late 1890s, George Alfred Henty and the aggressively militaristic authors who followed his example had, with their jingoistic tales of Victoria's warrior-heroes and their 'little' wars of empire, already partially eclipsed the earlier writers of straightforward adventure stories.[3] Now, at the beginning of the new century, they were themselves to some extent overtaken by writers who took as their theme the great war of the future – the war that would ensure the survival or annihilation of the British race. Like Henty, these authors saw their role as not simply providing thrilling entertainment, but as moulding the nation's youth, pointing out the dangers faced by the 'Island Race', and preparing boys and young men to play a major role in the defence of the empire. Thus Henty's glorification of war was combined with contemporary anxieties about the great struggle to come. And perhaps, more than any other single influence, it was the paranoia and commercial acumen of Alfred Harmsworth, later Lord Northcliffe, that helped to establish the theme of future war as a major ingredient of juvenile fiction.

It was Harmsworth who in the mid-1890s created a new, more sensational style of juvenile story papers. Between 1895 and 1903 he established a number of these, aimed specifically at boys and young men – *The Boys' Friend*, *The Boys' Realm*, *The Boys' Herald*, and so on. His stated purpose was to counter the malign influence of the long-established 'penny dreadfuls'. Cheaply-priced, with lurid cover illustrations, and packed with thrilling tales, he certainly succeeded in his aim; as A. A. Milne later pointed out, Harmsworth did in fact kill off the penny dreadful with the 'half-penny dreadfuller'.[4] But the publisher also intended that his papers would encourage 'physical strength, patriotism, interest in travel and exploration and pride in the empire among the younger generation.' They probably did, but in the process he visited his own xeno-phobia and paranoia on his readers. Harmsworth had a deep-seated distrust of foreigners, which after 1904 centred on the German Empire. From that point onwards, he became increasingly convinced that Germany was planning war or fermenting trouble within the empire. Every foreign policy initiative of the Second Reich was examined for its implications for British well-being, and every technological development was anxiously scrutinised for its warlike application, and for how it might undermine national and imperial security.[5]

A case in point was the invention of the aeroplane, and the subsequent first Channel crossing by air by the Frenchman Louis Bleriot in the summer of 1909. Harmsworth categorically refused to see aviation as evidence of human progress or as a major triumph in the development of communications, seeing instead only the potential of the flying machine as a weapon of war. What he found especially worrying was the implication that here was a machine that at one stroke undermined the supremacy of the Royal Navy – Britain's main defence against the threat of invasion. 'BRITAIN NO LONGER AN ISLAND', screamed the headline in the *Daily Mail*, and a number of specially-commis-sioned articles pointed out the fact that the Channel and the Fleet were no longer sufficient to safeguard British shores: an enemy airfleet would simply pass over them and strike deep inland at the heart of the nation.[6] Harmsworth's own fears, then, were clearly reflected in the editorial policies of his papers, and in the stories commissioned for his boys' papers. Their considerable success with juvenile readers spawned an almost endless stream of imitations in other papers, and later in the novels of more respected authors.

During the 1890s, the Harmsworth juveniles had relied on stories set during the imperial wars in Afghanistan, the Sudan and in Africa; exciting stories of 'plucky' young Englishmen building and holding an empire. By the end of the decade, however, the tale of the great war to come had to a large extent supplanted these tales of historical adventure. Typical of this new type of story was Hamilton Edwards' 'Britain in Arms', serialised in the *Boys' Friend* in 1897, and introduced by the editor as 'the story of how Great Britain fought the World in 1899 showing what Britons can do for their Queen and Country in the hour of need'.[7] In this story, it is the French and Russians who combine to bring down the British Empire. However, their invasion fleet is routed and Lord Roberts, Britain's most famous living soldier – and a figure often featured in such stories – leads the army against the French invaders, who are taught a lesson they will 'not soon forget'. Here the Harmsworth Press was expressing its concern at the recent Franco-Russian Alliance and the increasing imperial tensions between the Britain and France. Even in 1900, while public attention was mainly focused on the war in South Africa, the *Boys' Friend* still continued to publish articles such as 'What Will Happen in the Next Great War?'. This piece suggested that sooner or later Britain would be forced into a war with the French in order to safeguard the empire.[8] The Francophobia of the Harmsworth Press continued well into 1903, and ended with a splendid series of stories featuring 'Captain Strange' – a modern-day privateer who waged an unceasing private war against the French in the 'English' Channel. In the last story of the series, Strange foiled a French invasion of Gibraltar and thus prevented the enemy gaining control of the Mediterranean.[9] But the period 1904–5 saw an end to the tales of future war against France, for in the light of the 'Entente' of 1904 and improved Anglo-French relations, Harmsworth authors were now increasingly encouraged to portray Germany as the real enemy.

Fears of a possible German invasion of the British Isles had been expressed as early as 1903 in a *Boys' Realm* serial, 'A World at Stake'. This story related how German spies stole the latest designs for a British military airship, mass-produced the machines, and used them to carry an invading army across the Channel.[10] Quite why the Germans would want a British design when they had their own very successful Zeppelin machines is not explained. But the airship and aeroplane were indeed machines to capture the imagination of any boy, and between 1903 and 1914 they became an almost standard ingredient in the German invasion serials of the Harmsworth Press. Interestingly, it was also Harmsworth's *Daily Mail* that was instrumental in exploiting the so-called 'Zeppelin panics' which regularly occurred from about 1908 onwards, and which convinced gullible sections of the public that German airships were indeed hovering over British cities, mapping ports, arsenals, invasion routes and generally preparing for the great war to come.[11]

In the juvenile papers, the most spectacular of these stories came in 1912 in the serial 'War in the Clouds', published in the *Dreadnought*. Here, a German airborne invasion is helped along by devastating bombing raids on British cities which create panic among the citizens and disrupt communications. Shocking behaviour, indeed, as it directly contravened the Hague Peace Convention agreement of 1899, which prohibited the aerial bombardment of undefended cities. But, of course, such behaviour was typical of the barbaric German military. However, such calculated terror and the quite deliberate flaunting of the accepted rules of war also shocked some sections of German society, for the author tells us: 'German socialists and others could not believe that their government would unleash anything as diabolical as an attack on a defenceless city by air. But they had not reckoned on the German military party.'[12] After a hard-fought campaign that rages through the English countryside, the Germans are finally defeated and the British turn their attention to discover how such a disaster could have befallen them. The blame, of course, is firmly laid at the door of the British political establishment, particularly a weak Liberal government which had failed to provide the nation with an adequate means of national defence: 'What furious indignation there was in Britain against politicians who had failed to arm Britain with an efficient aerial navy.'[13] Harmsworth's sentiments exactly!

There is little doubt that these stories were intended to focus attention on what was believed to be Britain's precarious position in relation to the other Powers, and the government's allegedly feeble defence preparations. The editor's preface to 'War in the Clouds' leaves no doubt as to the purpose of the serial: 'This is no wild, impossible, and fantastic story.... "The War in the Clouds" teaches a great national lesson, conveys a grave warning, for the happenings chronicled here could easily occur and shatter for all time the hopes of the British Race....'[14]

In the last few years of peace, the juvenile papers published an enormous number of such stories. The titles are indicative of their subject matter – 'Kaiser or King?', 'The Invasion that Failed', 'Scourge of the Skies', and 'Legions of the Kaiser or the Mailed Fist'. The last, a serial of 1914, was indeed an interesting variation, for here we have a German invasion of Ireland. With Belfast in ruins and Dublin under siege, both loyalists and nationalists forget their political differences in order to unite with English troops and drive out the invader.[15]

These stories and serials all followed much the same formula: the British armed forces, starved of funds by shortsighted politicians, face an aggressive and expansionist German Empire ruthlessly pursuing her ambition to usurp Britain's premier position in the imperial league table; fantastic new weapons, and defeat narrowly averted by the courage and sacrifice of heroic young Britons ably led by an outstanding military commander – a role frequently filled by Lord Roberts, Britain's most famous living soldier and a leading spokesman for the conscription lobby.

But, according to the Harmsworth propagandists, it was not only the homeland that was in immediate danger, for the empire was equally at risk. 'The Fight for Empire', a *Boys' Realm* serial of 1903–4, is exemplary in this respect. In this adventure of heroic deeds, German agents incite another Mutiny in India – a rebellion that will rob Britain of her 'Jewel of Empire' and allow new masters to take control of the sub-continent.[16] And even when the Germans were not invading England or inciting rebellion throughout the empire, they were doing all manner of nasty things to undermine or embarrass the British. For example, after 1905 most of the really unpleasant villains in the public school or sporting serials were German. The 1911 tale by Norman Greaves, 'Flying to Victory', is a typical example. The hero of the story is a young British airman taking part in air races and flying exhibitions throughout Europe. However, before almost every race or demonstration, his machine is sabotaged by a German rival who cannot defeat the 'plucky English lad' fairly and must resort to underhand methods. The same German 'dirty tricks' are tried on the *Boys' Realm* hero, 'Dan the Airman'. Throughout the decade, young British sportsmen have to be constantly on guard against their 'unsporting' German opponents, while the ace detective Sexton Blake was continually unmasking German spies and sinister plots intended to weaken the nation.[17] Such stories reflected and reinforced contemporary Germanophobia. As Robert Roberts, growing up in Salford in the decade before 1914, later noted:

> Spy stories abounded. Germans who came here to "work", we were assured, could be spotted by a special button worn in the lapel. Each man had, we believed, sworn to serve Germany as a secret agent. With this, and innumerable myths of the same sort, the seeds of suspicion and hatred were sown....[18]

Clearly, then, young Britons exposed to a constant diet of such fictions could hardly fail to absorb the idea that the nation was poised on the brink of a great disaster, that Germany posed the single, most important challenge to the future security and well-being of the empire, and that a major war was inevitable.

The circulation of the Harmsworth juveniles was considerable – average weekly sales were in the region of 150,000 copies for each issue, and the total readership was probably far greater, for copies were loaned, swapped and traded and thus reached a much wider audience. The publishers believed that they were not simply providing exciting entertainment, but also performing a public service by drawing attention to the dangers faced by the nation and preparing young men for the time of trial that lay ahead. As the editor of the *Boys' Friend* smugly pointed out, shortly after the outbreak of war in 1914:

> For many years war serials have figured strongly in the *Boys' Friend* programme. For many years, through the medium of these serials, we have

spoken the words 'be prepared'. For that we have been condemned by many people.... But now as I sit at my desk, the grim day has come....[19]

The popularity and influence of these stories was such that by 1912 even the highly-respected authors of juvenile novels were beginning to reflect such themes; we find concern over defence issues and the idea of the great war to come in the fictions of Captain F. S. Brereton, Herbert Strang, Percy Westerman and Captain Charles Gilson. These authors had begun their literary careers with tales of high adventure and imperial warfare that took Henty's work as their model. Yet between 1911 and 1914 they increasingly began to reflect the paranoia over national security. Captain Brereton, for example, produced two novels, *The Great Aeroplane* and *The Great Airship*, both of which told of the invention of British superweapons which, despite numerous attempts by German agents to gain their secrets, were added to the nation's arsenal ready for the day when they will be needed to repel the invaders. In the first story, the marvellous flying machine, known as the 'Essex Ghost', takes part in a series of adventures across the world and is then hidden away at its base where: 'the crew ... guard the secrets of the "Essex Ghost" most thoroughly. They keep them, as it were, in trust for the nation, lest a time should come when England shall be glad of such a vessel.'[20]

Herbert Strang went even further. In *The Air Scout*, a novel of 1912, the author relates how the Chinese, encouraged of course by agents of the Kaiser, attempt to create a Pacific Empire and invade Australia. Only the ingenuity and daring of two plucky colonial lads using their Father's aeroplane delay the Chinese advance until a relief force arrives. Strang's intentions are made abundantly clear for, as he notes in the preface:

The ensuing story will have served its purpose if it succeeds in directing the thoughts of the boys of the present day, who will be called upon to fight our battles tomorrow, to the need for closing our ranks, to the benefits of training and co-operation, and to the unity of heart and mind which alone will preserve the goodly heritage our fathers have left us.[21]

The following year, Strang published a similar tale dealing with a Mongolian invasion of India. The sub-continent is almost lost, and only the costly sacrifice of British troops saves the day. However, the author pursues a familiar theme when he places the real blame on the British government who have risked the empire through their failure to provide adequate defence. In a preface, the author urges the authorities to increase defence expenditure and to develop and make use of the new weaponry that science has made available. Both novels were thoroughly endorsed by Lord Roberts, who wrote of *The Air Scout*, 'Your forecast is so good that I can only hope the future may not bring to Australia such a struggle as the one you so graphically describe'.[22]

Although these stories were written throughout the twenty or so years before 1914 and came from many pens, we can identify a number of common characteristics: the inevitability of war; an energetic and aggressive enemy poised to attack the homeland or create rebellion within the empire; complacency at home and a weak government unwilling to provide a military budget sufficient to ensure adequate national defence, and a refusal by the establishment to even consider the new weapons that science had made available – weapons which the 'enemy' will not hesitate to develop and use. Victory is eventually achieved, but only because of the daring, the ingenuity and the sacrifice of young Britons, under the command of a wise and heroic figure. And here, to lend authenticity to the fiction, real figures were often employed in this role – Lord Roberts, General Redvers Buller, or the airmen Claude Grahame-White and Gustav Hamel, for example.

The sheer quantity of such fictions and their obvious popularity clearly point to a paranoid style of juvenile literature in the last decades of peace before the Great War. Of course such stories, intended to warn and prepare young men for the coming struggle, compliment and reinforce the other manifestations of this expectation of war. Here one might include the public school cadet forces, the privately-sponsored Lads' Drill Association, the boys' rifle clubs advocated by Lord Roberts, and even Baden-Powell's Boys Scout movement which, as John MacKenzie has pointed out, was firmly located in mainstream Edwardian thinking by training young men in 'obeying orders from elders and superiors, training in firearms, acceptance of violence as part of the natural order [and] preparation for war'.[23] Such manifestations point to a general sense of unease in British society, a belief in impending catastrophe in the new century. In such a climate, all society could do was to warn its youth of the dangers to come and prepare them to play their part in the great struggle.

This literature and the other forms of propaganda inculcating such beliefs do not explain 1914, but they do go some way to help explain why the British declaration of war was greeted so enthusiastically by so many young men. As Roberts has written:

For nearly half a century before 1914 the newly literate millions were provided with an increasing flow of fiction based on war and the idea of its imminence.... Popular fiction and mass journalism now combined to condition the minds of the nation's new readers to a degree never possible before the advent of general literacy. In France and Germany, too, writings

in the same genre were equally successful in stimulating romantic conceptions about the carnage to come. When the final cataclysm did arrive,
response to such ideas set the masses cheering wildly through the capitals
of Europe. *Der Tag!* – The Day – was here at last! They could hardly
wait![24]

Tales of the great war to come had created a widespread belief among young
Britons that conflict was inevitable, and August 1914 simply fulfilled that
expectation; it was what British youth had been prepared for, and as such it was
welcomed by many as an end to uncertainty.

NOTES

1. On the growing rivalry between Britain and the German Empire, see
    Paul Kennedy, *The Rise of the Anglo-German Antagonism, 1860–1914*,
    London 1980.
2. I. F. Clarke, *Voices Prophesying War: Future Wars, 1763–3749*, Oxford
    1992.
3. On Henty and the imperialist school of authors, see Jeffrey Richards,
    Imperialism and Juvenile Fiction, Manchester 1989.
4. Quoted in the *Sunday Times*, 10th October 1948.
5. For Harmsworth's paranoia and xenophobia, see Reginald Pound and
    Geoffrey Harmsworth, *Northcliffe*, London 1959.
6. For example, see H. G. Wells, 'Of a cross-channel passage', *Daily
    Mail*, 27th July 1909.
7. Hamilton Edwards, 'Britain in Arms', *Boys' Friend*, 96, April 1897.
8. 'What will happen in the next Great War?', quoted in E. S. Turner, *Boys
    Will Be Boys*, London 1948. Turner's now-classic exploration of the
    juvenile papers still remains the only substantive study of the topic.
9. A number of 'Captain Strange' stories appeared in the *Boys' Herald*
    during 1903.
10. Reginald Wray, 'A World at Stake', *Boys' Realm*, 50–71, May-October
    1903.
11. On the Zeppelin panics, see Alfred Gollin, *The Impact of Air Power on
    the British People and Their Government, 1909–1914*, London 1989,
    Chapter 2, and Michael Paris, *Winged Warfare: The Literature and
    Theory of Aerial Warfare In Britain, 1859–1917*, Manchester 1992.
12. Colin Collins, 'War in the Clouds', *Dreadnought*, 26, 23rd November
    1912.

13. ibid.
14. ibid.
15. John Tregellis, 'Legions of the Kaiser', *Boys' Friend*, 679–93, June-September 1914.
16. Reginald Wray, 'The Fight for Empire', *Boys' Realm*, 72–92, October 1903 – March 1904.
17. See, for example, Norman Greaves, 'Flying to Victory', *Boys' Herald*, 441, 30th December 1911; Sidney Drew, 'Dan the Airman', *Boys' Realm*, 532, 12th August 1912, and 'Sexton Blake and the Airship Spy', *Boys' Herald*, 437, 15th December 1911.
18. Robert Roberts, *The Classic Slum: Salford Life in the First Quarter of the Century*, Manchester 1971, 181.
19. Editorial, *The Boys' Friend*, 690, 29th August 1914.
20. Captain F. S. Brereton, *The Great Aeroplane*, London 1911, 396. See also Brereton's *The Great Airship*, London 1913.
21. Herbert Strang, *The Air Scout*, London 1912, viii.
22. Herbert Strang, *The Air Patrol*, London 1913, ix; Strang, op. cit., iii.
23. John MacKenzie, 'The imperial pioneer and hunter and the British masculine stereotype in late Victorian and Edwardian times', in J. A. Mangan and J. Walvin, eds., *Manliness and Morality*, Manchester 1987, 176.
24. Roberts, op. cit., 179–90.

7

Bodies of evidence:
the case of Harold Frederic

Bridget Bennett

I

On Tuesday 25th October 1898, a short article appeared in a London paper, *The Daily Chronicle*. Headed 'The Late Mr Harold Frederic', it gives details of the cremation service of the American novelist and journalist Harold Frederic, who had died one week previously at the age of only forty-two. More precisely, though, it provides an account of the journey to that event. The article seems, initially, to be strictly to the point, detailed and fittingly restrained, but the narrative rapidly becomes dislocated, indirect, as it becomes guilty of indirection. In his end, then, is my beginning:

> The body was conveyed from … Waterloo by the quarter-past ten train yesterday morning, and a few friends of the deceased went down to Woking to attend the funeral service by the five minutes to one train. Two saloon carriages were placed at their disposal, one of the saloons being nearly filled with beautiful wreaths.… Unfortunately several friends of the deceased were directed to the wrong platform at Waterloo, and so lost the train which conveyed the rest of the mourners.
> Mrs Harold Frederic desires us to express her grateful thanks to the large number of her friends who have sent her letters and messages of sympathy in her bereavement.[1]

The wonderfully bathetic penultimate sentence transforms the unemotive prose which has preceded it, lending an unfortunate air of farce to the narrative. As readers, we enjoy the imagined spectacle and grimace at the sheer awfulness of it: the wrong platform; the missed or 'lost' train, as the paper calls it; the presumed horror of the mourners; the abandoned journey; the depleted funeral service; all of which mock the stateliness of the saloon 'nearly filled with beautiful wreaths', and radically de-stabilise the rhetoric of precision which is associated with the detail of the narrative (the carefully outlined train times), but which is also allied to the mode of cultural production, to the mechanics of newspaper journalism, to deadlines, limited spaces, and to that elusive concept, newsworthiness.

As readers we thrill to further possibilities, other variants of this story. What if the body had gone astray too and got sent off, not to Woking, but to Worksop, or even Worthing? Our glee and anxiety pivot upon these possibilities and focus on the unlikeliness of the route on which the narrative takes us, that unexpected journey. Like the hapless mourners, we find that we are sent off in the wrong direction, or in one which was not anticipated. The narrative has misdirected us, or perhaps we have misdirected ourselves through our anticipations; our evidence seems to have gone astray. The newspaper story turns out to be, at one level, a form of low comedy or grotesque humour, though it seemed at first to be something else. Ultimately that is exactly what it is: a story which is not what it seems, one which turns out to be about something else, or is available for multiple meanings or readings. It might be necessary to begin again, to retrace our steps and start upon a new narrative journey.

Yet before re-reading this short article we might be advised to take a step back, to stop ourselves and the body of Frederic in our disparate tracks, to reverse his journey to the other world and make him live once more, to recuperate our losses in order to begin again. First, then, we must diminish our expectations and stop ourselves imagining that we have privileged access to its meaning. We might then notice the disjunction between the first and the second paragraph. What exactly is the status of a comment like 'Mrs Harold Frederic desires us to...', followed by an account of her desires? Is the role of a newspaper of this kind to articulate the wishes of a bereaved woman, and, if not, what does this final paragraph do to the implied neutrality of the previous paragraph? What is the connection between the newspaper and Mrs Frederic? What sense can be made of this personal comment, which sits so oddly in an article whose rationale is suddenly under threat? As readers we must be alert to such nuances, must learn to interrogate our sources and recognise when the narratives which we expect transform themselves into ones which are unexpected. In this instance further investigation reveals that this account, like my account, is far from neutral. They each have their own biases.

Contemporary newspaper readers would have known that Frederic had separated from his wife Grace Frederic, but still visited her and their children regularly, and had been cohabiting with an American woman, Kate Lyon, for some years. This much had already emerged in the press in the few days that had elapsed since his death. They would have heard claims that Lyon, a devout Christian Scientist, denied Frederic medical help in his last illness, and that this contributed to, or possibly even caused, his premature death. They might have anticipated that Lyon and an American Christian Science healer, Athalie Mills, would be prosecuted for Frederic's manslaughter, for even in the days following his death the case against them looked plausible, at the very least. Knowing all of this, regular readers might have questioned the ideological stance of the passage above, particularly as it reveals itself in the final sentence which purports to know of the wishes of Grace Frederic. Readers might have intimated that an intellectual and ideological battleground was already taking formation, and that it was doing so in front of their eyes within the pages of their daily papers which covered the drama of unfolding events. Such detail in an article had its basis in the battle between conventional morality and a bourgeois norm, and in old and professional enmities: Frederic had never been afraid of making enemies amongst his colleagues, and old antagonists were starting to emerge and to take sides in the days following his death. Though this was gripping, what the papers were chiefly interested in, even more than the salacious details of Frederic's double life, was the growing influence of Christian Science in the final decade of the century, and of the significance of this as a symptom of fin-de-siècle decadence and malaise. The newspapers were overwhelmingly concerned that Frederic's death might turn out to be either a prolonged form of suicide (a sort of decadent death so common to the 1890s), or a marker in the emergence of a dangerous feminised cult that threatened society. Including an apparently personal comment by the widow of the deceased, in a manner which suggested that it was virtually an incidental (and certainly an innocent) comment, was part of a strategy of exposure. The cult would soon be dissected relentlessly, for it seemed symptomatic of an era in which cherished values were being abandoned. That multiple readings of Frederic's death were possible, and that they might be revealed in the spaces between public and private knowledge, was understood by his contemporaries.

What I am interested in investigating here is the question of how the literary scholar goes about filling in such gaps to produce an authoritative narrative of presence rather than absence, one which seeks to unite the disparate voices and sources of which it is comprised, and to unify them within what presents itself as a single privileged discourse. What I want to question further is whether that discourse can ever be privileged, or whether it can only ever be read as a piece of testimony, another disparate voice, another contingent or provisional part of the story, rather than an authoritative narrative or meta-narrative. I want to foreground the problematical rhetoric of discovery, revelation, analysis, and construction, and present a narrative which is quite deliberately seamed rather than seamless, patchy rather than patched up. The metaphors of journeys, absences and discoveries will be ones which I will draw upon throughout this essay.

In presenting the case of Harold Frederic, then, I am also demonstrating the processes by which I came to interrogate both his death and the way in which I should go about researching and writing about it. Even when I found the location of the body of Harold Frederic, a search which was not in itself difficult, but one which involved me in a journey to Northern New York, I found that the questions I had about his death were not solved. I had, it seemed, found the final resting place of the remains of his body – his ashes – since I had certainly found a tomb marked with his name. Yet other testimony suggested that his ashes had been interred a few thousand miles away, in England, where he had died. Having found what I thought was the end of his story, the end of the line and of my narrative journey, I found new texts which preoccupied me – that of the possibly misleading inscription on his tombstone, and then, as I investigated that, the texts proliferated and I found myself immersed in cemetery records and city directories, notices of births and deaths, and details of cemetery purchases. I was left attempting to construct a body of evidence which would help me ascertain the circumstances of his death, and trying to find the 'real' location of Harold Frederic. I found myself wanting to construct the narrative I resisted, the definitive text, the last word. Yet I knew that this was impossible and that I must go about my search without making special claims for myself. In doing this, I found that I had to return to the newspaper accounts of his death which had appeared in papers in two continents, to correspondence, memoirs and diaries, and to the evidence which I had managed to put together about his coded and complex double life, a life which had taken him on a long journey from Utica, New York, to London and a death which, it seemed, had returned him to Utica, a transformed figure, a handful of dust.[2] His body had formed, and had provided, the evidence of these journeyings. His body, the subject of an autopsy after his death, and of anecdotes and accounts which centred upon it, was to some degree the key evidence in the manslaughter trial which followed his death. The mute body, mutilated after the doctors had finished their final examinations, was made to speak – and it told of a life of excess. Yet it did not respond to questions of a pressing nature, did not tell whether it was that of a suicide or that of a man who had been killed by another or other parties. The body did not provide evidence for either argument, and it was clear that other documentation or forms of evidence would have to be resurrected if the case of Harold Frederic was to be solved. The body of Harold Frederic, a site of competing articulations and accounts, did not speak for itself, and indeed could not.

What did speak, sometimes after silences of sixty years, were the testimonies of his children, both legitimate and illegitimate, who were traced and approached for information in the late 1950s and early 1960s. As they moved toward their own deaths, they broke through the silence of decades and revealed their conflicting memories of their lives in the 1890s. It is in their broken and incomplete stories, told out of lonely old age, that I turned, to try, finally, to answer some of the questions I had about this case. Did Frederic, as some believed, will his own death? Suicide was believed by some to be reaching epidemic proportions in the 1890s, and Frederic himself had publicly contributed to the debate surrounding one of the most famous British suicides of that decade by writing a long letter to *The Daily Chronicle* about the death of Ernest Clark.[3] Stephen Crane thought not, writing almost a year after Frederic's death to his brother William Howe Crane that:

> the rumpus about H. continues. As I have told you he had enemies. He did not kill himself and if his ladylove killed him she picked one of those roundabout Sherlock Doyle ways of doing it. It is simply too easy to call a man you don't like a suicide. Mrs Frederic [Grace Frederic] loved H. maybe. She has taken precious little trouble to put him right with people since May. Neither do I much like Mr James' [Henry James] manner. He professed to be er, er, er much attached to H. and now he has shut up like a clam.[4]

Crane is somewhat unfair. Grace Frederic had died on 17th March 1899 and, save an intervention from the grave, a ghostly narrative perhaps, there was little she could do to rescue Frederic's reputation.[5] Despite these reservations, Crane's view of Frederic's death was held by some of his closest friends. If Frederic had not effectively killed himself, and it seems unlikely that he had, then was it the case that others had killed him? Had Kate Lyon and Athalie Mills been 'concerned together in feloniously killing and slaying one Harold Frederic, by neglecting to supply him with proper medical attendance', as they were charged?[6] I found that to start to answer these questions I had to turn to every source I could trace. The body of evidence would have to be built from the scraps and fragments which had survived family censorship, incendiary bombing in the 1939–45 war, and the general decay of one hundred years.

The object of this essay, then, is both to discuss a particular case which had peculiar resonances for the public in the 1890s, and to locate it within the matrix of contemporary fin-de-siècle discourses and currents. I wish to set the processes of this research up, and move towards examining the ways in which they might operate as a paradigm of a specific sort of historicising scholarship. So my investigations and representations are twofold: I want to investigate the case of Harold Frederic and offer, by example rather than explicitly, a case study of how I went about reconstructing it. Through this I hope to be able to produce an argument which works through two main narratives, one which is particular and specific, the other more general.

II

Two telegrams play striking roles in the case of Harold Frederic. The first, from Kate Lyon, is dated 16th August 1898, and was the subject of close scrutiny at Frederic's inquest and the manslaughter trial of Lyon and Mills: 'Victory! Send someone to stay immediately – must be strong and wise – not Mrs Boyd's healer – send at once – terribly urgent – FREDERIC.'[7] The second echoes the first and was sent some time later by Frederic's daughter Ruth: 'Victory! Doctors in. Please tell at old house.'[8] The battle which these two reveal is one which was fought over the body of Harold Frederic, and between two differing discourses, that of Christian Science healing and the male domain of conventional medicine. It was, in more than one way, a conflict between legitimacy and illegitimacy, between a lover and a wife, between two radically different ideologies, and between two nations. What was being played out over the body of the dying man articulated two notions of late-Victorian society, and this was seen quite clearly by the newspapers which covered Frederic's death, as I have already suggested.[9] But before these can be discussed, I will briefly outline the circumstances which led up to his death.

Harold Frederic moved to London from Albany, New York in 1884. He had resigned from the editorship of the *Albany Evening Press* on a matter of political principle, and became the London Correspondent of the *New York Times*, a position he held until his death. His brief was to produce a weekly 'cable letter', a narrative which would translate the events of British life for an American readership. In effect he would do exactly what I am challenging here: he would produce what he represented as an authoritative narrative of British life. He would write from the position of supreme knowledge. My anxiety about the possibility or desirability of such authority would have been profoundly antithetical to him. Frederic brought his wife and their two children with him. Together they were to have a further two surviving children. He had started to write fiction before he arrived in London and he consolidated this with a series of novels, short fiction and unpublished plays. He established a reputation for himself as a distinguished journalist within weeks of arriving in England, and soon he was well known as a writer of fiction. In 1896, his novel *The Damnation of Theron Ware* (published in England as *Illumination*) was a bestseller. At the time of his death he was a public figure with a wide range of friends and acquaintances who were mainly writers and politicians.

In Frederic's surviving correspondence, most of which relates to his life in England after 1884, references to his wife decrease as time went on. Since most of his surviving correspondence deals largely with business, it is difficult to explain the gradual breakdown of his marriage. It was in 1889 (or 1890 at the latest) that he met Kate Lyon, an American with a strong belief in Christian Science. At some point in their relationship, the pair set up some sort of home together at Furnival's Inn, London, where Charles Dickens had begun his married life. At first, Kate Lyon would be as invisible to others as Dickens's lover Ellen Ternan was to his adoring readership. At this time only Frederic's closest friends knew about this relationship and many of them were unhappy with the situation. In 1893 the couple moved to Homefield in the village of Kenley, Surrey. Here Lyon was known as 'Mrs Frederic', a name which outraged some of Frederic's acquaintances who had met a quite different 'Mrs Frederic' a short time earlier. Initially, they were secretive about their relationship, but by 1895 Frederic was more open about his second family – the pair eventually had three children together. Nevertheless he remained sensitive to the difficulties of the situation. On 20th February 1895, he wrote to his main English publisher, William Heinemann, referring to the Homefield address as 'the address which isn't mentioned to the *hoi polloi*', and marking the letter '"personal"'.[10] On 1st March he wrote to the Editor of *Black and White* magazine, saying: 'this address of mine relates to an intimately personal phase of my life which isn't talked about. I do all my work here, and never see anybody about me whom I don't wholly like.'[11]

The invocation of silence and utilisation of censorship has inevitably had consequences in terms of what is available for researchers. Frederic's unwillingness to talk about this relationship is understandable, and it is significant that it is one of the only aspects of his life on which he was silent. He was notoriously voluble. Though he had friends who cohabited (sometimes openly) with their lovers, his relationship with Lyon was complicated by the existence of his legitimate family who were entirely dependent on him. He divided his weeks into two parts, spending weekends with his wife in Brook Green, London (who knew about and greatly resented his other relationship), and weekdays with Kate Lyon in Surrey. Correspondence from his son and daughter by Grace Frederic – Harold Frederic Jr. and Ruth Keen – suggests that in both households Frederic was an aloof figure who spent much of his time in his study, writing.[12] One acquaintance claimed in his memoirs that Frederic had told him that he had to earn £1,400 per annum to support the two families. It is quite certain that the stresses caused by the prodigious quantity of writing he was producing in this period contributed to his illness and death.

His cohabitation with Lyon was not a political statement, not a willed challenge to convention, but an awkward compromise. Earlier, Grace Frederic had refused him a divorce, which he wanted on the grounds of incompatibility. During his final illness she changed her mind and a divorce writ was served through the open window of Homefield. Frederic was not told of this. This may have been calculatedly vindictive, or the despairing action of a wretched woman. It is very possible that she wished to secure a settlement for her children, realising the severity of her own illness. By this time she was already suffering from the cancer which would kill her. The situation cannot have been easy for any of the participants. It may have been most difficult for Grace Frederic, the quiet and lonely woman who had been first eclipsed and then rejected by her ambitious husband. Her daughter Ruth wrote, in 1960, that her mother became virtually a recluse and entertained or left her house very rarely. She remained the ghost of Frederic's American past embodied in a woman who was never 'at home' in England. Yet after Frederic's death Kate Lyon, who had braved convention and had been scorned by vicious neighbours and a hostile press, was forced to change her name and that of her children and to return to the United States, for it would have been impossible for her to live quietly in England and support her children.[13]

From spring until early summer 1898 Frederic was continually plagued by poor health. He lost weight rapidly in March and an illness which he put down to food poisoning in early summer led to what was probably a minor stroke. On 13th August he had a severe stroke in Kenley, though he did not see a doctor until the following day.[14] This delay suggests fright, perhaps, or obstinacy, either on his behalf, or on that of Kate Lyon. Frederic was notorious for his dislike of doctors, though the cause of the low esteem in which he held them has never been clear from his correspondence, or from what contemporaries have written about him. At the manslaughter trial it was agreed that he abused doctors regularly, but this was countered by a claim, commonly accepted, that in fact he abused everybody. The lawyers indulged themselves in some playfulness; when, for instance, one asked whether Frederic abused the legal profession, he was told that Frederic had not heard that particular lawyer's method of cross-examination. What became crucial in the months that followed his stroke and death was the issue of who the controlling mind was in the house he shared with Kate Lyon. Issues of control (specifically mind control, but also control of passions and social control), and of influence, were what chiefly interested commentators. Both were implicitly associated with mesmeric healing as well as Christian Science, and were set up as antitheses to conventional medicine and to the conventions of well-regulated society. They were also associated with the fin de siècle, with the breakdown of established systems of belief, the rise of new and threatening patterns of behaviour, and a cult of personal pleasure which was built into decadence. Narratives of the trial are always framed by these other, implied narratives.

On 16th August Kate Lyon telegraphed for a Christian Science healer to attend Frederic. Athalie Mills arrived with her husband and talked to Frederic about the possibility of healing him. She assured him that her treatment could only be successful if the doctors stopped treating him. Frederic demanded that she should leave his room, and his doctor travelled to London with her by train in a vain attempt to persuade her not to attend Frederic. On 17th August Frederic demanded the presence of a friend who was a solicitor and dictated his will, despite Kate Lyon's reluctance. The solicitor persuaded her that this would pacify Frederic, but she remained insistent that Grace Frederic should inherit Frederic's estate, threatening to tear up the will if Frederic did not acquiesce; yet he did not, and nor did she. His will was a potent symbol of the double life which he had led for many years: a final, formal, division. His American copyrights and property were to go to 'my very dearly beloved and faithful Kate Lyon and to her children', while the house and effects of 101 Brook Green and the English copyrights went 'to Mrs Frederic and my daughter Ruth in general trust for themselves and my other children now residing or generally residing with them'.[15] Ruth was to have a piano for herself (an earlier gift which was formalised here) and was to choose any books which she wanted from Brook Green for herself, or which 'she may consider of use in the education of her sister and brothers'. The other books were to be moved to Homefield. The English copyrights and most of the furniture in Brook Green were all mortgaged. In financial terms his bequests meant little. Frederic's tone matches the coldly formal wording of the will. He offers no apologies, or explanations for his life, even though the gravity of his situation must have been clear to him, and is oddly indifferent to his children, with the exception of Ruth.

On 17th August a specialist was called in at the insistence of Frederic's doctor, and between this date and 20th September two further doctors attended him, making four doctors in all. Evidence from the manslaughter trial shows that throughout the two months of Frederic's final illness the house at Kenley was so full of human traffic that it resembled a railway station. A series of doctors arrived, examined Frederic and were soon told to leave the house. After 20th September the doctors were sent away altogether and were only recalled on 17th October at the insistence of Cora Crane, who lived nearby. In the last month of Frederic's life he was attended by Athalie Mills who sat with him, reading from Mary Baker Eddy's *Science and Health With a Key to the Scriptures* (1875), and arguing with him about the Bible. After she was finally dismissed he announced, though he could barely speak, '"I never said that this

Christian Science would do a -- bit of good, and this -- woman Mills bores the head off my shoulders"'. In the early hours of 19th October he died.

The first hint of a scandal that would receive extensive press coverage appeared almost immediately. On 21st October the *New York Times* announced the forthcoming cremation. A line adds that he had 'been in the hands of Christian Scientists'. This was the start of a sustained campaign against Christian Science – 'the protean monster', or 'this wretched delusion', as it was dubbed. Over the next two months the Frederic case was covered in detail by the *New York Times*, as Frederic's former employer, but also by the international press. The *New York Times* published letters denouncing faith-healing, and stories about Christian Science healers whose patients had died while under their care. The paper's tone was seldom neutral, and was sometimes outraged, sometimes scoffing. The case was also covered in England, for another sect, the 'Peculiar People', was acquiring a similar notoriety. The Frederic case had captured the public imagination; Canon Eyeton preached a sermon against Christian Science in Westminster Abbey. Later, along with a group of illustrious names, he would become a member of a committee established to collect money for Grace Frederic and her children.[16] The subscription letter was sent out under the name of W. J. Fisher, the assistant editor, soon to be editor-in-chief of *The Daily Chronicle*, the newspaper from which I quoted at the beginning of this essay. As I suggested above, that paper had an explicit agenda of backing Frederic's wife – this was not a case which inspired neutrality.

The case of Harold Frederic was read by contemporaries as one with a particular moral for the 1890s. It proved that a man known for his bluntness, his scepticism and love of argument, and his hatred of pretence, could still become the victim of 'delusion', of what was seen to be a dangerous and faddish cult. How could he have been taken in? If he could, who else might be? Crucially, the newspapers mediated the disaster which befell Frederic through his relationship with Kate Lyon, and the fact that two women, traditionally carers, had seemingly brought about this man's death through lack of care.[17] So the underlying preoccupation of the press was the question of what happens when an unconventional system of beliefs (Christian Science, cohabitation outside of marriage) is invoked and acted upon. The fate of Harold Frederic revealed the physical vulnerability of a man who had been celebrated for his great physicality, the mental vicissitudes of a man renowned for an unusual degree of mental resilience. The consequences of his actions for his seven children was also the subject of great indignation. Since Frederic was already dead, Kate Lyon could easily be, and usually was, blamed for the penury of these innocent victims, as they were portrayed. What was shocking to his contemporaries was that if this particular man could prove susceptible, then surely unconventional belief systems might undermine any of them, and equally might threaten the tenor of late-Victorian life. That your lover might also be your killer was a neat moral twist too: break your marital vows and you might not live to regret it. Some of the elements of the moral interpretations of the case of Harold Frederic are familiar to us all in a post-AIDS age. The sense of cataclysm which Frederic's death seemed to encompass and to trigger was read, however, as one peculiarly of the period. A man uniformly described in masculine terms had fallen victim to a religion founded by a woman and largely administered by women healers. Death seemed to be domesticated in the case of Frederic, as it had been a decade previously, in the celebrated case of James Maybrick; it could creep up upon the unsuspecting in the form of a smiling woman.[18] If this is a specifically fin-de-siècle narrative, then it is one which still has resonances as we move towards the millennium. We are all familiar with cults which threaten, sexual scandals which titillate, court cases which capture the public imagination. Yet what marks this narrative as being of the turn of this century, rather than the last, is its uncertainty, its provisionality and its halting nature. Though my narrative is one which makes editorial choices, and mediates between different voices and other versions of events, it can only be contingent, can only present and arbitrate between the many varied voices, including my own, which make up the case of Harold Frederic.

NOTES

This essay emerges from an extended piece of work, *The Damnation of Harold Frederic*, and appears with the permission of Syracuse University Press.

1. 'The Late Mr Harold Frederic', *The Daily Chronicle*, 25th October 1898, 3.
2. John Scott Stokes makes a similar point when he describes the cremation as follows: 'The furnace door flew open, revealing a long iron chamber glowing red. In another second the door had closed, and two hours afterward a mere handful of ashes was all that remained of our great friend; gone at forty-two, he who ought to have had years before him, he who did such great work in fact and fiction, and who had it in him to become one of the greatest writers of the present century': 'The Sirdar's Return', *New York Times*, 30th October 1898, 19.
3. Letter to *The Daily Chronicle*, 20th August 1893, in Harold Frederic, ed. George E. Fortenberry, Stanton Garner, and Robert H. Woodward, *The Correspondence of Harold Frederic*, Fort Worth, Texas 1977, 340–45.

Interestingly, Frederic writes, 'I go to the full with your leader in hating as cowardly and mean the suicides which leave burdens of debt or poverty in injustice to others'. For more on suicide and the Ernest Clark case, see John Stokes, *In the Nineties*, Chicago 1989, 115–43.

4. Letter to William Howe Crane, 10th August 1899, in Stanley Wertheim and Paul Sorrentino, eds., *The Correspondence of Stephen Crane*, New York 1988, 496.

5. After the deaths of Frederic and Crane, friends of both men held a séance, hoping to extract messages from the pair. They were unsuccessful.

6. This formal charge was repeated in most newspaper reports of the case.

7. 'Mr Harold Frederic's Death', *Croydon Advertiser and Surrey County Reporter*, 29th October 1898, 3.

8. 'Mr Harold Frederic's Death', *Croydon Advertiser and Surrey County Reporter*, 5th November 1898, 5. She was the daughter of Grace and Harold Frederic. The words 'the old house' refer to the house she shared with her mother.

9. John Scott Stokes discusses the battle over Frederic's body in terms of possession. See Scott Stokes, op. cit., 19.

10. Letter to William Heinemann, 20th February 1895, in Frederic, op. cit., 390.

11. Letter to James N. Dunn, 1st March 1895: ibid., 392.

12. Letter to Hoyt Franchere from Ruth [Frederic] Keen, 4th August 1960; letter to Hoyt Franchere from Harold Frederic Jr., 18th September 1960. Both are in the collection of the Harold Frederic Edition held in the English Department in Lincoln, the University of Nebraska. I would like to thank Norm Hostetler and Bob Burgess for giving me access to the collection.

13. George Gissing wrote to H. G. Wells on 2nd January 1899 that: 'the children are away in the country, in good hands, and we want to secure them there for a day or two, till it can be seen what Kate Lyon can do. Of course their identity has to be concealed – else the sweet neighbours would make life impossible for the people who take care of them/ Grrrr!!': George Gissing and H. G. Wells, ed. Royall A. Gettman, *George Gissing and H. G. Wells: Their Friendship and Correspondence*, Urbana 1961, 132.

14. This account of Frederic's illness and death is drawn from a huge number of sources. The specifics come from accounts of the manslaughter trial in *The Daily Graphic*, the *New York Times*, the *Croydon Advertiser and Surrey County Reporter*, the *Utica Daily Press*, the

London *Times*, the *Croydon Chronicle*, the *Caterham, Oxted, and Godstone News* and the *East Surrey Advertiser*, the *Croydon Guardian and Surrey County-Gazette*, and *The Daily Chronicle*.

15. The will is in the Harold Frederic Papers in the Library of Congress, Washington D.C.

16. The other men included: H. H. Asquith, J. M. Barrie, A. T. Quiller-Couch, Charles Dilke, A. Conan Doyle, William Heinemann, Henry Irving, Arther Wing Pinero, Brandon Thomas, and T. P. O'Connor.

17. A. B. Walkley wrote that: 'Good women have control of our sick rooms; we men trust them and know well that in the long run our trust is not misplaced. In the long run, I say, because there is danger which comes from weakness of good women for religious sentiment divorced from knowledge and working in the wrong place.' From *The Daily Chronicle*, cited by John Scott Stokes, op. cit., 19.

18. In 1889 an American woman, Florence Maybrick, was accused of poisoning her husband, a wealthy Liverpool businessman. After a sensational trial, which was reported widely in the press, she was sentenced to death, although eventually she served a fifteen-year jail sentence. She was defended by Frederic's good friend Charles Russell, who later became Lord Chief Justice, and the outcome of the case was covered extensively by Frederic in the *New York Times*. For Frederic's public response to the case, see 'Mrs Maybrick Guilty', 8th August 1889, 5, and 'Mrs Maybrick's Doom', 11th August 1889, 1. Frederic announced that most commentators did not care whether she had poisoned 'the tiresome old fool', her husband, but were outraged at a judicial system that did not allow a person accused of murder to testify in their own defence. He argued that she had been, in effect, convicted because of her acknowledged adultery, and linked the case to the agitation over divorce laws. What emerged from the case was the inequity of the sexual double standard: James Maybrick had maintained a second household prior to and during his marriage, and had five children by this other relationship. It was her discovery of this fact that had estranged Mrs Maybrick from her husband. The case provided another narrative by which Frederic's own death could be read.

8

'A child of realism who is not on speaking terms with his father': Meredith in the nineties

Sue Zlosnik

At one point in *The Ordeal of Richard Feverel*, Meredith's first major novel, published in 1859, the narrator envisages a readership of the future:

> an audience will come to whom it will be given to see the elementary machinery at work; who, as it were, from some slight hint of the straws, will feel the winds of March when they do not blow. To them nothing will be trivial.... They will see the links of things as they pass, and wonder not, as foolish people now do, that this great matter came out of this small one.[1]

The anxiety of readership suggested by this quotation is characteristic of all George Meredith's novels and it is the purpose of this essay to suggest that his fiction, after almost a century of relative neglect, might be revisited through new reading strategies by a new 'audience'.

During his long writing career, from the 1850s into the present century, Meredith moved from obscurity to the status of Grand Old Man. His reputation has, as John Lucas pointed out in 1971, suffered from peaks and troughs: the adulation which he enjoyed at the turn of the century was superseded by an equally strong rejection.[2] He was, it appears, too Victorian for the modernists, nor did his work fit him for entry into Leavis's morally-determined 'Great Tradition'. As early as 1966, C. L. Cline suggested that the time had come 'to re-examine Meredith's novels in the light of contemporary standards of criticism. Only when this has been done can Meredith take his rightful place in the canon.'[3] Since Cline wrote these words, 'standards of contemporary criticism' have undergone radical changes, to the extent that the concept of 'canon', let alone a 'rightful place' in it, has become highly contentious. This essay will argue that the insights of feminist criticism in a postmodern context provide critical paradigms that generate interesting new readings of Meredith's novels which demonstrate the aptness of Wilde's comment that he was 'a child of realism who was not on speaking terms with his father'.

Wilde makes this comment in his essay, 'The Decay of Lying', which appeared in 1891, the same year as Meredith's *One of Our Conquerors*, a late novel.[4] Wilde's essay and Meredith's novel were written at a point in the nineteenth century when gender relations, an enduring theme of Meredith's writing, were becoming vexed. Whereas Meredith's first major novel, *The Ordeal of Richard Feverel*, was published in the same year as Eliot's *Adam Bede*, such was the length of his writing career that his later work appeared during a period in which, to quote Sally Ledger, 'the recurrent theme of cultural politics ... was instability, and gender was the most destabilizing category'.[5] The challenges to the illusory fixities of literary realism which heralded modernism may be seen as part of a wider destabilisation and, as Elaine Showalter demonstrates at length in *Sexual Anarchy*, this was most apparent in the way that 'all the laws that governed sexual identity and behavior seemed to be breaking down'.[6] Wilde's comment is particularly perceptive in identifying Meredith's vexed relationship with narrative form but, in its evocation of what has since been called 'the anxiety of influence', also points to issues related to paternal models of authorship which are of interest to a contemporary feminist critic.

Twentieth-century literary criticism absorbed the tenets of modernism in valorising the coherence of literary form in the face of the 'anarchy' which Showalter and Ledger document, and it has taken a long time to adopt the postmodernist stance which valorises irony, disruption and dislocation in texts.[7] Recent feminist criticism, in particular, has sought to value such disruption in destabilising those gender relations which have been disabling to women, and in challenging paternal models of authorship. In Meredith's fiction, feminist critics can find ample evidence of such creative disruption.

Meredith was a 'child of realism' in the sense that he never abandoned his commitment to the representation and critique of a recognisable social world: his plots never step outside the bounds of social possibility. His social critique led him to identify the relationship between the sexes as being at the heart of the social malaise he recognised in the England of his day, a malaise characterised by the twin vices of sentimentalism and egoism. Greater equality for women, he believed, was the only way to bring about what he called 'civilisation'.[8] However, his commitment to the representation of the knowable social world presents a problem with his much-written-about heroines: Clara Middleton in *The Egoist*, for example, liberating herself only to choose a more suitable man. The debate over whether he might be described as a feminist continues; traditional criticism applauds his creation of strong heroines: Emilia in the Italian novels and Diana in *Diana of the Crossways*, to name but two. More recent work laments that these strong women dwindle into wives – Kate Millett raises this point, although of course it is not actually true of Emilia, who survives to be a strong widow.[9] In the later novels, those of the eighties and nineties, Meredith, like Hardy, dares to venture into the territory of challenging moral orthodoxy and endorsing relationships which are not contained by it. Meredith's treatment of gender is much more subtle than this, however: it is a masculine authority that he undermines in his textual practice. In various ways, he valorises the feminine over the masculine. He repudiates the authority of the father, at a thematic level by the representation of problematic father figures (the list is long: Sir Austin Feverel, Mr Pole in *Sandra Belloni*, Dr Middleton in *The Egoist*, Richmond Roy in *The Adventures of Harry Richmond*), and at the level of form by challenging patriarchal discourses, particularly those of the omniscient narrator and the closure of conventional plot structures. Virginia Woolf claimed that 'he has destroyed all the usual staircases by which we have learnt to climb'.[10]

For Meredith's social critique, informed by the realist concern with the immanent social world, pushes constantly into a concern with the authority of representation. To endorse his own authority as author would ironically vindicate those aspects of social behaviour which he believed to be so damaging: it would turn him into the egoist. The authorial presence, therefore, is characterised by an ironic stance, sceptical of its own role, and the novels demonstrate a constantly vexatious relationship with the forms of realism: the omniscient narrator is parodied in various ways, the 'stable ego' of character, as Lawrence described it, is undermined, and closure is problematised by endings which either refuse to conform to realist expectations or which parody them. The later novels refuse to conform to realist expectations of beginnings also; they adamantly refuse to launch the reader into the plot. *Diana of the Crossways*, for example, has a lengthy opening chapter which expounds upon the inadequacies both of 'rose pink' sentimental fiction and the 'dirty drab' that realism has now become, concluding that 'the brainstuff of fiction is internal history'.[11]

The overt challenge to the authority of the author over his text which is presented by this ironic stance is also an invitation to the reader to engage in a dialogic which involves an ironic mode of *reading*. Two important works of the 1980s, by Joseph Moses and Gary Handwerk, see irony as the key concept in reading Meredith. In the only book of the 1980s entirely on Meredith's work, Moses places an ironic sensibility at the heart of his writing and sees this, not as a didactic tool, but as a constantly questioning and disrupting ironising self-consciousness which anticipates the fragmented subject of modernist literature.[12] Handwerk, in *Irony and Ethics in Narrative Structure*, published two years later, argues that Meredith's fiction presents a model of the subject which has only come to be theorised in the twentieth century in the work of Lacan.[13]

Handwerk's approach involves an examination of the language of the dialogue and the interaction between characters in the novels which, he claims, 'display an acute awareness both of the subjective nature of knowledge and of the linguistic detours through which alone such knowledge can be attained'. It is the representation of social interaction which particularly concerns him. He acknowledges that 'Meredith is ironic ... in his undermining of literary conventions and current ideas', but states that this is not the irony with which he is most concerned.[14] Handwerk's model of intersubjectivity may, however, also be applied to a model of reading in which the 'undermining of literary conventions' becomes central. He admires Judith Wilt's 1975 study of Meredith because its argument recognises the intersubjective imperative, but Wilt's recognition of the intersubjective imperative extends, however, to the relationship between the novelist and his implied reader.[15] Such a relationship is the focus of Stanley Fish who, in a persuasive essay entitled 'Short people got no reason to live', argues that irony is located in the interpretive community rather than in the text and that we always 'know' an irony but what we know will change according to our interpretive community.[16]

For neither Handwerk, nor Wilt, nor Moses is the question of gender particularly significant. Meredith's novels, however, far from being 'gender blind', may be seen as foregrounding problems of experience differentiated by gender; relationships between men and women are central to the fiction. They depict a contemporary society in which sentimentalism and egoism are most apparent in the sexual relationship: the narrator of *The Egoist* asserts that 'the love season is the carnival of egoism'.[17] Rachel Blau DuPlessis, in *Writing Beyond the Ending*, describes the work of late-nineteenth-century women novelists as being concerned with 'the examination and delegitimization of cultural conventions about male and female, romance and quest, hero and heroine, public and private.'[18] This is also what the novels of George Meredith, from the polyphonic *The Ordeal of Richard Feverel* onwards, are engaged in doing through their interrogation and subversion of fictional conventions. Elaine Showalter suggests that:

> the scriptures of sexual difference had been part of the infrastructure of Victorian fiction, which had "produced a great tradition of narrative controlled by difference, by the discrete separation of subject and object, public and private, active and passive – categories intimately linked to the radical dualism of masculine and feminine."[19]

It is such 'difference' that the novels of George Meredith deconstruct through an interrogation of the form of the novel itself. As well as opening the way for later modernist experiments, this exposes the provisional nature of gender. The realist novel with its plotted action and definitive narrative closure constructs a teleological view of human experience; Meredith's destruction of the narrative 'staircases' refutes this view. In his novels, the representations of gender identities, the conventions of plot (realist and romantic) which enforce what he saw as damaging stereotypes (damaging both to women and to society itself) are constantly subverted and the patriarchal authority of the omniscient narrator is undermined. Consequently the discourse of 'difference' too is subverted.

The community of belief which Handwerk characterises is recognised as just that by Meredith: his novels, in their presentation of ironic incongruity, challenge any notion of immutable truth. They thus offer to the reader some limited possibilities of liberation for his female 'characters' from the constraints of gender at the level of plot, but more importantly, a potentially liberating disruption of the fixities of gender identity as they are reinforced through conventional narrative. In a sense, his work is political in that it envisages the possibility of an alternative order in which sentimentalism and egoism are eradicated. This can only happen, however, through a realignment of gender roles; his fiction stops short of being utopian and maintains a mimetic commitment to realism, however strained. We see no more than intimations of such a new order – Aminta abandoning her ambiguous role as wife to the admiral and diving into the sea and swimming to meet the 'new man', Matthew Weyburn, for example.[20] Read in the realist mode, the later novels offer limited possibilities for change even though they appear to be challenging social orthodoxy; their radicalism lies rather in the way in which such a commitment to mimetic realism is foregrounded as being under strain through the narrative strategies. Indeed, it is these strategies which open up a space which the contemporary feminist reader may occupy in her recuperation of the texts. In reading the incongruities and disjunctions ironically, she may perceive the challenge they represent to the illusory gender fixities of mid- and late-nineteenth-century culture. It is the readiness of the feminist critic to read ironically which offers the prospect of re-evaluating the place of Meredith in a revised literary history.

Critical paradigms of the late twentieth century accommodate such a mode: irony is arguably the key characteristic of the postmodern critical world. It was Cleanth Brooks who suggested in 1949 that 'irony' was in danger of becoming a catchword for the times,[21] but it is Umberto Eco has produced the most vivid and entertaining illustration of postmodern irony. It is worth quoting in full:

I think of the postmodern attitude as that of a man who loves a very cultivated woman and knows he cannot say to her, "I love you madly", because he knows that she knows (and that she knows that he knows) that these words have already been written by Barbara Cartland. Still, there is a solution. He can say, "As Barbara Cartland would put it, I love you madly." At this point, having avoided false innocence, having said clearly that it is no longer possible to speak innocently, he will nevertheless have said what he wanted to say to the woman: that he loves her but he loves her in an age of lost innocence. If the woman goes along with this, she will have received a declaration of love all the same. Neither of the two speakers will feel innocent, both will have accepted the challenge of the past, of the already said, which cannot be eliminated; both will consciously and with pleasure play the game of irony.... But both will have succeeded, once again, in speaking of love.[22]

We can find something approaching such a postmodernist stance in Meredith's work. His novels foreground the way in which experience and understanding is mediated through texts. The 'invitation to subversion' that the novels offer involves the hope of a mutual recognition on the part of reader and writer that while 'it is no longer possible to speak innocently', this does not involve the repudiation of all meaning. If the feminist critic is 'the very cultivated woman', she can answer him back!

Feminists can adopt the sceptical practices of postmodernism in order to assert their own difference as readers. This in itself involves a transfer of authority from author to reader. Linda Nicholson alerts us to the dangers of polarising postmodernism and feminism and suggests that:

each of the two perspectives suggests some important criticism of the other. A postmodernist reflection on feminist theory reveals disabling vestiges of essentialism while a feminist reflection on postmodernism reveals andro-centrism and political naïveté.

She goes on to consider how we might combine a postmodernist incredulity towards meta-narratives with the social-critical power of feminism, and proposes a pragmatic set of practices 'made up of a patchwork of overlapping alliances, not one circumscribable by an essential definition'.[23] The adoption of postmodernist assumptions and practices may be seen as liberating the feminist as reader, allowing her to exercise authority over the text in the pursuit of a woman-centred critique of narrative form. Thus what Linda Hutcheon calls the 'potential quietism of the political ambiguities or paradoxes of post-modernism' may be transformed into an empowering critique of the ways in which narrative conventions, while promoting cultural meanings, are not necessarily monolithic in their authority.[24] The perception of irony is the agent of empowerment, and one which Donna Haraway, for example, would like to see figuring much higher on the agenda of feminism:

> Irony is about contradictions that do not resolve into larger wholes, even dialectically, about the tension of holding incompatible things together because both or all are necessary and true. Irony is about humor and serious play. It is also a rhetorical strategy and a political method, one I would like to see more honoured within socialist feminism.[25]

Following Richard Rorty, I believe that an ironic view of the world is not inconsistent with solidarity and can be liberating in its acknowledgement of the provisional nature of vocabulary.[26] If vocabularies may be displaced, they may be displaced by vocabularies we find more congenial – at least for the time being. Such an assumption allows us to be more sensitive to this process in texts from the past. To read an irony is to be quite conscious of incongruity, of the point where different vocabularies, different ways of seeing the world compete and challenge one another without either establishing mastery. Reading irony is thus a pragmatic activity and a self-conscious one: we always 'know', says Stanley Fish, when something is ironic.[27] That knowledge can be the starting point for interpretation in a feminist criticism which grounds itself in close reading of the literary text. Whatever the biological sex of an *author*, an ironic reading practice is an empowering process for the feminist *reader*, enabling her to occupy the space opened up by the ironic disjunctions of fractured texts. Irony as a reading strategy is therefore not incompatible with the social and political aims of feminism; it is an agent of empowerment. In drawing power from it, the contemporary feminist reader can usefully assimilate and appropriate insights from the variety of feminist critical practices which have been developed by her predecessors. Meredith is a good subject for such an ironic reading because his fiction challenges the reader to question the authority of the author, or to put it the other way round, does not make it easy for her to accept it.

One of Our Conquerors was published in 1891 when its author was sixty-three. Meredith had at last achieved popular success six years before with *Diana of the Crossways*, but *One of Our Conquerors* was hardly calculated to appeal to a popular audience. Described by Meredith's biographer, David Williams, as 'the most stylistically opaque and tortured of all his novels', it, to quote a contemporary reviewer, made its 'appeal through a sense of pain'.[28] It demonstrates both the acceptance of the realist tradition and a repudiation of it. Its dislocations and ironies can be revisited from the fin (as it were) of this siècle and read as metafictive experiments. From a historical perspective, we can see how it exemplifies the fragmentation of what Lyotard has called the *grand récit*, those mastering narratives which informed history until the end of the nineteenth century. The self-ironising stance which Meredith exhibits in all his fiction is very much in evidence here, in a novel which explores the instability of meaning.

The plot of the novel verges on the melodramatic. Its 'hero', Victor Radnor, the ironically named 'conqueror' of the title, is now in early middle age. As a young man he had married a much older woman, but had fallen in love with and eloped with her companion, Nataly. These two have lived together as man and wife for many years and have a daughter, Nesta, who is now a young woman, ripe for marriage. Her parents, however, remain unmarried as Victor's legal wife (whom he always refers to as Mrs Burman) unco-operatively refuses to die. Victor has become a very rich man and, close to the centres of financial power, he also seeks political power through election to Parliament. His equilibrium, however, is constantly threatened by the fear that his unorthodox domestic life will be exposed. This fear is felt much more keenly by Nataly and her life comes to be dominated by it. The couple have had to move twice from comfortable country houses they have lived in because rumour has begun to do its work. Nesta is 'courted' by the heir to an earldom who is discouraged when he finds out about her illegitimacy, and withdraws completely when she befriends a young woman who is the mistress of an army officer. Progressively driven into silence and despair, Nataly dies at this point and, ironically, is survived by Mrs Burman for only a few days. Victor becomes deranged by grief and lives a few years longer. The novel ends with Nesta, away in Europe, marrying Dartrey Fenellan, an ex-soldier and brother of one of Victor's friends, who is an older and wiser man after an unhappy marriage that had ended with his spouse's death. She is poised ready to return to England, presumably to inherit the country house of all country houses, Lakelands, (an 'English architect's fantasia'), built from Victor's dreams for his family but never realised.

One of Our Conquerors is both thematically and linguistically about deferral. Victor attempts to control his circumstances and to build the future; both desires are doomed to failure. Characterised by his name as a Celt rather than a Saxon (a contrast much favoured by Meredith), he has many valuable qualities. His desire for control, however, sets him up as an analogue for the author who grapples with his text; this is the extended metaphor of the whole novel. The opening chapter, whose sole event is Victor slipping on a banana skin on London Bridge, demonstrates vividly the vexed relationship between the two, operating as it does through a stream of consciousness in which language becomes more and more slippery and meaning evasive. The one word which is foregrounded in the chapter is not supplied by this stream of consciousness but by something external to it, the man who has helped Victor to his feet. Victor's complaints that his pristine waistcoat has been besmirched by 'the smutty knuckles' of 'the member of the mob' who helped him to his feet is greeted by the retort: 'And none of your dam punctilio.'[29] The word takes on a new significance as it reverberates through the novel and returns to haunt Victor, to remind him in roundabout ways of his vulnerability. Ironically, in opposition to its meaning of exaggerated politeness, the phenomenon of a society well-ordered by etiquette, it comes to signify for Victor a periodic irruption of all that he finds disruptive and disquieting.

It is a central irony of the text that Victor, in attempting to exercise the control he enjoys in public life over the private sphere, is exposed as controlled rather than controlling. His personal life is entirely dependent on his relations with women, and it is the representation of women that might be one of the focuses for the feminist reader. The feminist reader who accepts the realist dimensions of the novel might point to the constraining nature of late-Victorian morality. Viewed from this perspective, the text is an indictment of the human misery caused by restrictive codes, and Nataly may be seen as a victim of patriarchal society, a woman without 'a tongue to speak and contend', and hence marginalised by its discourses to the point of silence. Mrs Burman may also be understood as a victim, reviled to the extent of being demonised, the 'withered' old woman abandoned by her young husband. Nesta only is offered some hope, but her happy ending consists of marriage to a reasonable and attractive man, a fate which many contemporary feminists would find diminishing, and indeed one to which Meredith's feminist contemporaries might have offered alternatives.

However, there are other ways of approaching the representation of women in the text. The ironic reader might see it as part of the ironic scheme of a novel which progressively decentres its hero. Victor, like the realist novelist, works within the logic of temporality: in the public sphere he is represented as one of the makers of history; in the private he is undone through his own history. Yet the opening of the novel gives a clue to the spatial dimension of the novel, a crucial dimension. Crossing London Bridge, his fall is literal, physical; the telling of the event, however, repudiates the exteriority of realism and places the reader inside Victor's head in a stream of consciousness more characteristic of modernist writing. This is the first of a series of interior monologues inviting an ironic reading which involves both empathy and distance. Victor's belief in his ability to control events becomes increasingly illusory as the novel progresses to a point where his own death itself does not create closure. Instead, the vision of Lakelands remains as possibility, a deferred vision of utopian space, a space for the development of feminine potential, which seems likely to be fulfilled through feminine rather than masculine agency. Looked at from this perspective, Mrs Burman becomes a much more ambiguous presence in the novel, a figure of the past who is also very much in the present. She presents a threat to patriarchy rather than being its victim: a symptom of patriarchal anxiety in her construction as both a grotesque castrating female figure and an ironic inversion of patriarchal power. Nataly represents the silence which is the price of a dominant discourse, and that which the mastering discourses of Victor's public life suppress; her refusal of Lakelands suggests that what it metaphorically represents cannot be within the gift of Victory. Only with Nesta, at the very end of the novel, does Lakelands, beyond the plotting of the dead Victor, seem within reach. Its achievement involves both writing and reading beyond the ending.

NOTES

1. George Meredith, *The Ordeal of Richard Feverel*, London 1859, 233–4.
2. John Lucas, 'Meredith's reputation' in I. Fletcher, ed., *Meredith Now*, London 1971, 7.
3. C. L. Cline, 'George Meredith', in L. Stevenson, ed., *Victorian Fiction: A Guide to Research*, Cambridge, Mass. 1966, 344.
4. Oscar Wilde, 'The Decay of Lying', in *The Complete Works of Oscar Wilde*, London 1976, 976. George Meredith, *One of Our Conquerors*, London 1891 (Mickleham edition, 1924). Only two complete novels were to follow, *Lord Ormont and his Aminta*, London 1894, and *The Amazing Marriage*, London 1895, from the prolific writer who produced fourteen novels as well as essays and several volumes of poetry.
5. Sally Ledger, 'The New Woman and the crisis of Victorianism', in Sally Ledger and Scott McCracken, eds., *Cultural Politics at the Fin de Siècle*, Cambridge 1995, 22.
6. Elaine Showalter, *Sexual Anarchy: Gender and Culture at the Fin de Siècle*, London 1991, 3.
7. An interesting example of this in relation to Meredith criticism is provided by the American critic Donald Stone, who in 1972 dismissed *Diana of the Crossways*, Meredith's 1885 novel, as 'the product of an exhausted man', but in 1988, after he had discovered Bakhtin, admitted to changing his mind and acclaimed it. See Donald D. Stone, *Novelists in a Changing World: Meredith, James and the Transformation of English Fiction in the 1880s*, Cambridge, Mass. 1972, 153, and

'Meredith and Bakhtin; polyphony and Bildung', *Studies in English Literature 1500–1900*, 28 (1988), 693–712.

8. George Meredith, *An Essay on Comedy*, London 1877, 91.
9. Kate Millett, *Sexual Politics*, New York 1970, 139.
10. Virginia Woolf, *The Common Reader*, London 1986, 228.
11. George Meredith, *Diana of the Crossways*, London 1885, 15.
12. Joseph Moses, *The Novelist as Comedian: George Meredith and the Ironic Sensibility*, New York 1983.
13. Gary J. Handwerk, *Irony and Ethics in Narrative Structure*, New Haven and London 1985.
14. ibid., 91–3.
15. Judith Wilt, *The Readable People of George Meredith*, New Jersey 1975.
16. Stanley Fish, 'Short people got no reason to live: reading irony', in *Doing What Comes Naturally*, North Carolina 1989, 186–96.
17. George Meredith, *The Egoist*, London 1915, 130.
18. Rachel Blau DuPlessis, *Writing Beyond the Ending*, Indiana 1985, ix.
19. Showalter, op. cit., 17.
20. George Meredith, *Lord Ormont and his Aminta*, London 1916, 319–20.
21. Cleanth Brooks, 'Irony as a principle of structure', in H. Adams, ed., *Critical Theory Since Plato*, New York 1971, 1041–8.
22. Umberto Eco, 'Postmodernism, irony and the enjoyable', in P. Brooker, ed., *Modernism/Postmodernism*, Harlow 1992, 227.
23. Linda Nicholson, 'Social criticism without philosophy', in Linda Nicholson, ed., *Feminism/Postmodernism*, London 1990, 20–35.
24. Linda Hutcheon, *The Politics of Postmodernism*, London 1989, 22.
25. Donna Haraway, 'A manifesto for cyborgs: science, technology and socialist feminism in the 1980s', in Nicholson, ed., op. cit., 190.
26. Richard Rorty, *Contingency, Irony and Solidarity*, New York 1989, 79.
27. Fish, op. cit., 186–96.
28. David Williams, *George Meredith: His Life and Lost Love*, London 1977, 161.
29. Meredith, *One of Our Conquerors*, 2–3.

9

Oscar Wilde and the 'daughters of decadence'

Sally Ledger

It is no coincidence that the New Woman materialised alongside the decadent and the dandy. Whilst the New Woman was perceived as a direct threat to classic Victorian definitions of femininity, the decadent and the dandy undermined the Victorians' valorisation of a robust, muscular brand of masculinity deemed to be crucial, at the turn of the century, to the maintenance of the British Empire.[1] The perceived connection between the New Woman and decadence meant that the fate of the New Woman was inextricably linked to the public disgracing of Oscar Wilde. On 25th May 1895, Wilde was sentenced to two years' hard labour for committing acts of 'gross indecency';[2] on 21st December 1895 *Punch* triumphantly announced 'THE END OF THE NEW WOMAN – The crash has come at last'.[3] Victorian feminism, for this most misogynist of Victorian journals, was on the run. An enormous number of New Woman novels had been published and widely read in the early 1890s, concomitant both with the rise of mass-market fiction and with the resurgence of interest in the Woman Question at the fin de siècle. But this deluge of popular New Woman fiction dwindled dramatically after 1895, confirming *Punch*'s prediction at the close of that year. The fictional New Woman was almost certainly a victim of the moral rearguard action which followed the Wilde trials.

Although ideologically they had surprisingly little in common, the New Women and the decadents of the fin de siècle were repeatedly lumped together in the flourishing periodical press of the 1890s. In 1895 the *Speaker* asserted that:

> for many years past Mr Wilde has been the real leader in this country of the "new school" in literature – the revolutionary and anarchist school which has forced itself into such prominence in every domain of art.... The new criticism, the new poetry, even the new woman, are all, more or less, the creatures of Mr Oscar Wilde's fancy.[4]

This radical conjunction of the 'new' was seized upon by conservative writers of the period as a threat to the dominant moral, socio-sexual and aesthetic codes of the Victorian age. Eliza Lynn Linton, in an onslaught upon 'The Partisans of the Wild Woman', yoked together the New Journalism, the New Woman and decadence into an unholy trinity of radical degeneration.[5] As Elaine Showalter has put it: 'to many outraged male reviewers, the New Woman writers were threatening daughters of decadence. They saw connections between New Women and decadent men, as members of an avant garde attacking marriage and reproduction.'[6]

What most obviously linked the New Woman with the Wildean decadents of the 1890s was the fact that both overtly challenged Victorian sexual codes. The New Woman fiction is generally characterised by a sexual candour which was also a feature of literary decadence. Whereas George Egerton's short stories explore the *terra incognita* of woman – the often erotic dimensions of a woman's life unknown to men – Sarah Grand's best-selling novel, *The Heavenly Twins*, explores the subject of male sexual licentiousness, confronting the problem of syphilis head-on. A writer for the *Westminster Review* speculated that the dominant note of sexuality in all literature of the 1890s was 'a sign that English fiction has entered a stage of decadence'.[7] The trials of Oscar Wilde in April and May 1895 crystallised in the general cultural psyche the challenge to gender definitions posed by the decadents and the New Woman, and the immediate result was an attempt both to ridicule and to silence them. The second Wilde trial began on 26th April 1895, and on 27th April *Punch* published a diatribe against 'Sexomania', written 'By an Angry Old Buffer':

When Adam delved and Eve span
No one need ask which was the man.
Bicycling, footballing, scarce human,
All wonder now, "Which is the woman?"
But a new fear my bosom vexes;
Tomorrow there may be no sexes!
Unless, as end to all the pother,
Each one in fact become the other.[8]

New Women on bicycles, garbed in bloomers – a product of the campaign for rational dress at the fin de siècle – fill this Old Buffer with fears that the counterpart of the effeminate man was the unwomanly woman. Max Beerbohm remarked in a light-hearted vein that the amalgamation of the sexes was 'one of the chief planks of the decadent platform'.[9] New Women and feminists in general were often constructed in the periodical press as mannish, overeducated, humourless bores. The Girton Girl was much maligned and ridiculed throughout the period. Severely-dressed, wearing college ties, and smoking, the New Woman as she frequently appeared in the pages of *Punch* decidedly lacked the attributes of classic Victorian femininity.

Where the New Woman was not figured in discourse as a 'masculine' figure, she tended to be represented instead as an oversexed, threatening, vampiric figure. George Egerton had represented the New Woman positively as a sensuous, erotic being, but less sympathetic, anti-feminist writers distorted this construction, so that in Bram Stoker's *Dracula*, for example, the New Woman's sexuality is figured as a dangerous aberration which must be extinguished. The New Woman was also constructed as a sexually decadent, vampiric figure in Marie Corelli's best-selling novel from 1895, *The Sorrows of Satan*. Sybil Elton, the New Woman of the piece, is described as 'a harpy – a vulture of vice'.[10] She has an enormous sexual appetite which terrifies and disgusts the man she marries, and in her suicide note she blames the New Woman fiction and the poetry of Swinburne – 'this satyr songster' – for her own moral corruption.[11]

Writers such as Bram Stoker and Marie Corelli, among many others, were very confident, in the 1890s, about the association between Wildean decadence and the New Woman. And yet there was much which divided these cultural phenomena. The sexually-charged heroines of George Egerton's stories were not typical of fictional representations of women by the New Woman novelists, and many of the activities of the late-nineteenth-century women's movement were antithetical to the sexual politics of decadence. Oscar Wilde, though, did have one or two feminist credentials. Most obviously, in connection with the rise of the New Woman at the fin de siècle, Wilde edited the *Woman's World* for two years, changing the title from the *Lady's World* and insisting that the paper become less frivolous. But his editorship was by no means uncomplicatedly feminist, as Laurel Brake has illustrated in her fascinating account of Wilde's influence on this woman's magazine.[12]

Whilst the *Lady's World* had been dominated by articles on fashion, household management, fancy cooking and needlework, music and visual art, the *Woman's World* comprised a much more varied compendium of discourses on, for example, aestheticism, higher education for women, the 'woman question', prospective professions for women, working women, women abroad, fashion and its history, drama and Ireland. It was also notable for its dissemination of women's writing.[13] In two letters concerned with his editorship of the *Women's World*, Wilde's credentials seem impeccably feminist. Writing to a potential contributor he wrote of the magazine that: 'I am anxious to make it the recognized organ through which women of culture and position will express their views.'[14] In a letter to his (probable) forbear as editor, Wemyss Reid, Wilde had written that he wanted to get rid of the *Lady's World's* preoccupation with women's fashion in the interest of greater intellectual seriousness.

As Brake has remarked, it is somewhat curious to witness Wilde decrying fashion – he relegated the fashion column to the back pages of the *Woman's World* – just as it is rather amusing to see him purging the magazine of its gossip column.[15] For in Wilde's own writings such 'trivia' are valorised rather than decried. The attribution of moral seriousness to women constitutes, on one level, an ostensibly 'feminist' inversion of Victorian gender codes (normally it would have been women who were associated with trivia, and men with intellectual and moral seriousness). But Wilde's sincerity apropos of the inversion becomes questionable on a close examination of the very first edition of the new magazine. The fashion slot which had taken pride of place in the opening pages of the *Ladies World* was usurped, in the first edition of the *Woman's World*, by a piece on a theatrical subject, 'The Woodland Gods', which is heavily illustrated with plates of comely, emphatically 'effeminate' young men in costume.[16] Wilde clearly preferred a display of aesthetically adorned male bodies to a similar display of women.

Wilde's editorship of the *Woman's World* could sustain a very detailed analysis, and some interesting work has also been undertaken on his relations with actresses and women directors.[17] It is probably in *The Picture of Dorian Gray*, though, that he has most come under critical scrutiny in terms of his relationship with feminism at the fin de siècle. The general critical consensus in the 1890s was that the decadent aesthetic represented a 'feminisation' of literature through its disestablishment of traditional models of male bourgeois identity. Industry, thrift, utility and moral uprightness – these were the qualities ascribed to bourgeois masculinity. Industry, thrift, utility and moral uprightness – these are not epithets which come to mind when reflecting on *The Picture of Dorian Gray*.

Wilde's novel concerns itself with a sphere of art and idleness in which traditional 'masculine' virtues are rejected in favour of the aesthetic. The novel's critics were appalled. According to Regenia Gagnier, the novel was seen as 'decadent' both because of 'its distance from and rejection of middle-class life', and because 'it was not only dandiacal, it was "feminine"'.[18] And yet Dorian Gray's identification with the 'feminine' in the novel does *not* coincide with a valorisation of 'woman': quite the reverse is true. Rita Felski has clearly articulated the contradictory gender ideology of the novel: 'Feminine traits, when adopted by a man, are defamiliarized, placed in quotation marks, recognized as free-floating signifiers rather than as natural, God-given, and immutable attributes ... whereas feminine qualities in a woman merely confirm her incapacity to escape her natural condition.'[19] 'Femininity' in *The Picture of Dorian Gray*, is accredited value as a 'free-floating signifier' – as part of a pose, a performance – which clearly belongs to the world of 'art'; 'woman', by contrast, is represented in the novel as hopelessly corporeal, physical, and leadenly material. The aestheticisation of homoerotic desire is accompanied in the novel by an overt misogyny. Women represent for Wilde's dandies a gross physicality. As Lord Henry Wotton puts it: 'no woman is a genius.... Women represent the triumph of matter over mind, just as men represent the triumph of mind over morals.'[20]

It is in the account of Dorian's rejection of Sybil Vane, and her subsequent suicide, that a repulsion towards women – and in this instance towards women's sexualised bodies in particular – can be traced in the novel's discourses. The rejection of Sybil is clearly an important staging post in the development of Dorian Gray's homosexual identity, an identity which is predicated on an aversion to 'woman'.

If Wilde's attitude to 'woman' and to feminism was less than unambivalently positive, he was nonetheless a lot more generous to the feminist movement than the feminist movement was to him. Altogether typical of the response of the feminist press to Wilde's criminal conviction was an article in the *Woman's Signal* which welcomed 'the fall of Mr Oscar Wilde and the malodorous decadents', which, the columnist wrote, 'must hearten every mother who, in the love of God, is training her sons to habits of purity and manliness'.[21]

The mainstream feminist movement was anxious to distance itself from Oscar Wilde and his followers, and in pragmatic terms it is easy to see why this should have been the case. To have aligned themselves with Wilde, who had been publicly disgraced as a sexual deviant, would almost certainly have damaged the feminists' claims for civic and constitutional rights. But the series of outraged denunciations of Wildean decadence in the feminist press of the 1890s is also symptomatic of the absence of any fully-articulated discourse on female sexuality within the mainstream women's movement of the late nineteenth century. Feminists were concerned less with female sexuality than with male sexuality, which they condemned as an oppressive pollutant of society. It was through the campaigns against the Contagious Diseases Acts and, later, through the wider Social Purity movement of the 1880s, that feminism made an assault on male sexuality (and this included male homosexuality). The feminist campaigners against the CD Acts and the leaders of the Social Purity movement were largely responsible for the legislation – the Criminal Law Amendment Act of 1885 – which subjected Wilde to two years' hard labour in 1895.

Sarah Grand's best-selling New Woman novel from 1893, *The Heavenly Twins*, clearly grew out of the concerns of the social purity movement.[22] It is, though, a lot more than a narrowly political novel. For whilst it explicitly condemns the rampant form of male sexuality which spread syphilis and hereditary disease, its exploration of female sexual desire, its interrogation of gender roles and tentative exploration of same-sex relationships, confirm its status as a challenging feminist critique of Victorian sexual ideology.

When students come to read *The Heavenly Twins* in the late twentieth century, its somewhat unwieldy, seven-hundred page, three-volume format means that it is easy to forget – or difficult to believe – that this novel was a phenomenal success from 1893. Whilst *Tess of the D'Urbervilles* was the best-selling novel of 1892, in 1893 *The Heavenly Twins* could make the same claim to literary fame. If Hardy's novel had provoked often heated debate, the sexual politics of Grand's third novel created nothing less than a scandal. In an interview one year after the publication of *The Heavenly Twins*, Grand was quite explicit about the sexual politics of the novel, in which a young woman, Evadne Frayling, refuses to consummate her marriage when she discovers, on her wedding day, that her husband has a dubious sexual history (he finally dies of syphilis). Clearly referring to the feminist campaigns against the CD Acts, Grand revealed in 1896 that her impetus for writing the novel derived from her perception that: 'men endeavour to protect themselves from disease by restrictive laws bearing on women, but nothing has yet been done to protect the married woman from contagion.' She added to this observation her hope that 'we shall soon see the marriage of certain men made a criminal offence'.[23]

There are two main plot strands in *The Heavenly Twins*. The first, main strand concerns Evadne Frayling's mutiny against the syphilitic male body. The second plot line involves cross-dressing and an interrogation of same-sex relationships. It was the first which caused the critical brouhaha, but arguably the second which gives the book its sexually radical edge. If Sarah Grand could in any way be aligned with Oscar Wilde (and the association is at best dubious), it is in her narrative of 'The Tenor and the Boy' that she comes closest to Wilde, the apostle of decadence with whom New Woman novelists were so glibly categorised at the fin de siècle.

Evadne Frayling's credentials as a social purity feminist are impeccable. In refusing to consummate her marriage, she reflects that to submit to her husband would be tantamount to 'countenancing vice, and ... helping to spread it'.[24] Although the sexual ethics of social purity as they manifest themselves in the novel hardly mark Grand as a sexual radical, nonetheless *The Heavenly Twins* is most interesting in the way that it inverts contemporary sexual ideology. The Contagious Diseases Acts were predicated on the idea that the (fallen) female body pollutes society. Grand turns such a notion on its head, so that it is now the (syphilitic) male body which infects the wider social body; this is arguably a discursive manoeuvre of the highest feminist order. And on another level, the 'social question', which had been cast in class terms in nineteenth-century novels as chronologically disparate as Elizabeth Gaskell's *Mary Barton* (1848) and George Gissing's *Demos* (1886), is recast in *The Heavenly Twins* in gender terms. In the feminist fiction of the 1890s, it is the male body, rather than the working-class body, which threatens English society with instability and potential ruination. Historically, I would claim that this represents a fictional expression of the general shift, in writings of the 1890s, away from 'class' as a locus of social disruption, towards a focus on gender.

Critics have had no difficulty in commenting on the sexual politics of Evadne's narrative in *The Heavenly Twins*, but have had much more difficulty with the 'heavenly twins' themselves.[25] The twins' names immediately suggest a parody of the feminine/masculine binary opposition, and this is accompanied by a gender inversion in the twins' physical and mental characteristics: Angelica is taller, stronger and cleverer than Diavolo. The twins' cross-dressing – they swap clothes at Evadne's wedding – also playfully suggests a gender inversion. Angelica and Diavolo refuse a gendered education – their father concedes the point and allows his daughter to share his son's tutor – and at fifteen years old, Diavolo shows himself to be something of a 'New Man', complaining to his tutor about the misogyny of classical literature (272).

The most significant section of the novel with regard to gender roles is the curious hundred-page episode called 'The Tenor and the Boy – An Interlude'. The tenor in the cathedral choir with whom Angelica, dressed as a boy, forms a relationship, is a virgin male, and virginity in Victorian terms was of course a 'feminine' gender attribute. The chaste tenor is emphatically *not* decadent, and if his relationship with the 'Boy' is based on same-sex desire, as it appears to be, it is nonetheless a far cry from the more sexually-charged homoeroticism of *Dorian Gray*. In a confused way, the Tenor desires the androgynous 'Boy', feeling towards him 'a something of that something which he knew he needed but could not name' (382), which is strongly suggestive of the love that had no name in the English language until the early 1890s, the love that dare not speak its name.[26] If same-sex desire is hinted at in the relationship, it is not clear-cut, for the appeal of the Boy for the tenor is that 'he' appears to be androgynous. He tells Angelica that:

> when you play [the violin] you are like that creature in the 'Witch of Atlas':
> "A sexless thing it was, and in its growth
> It seemed to have developed no defect

Of either sex, yet all the grace of both" (403).

The appeal of the relationship for both the Tenor and Angelica is that it is free from the gender constraints of society. As Angelica puts it, when her sex is revealed:

> "The charm – the charm," she faltered, "has all been in the delight of associating with a man intimately who did not know I was a woman. I have enjoyed the benefit of free intercourse with your masculine mind undiluted by the masculine prejudices and proclivities with regard to my sex" (458).

Such freedom could not possibly have been achieved in the emphatically heterosexual unions figured in the main narrative; this 'other' narrative contains that which could not be articulated within the dominant discourse on gender.

What Angelica wants from her cross-dressing is very different from what the Tenor desires, however. He has been in love with the 'Boy', and when the 'Boy' disappears, he is heartbroken and dies an exaggeratedly romantic death, full of sentiment and pathos. But Angelica seeks with the tenor a heterosexual friendship which has the equality of a brother/sister relationship, the sort of relationship she has had with her brother until convention insisted he go to Sandhurst for an army career. The desire for the equality of a brother/sister relationship can be compared to the (equally doomed) union between Sue Bridehead and Jude Fawley in *Jude the Obscure*, published two years later.

Neither of the possibilities explored in 'The Tenor and the Boy' – same-sex love and a brother/sister relationship – is realisable in the pages of this ultimately morally conventional novel, and Angelica collapses into what Grand calls an 'ideal' marriage with her twenty-years-senior husband, whom she calls 'daddy'. The central female characters of the novel, Evadne and Angelica, both end up in conventional marriages with 'respectable' men. But there is no romantic closure: Evadne, now married to the morally correct Dr Galbraith, is more his patient than his wife. Pregnant with their child, she attempts suicide because of an (irrational) fear that their child will bear some kind of hereditary taint. Evadne's hysteria – Galbraith diagnoses it as such – seems to stem from a residual fear of the pollutant effect of male sexuality that has persisted after her first husband's death. It is a fear which haunts Grand's novel and which means that, in the final analysis, the epithet of 'decadent lady novelist' which had been so frequently applied to New Woman writers such as Grand, hardly seems to have been appropriate.[27]

NOTES

1. Studies of the New Woman include: Ann Ardis, *New Women, New Novels: Feminism and Early Modernism*, New Brunswick and London 1990; Gerd Bjorhovde, *Rebellious Structures: Women Writers and the Crisis of the Novel*, Oslo 1987; Ruth Brandon, *The New Women and the Old Men*, London 1990; Lyn Pykett, *The Improper Feminine: The Women's Sensation Novel and the New Woman Writing*, London and New York 1992; Elaine Showalter, *Sexual Anarchy: Gender and Culture at the Fin de Siècle*, London 1991, chapters 3 and 9.
   For a discussion of the relationship between imperialist politics and sexual politics at the fin de siècle, see Vron Ware, *Beyond the Pale: White Women, Racism and History*, London and New York 1992; Nupur Chaudhuri and Margaret Strobel, eds., *Western Women and Imperialism: Complicity and Resistance*, Bloomington and Indianapolis 1992; Ronald Hyam, *Empire and Sexuality: the British Experience*, Manchester 1990; Joseph Bristow, *Empire Boys: Adventures in a Man's World*, New York 1990; and Jeffrey Weeks, *Coming Out: Homosexual Politics in Britain, From the Nineteenth Century to the Present*, London, Melbourne and New York 1977, 18.

2. For an account of the two trials see Richard Ellmann, *Oscar Wilde*, New York 1988, 462–78.

3. *Punch*, 21st December 1895, 297.

4. *Speaker*, 13th April 1895, 403, quoted by John Stokes, *In the Nineties*, Hemel Hempstead 1989, 14.

5. Eliza Lynn Linton, 'The partisans of the Wild Woman', *Nineteenth Century*, 31 (1892), 463.

6. Elaine Showalter, *Daughters of Decadence*, London 1993, ix.

7. Thomas Bradfield, 'A dominant note of some recent fiction', *Westminster Review*, 142 (1894), 543.

8. *Punch*, 27th April 1895, 203.

9. Max Beerbohm, 'A defence of cosmetics,' *Yellow Book* 1 (1894), 78.

10. Marie Corelli, *The Sorrows of Satan*, London 1895, 301.

11. ibid., 406.

12. Laurel Brake, *Subjugated Knowledges: Journalism, Gender and Literature in the Nineteenth Century*, Basingstoke 1994, 127–48.

13. ibid., 138-9.

14. Oscar Wilde, 'A.L.S to "Madam"', (London, Summer 1887), Henry W. and Albert A. Berg Collection, The New York Public Library, Astor, Lenox and Tilden Foundations. Quoted in Brake, ibid., 134.

15. ibid., 142.

16. See ibid., 132–3 for examples of these illustrations.

17. See, for example, Kerry Powell, 'Oscar Wilde, Elizabeth Robins and the theatre of the future', *Modern Drama*, (Spring 1994), 220–38; and Joel H. Kaplan and Sheila Stowell, *Theatre and Fashion: Oscar Wilde to the Suffragettes*, Cambridge 1994.

18. ibid., 65.

19. Rita Felski, 'The counter-discourse of the feminine in three texts by Huysmans, Wilde and Sacher-Masoch', *PMLA*, 106:5 (1991), 1099.

20. Oscar Wilde, *The Picture of Dorian Gray*, Harmondsworth 1985, 72. Further references are to this edition and given in the text.

21. 'Death of a decadent', *Woman's Signal*, 3 (May 1895), 289.

22. For recent feminist readings of the novel see Ardis, op. cit.; Bjorhovde, op. cit.; Pykett, op. cit.; and Elaine Showalter, *A Literature of Their Own: British Novelists From Brontë to Lessing*, London 1978, and *Sexual Anarchy*, op. cit. For an excellent account of the importance of women's reading in *The Heavenly Twins* and of the novel's reception by the feminist press, see Kate Flint, *The Woman Reader 1830-1914*, Oxford 1993.

23. Sarah A. Tooley, 'The woman's question: an interview with Madame Sarah Grand', *Humanitarian* 8 (1896), 160-9.

24. Sarah Grand, *The Heavenly Twins*, 1893; repr. London 1894, 79. All further references to the novel are to this edition, and will be given in the text.

25. Much the most convincing reading of the 'Tenor and the Boy' interlude to date is Lyn Pykett's brief commentary in Pykett, op. cit., chapter 17. Whilst Pykett ponders the sexual ambiguity of the relationship, Gerd Bjorhovde rather lamely regards the twins' role as 'comic relief' and 'a standard by which other characters are judged'. Bjorhovde, op. cit., chapter 4.

26. The term 'homosexual' was first translated from German into English in 1892.

27. See, for example, Hugh Stutfield, 'Tommyrotics', *Blackwood's Magazine* 157 (June 1895), 833-45.

10

'Sphinxes and secrets':
women poets of the 1880s and 1890s

Deborah Tyler-Bennett

> Come forth my lovely seneschal! So somnolent, so
> statuesque!
> Come forth you exquisite grotesque! Half woman
> and half animal![1]

So wrote Oscar Wilde in 'The Sphinx' (1894) a poem which, by conflating images of hostile and unknowable female fatalism, can be used as a point of reference, both for images of 'feminine' decadence, and for indications of fin-de-siècle socio-sexual anxiety. Wilde's poetry is often used as a critical marker for other works written in the 1880s and early 1890s, so beginning with his aesthetic appears to be essential when attempting to reclaim 'lost' works by women poets of the period, as one can then endeavour to outline which aspects of his aesthetic were developed or rejected by women poets. In Wilde's poem, the Sphinx is at once sexually unknowable – the poet constantly questioning her sexual preferences – and a site of conjecture: Wilde depicts her as consorting with mythic and known animals, Egyptian gods, heroes, and also manages to present her as asexual. Wilde's text, which is only one example of his use of a degenerate female archetype, fluctuates between a specifically Christian imagery, of the one God whose symbolism is of human suffering, but in whom the poet cannot wholly believe, and pagan sensuality which, by implication, the poet both desires and fears. In conclusion, the poet rejects the Sphinx, via a similar terminology to that used by writers representing the expulsion of the fallen woman: 'False Sphinx! False Sphinx!/ Go thou before, and leave/ me to my crucifix!'[2] It is interesting to note how the figure of the Sphinx came to be employed by both male and female poets to represent concepts of 'suspect' femininity, both questioning and falling into the orientalist stereotype of mystical androgyny and female fatalism. In many of these revisions of Eastern myth, Western ideologies (either the Western version of Christ the Redeemer, or new European philosophical structures) replace or destroy the mythological archetype.

119

However, in Wilde's case, Christ cannot redeem, but passively 'weeps for every soul in vain', thus rendering the Sphinx's imagined sexual activity the more powerful and terrifying.[3] Likewise, in 'The Harlot's House' (1885), where the Harlot magically renders both clients and other prostitutes into automata, her house is known but she remains an enigma.[4]

In both early and later works, Wilde uses imagery of female fatalism to locate his own desires, where the gentle sensuality of Charmides works in opposition to the fierce beauty of the Sphinx, and to outline fears occurring at the end of a century. These fears are exemplified by the Sphinx, a reconstituted woman, both animal and human, which questions the concept of gender difference itself. As Alan Sinfield argues, gay readings of Wilde serve to reveal the complexity both of context and content, pointing to questions concerning culture and sub-culture.[5] Whilst my argument is influenced by critiques of nineteenth-century homosexual culture such as Sinfield's, I wish to employ images of 'decadent' female sexuality created by Wilde and others to accompany discussion of a 'women's aesthetic' which provides alternative readings of these images. Of course, the term 'woman's aesthetic' is not intended to be taken as fixed, but rather is used to imply a series of strategies open to women poets of the period.

Wilde's Sphinx and Harlot are not isolated figures in male representations of female sexuality; such animalistic *femme fatales* occur in works published in the 1880s and 1890s by Swinburne, Ernest Dowson, Lord Alfred Douglas, Francis Thompson, Aubrey Beardsley, John Davidson, and others. Dowson's Cynara (1896), who renders the poet 'sick of an old passion', and John Gray's translation of Baudelaire (1893), where damned women signify a sadomasochistic blending of pleasure and pain, are two well-known examples of this trope.[6] It is worth remembering in this context that opiates and alcohol were likewise linked to female sexuality in this period, in both dominant European cultures and sub-cultures, as Barnaby Conran's work on absinthe, commonly known as 'the Green Fairy' demonstrates.[7] As Bram Dikstra, Nina Auerbach, and Shearer West suggest, portrayals of the demonised woman are common to both visual and verbal art in the late nineteenth century.[8] What I wish to indicate here is how women poets of the 1880s and 1890s subverted these familiar female archetypes, whilst contributing to a body of literature using mythological figures.

In *Teleny* (1893) the 'pornographic'/erotic work penned possibly by Wilde and others, homosexuality is termed 'the reverse of the medal'.[9] By implication, the medal's front is heterosexuality, thus leaving no place for the possibility of either lesbianism, or female desire outside of the framework of a male/female relationship. This view of sexuality can also be observed in other works spanning the 1880s and 1890s. However, in poems by women, desire is signified via a complex series of tropes and reversed archetypes. Its presence implies, not the reverse of a medal, but the re-casting of it. In works prior to the period, such as the poem 'The World' by Christina Rossetti, unleashed female passion is depicted as a monstrous spectre, a figure to be denied at all costs.[10] As developed in the poetry of Mary Elizabeth Coleridge, this figure has become impossible to contain, and thus the demonic woman is openly acknowledged as an alternative version of the self. In 'The Other Side of a Mirror' (1896), the vision of female sexuality which the narrator sees reflected in her looking-glass is conveyed via menstrual images: 'the hideous wound/ in silence and in secret bled.'[11] The wound is hideous, Coleridge implies, not because it exists, but because its presence remains unspoken. Likewise, the reflection of suppressed female desire is demonic, not due to desire itself, but because it remains hidden. Similarly, the female satanist in 'The Witch' who, as with many vampiric women also depicted in poems by male writers is 'let' into the narrator's house, pleads 'for her heart's desire', thus outlining society's denial of female desire as the greater evil.[12]

As many feminist scholars working on the subject of mythology indicate, myth can be adapted to imply gender difference. Sirens both ancient and modern, who often embody doom in Pre-Raphaelite (and later in decadent) writings are transformed in many poems by women. The idea of 'low' female music, which accompanies the dead Queen in Lionel Johnson's 'The Last Music' (1895), is used to different effect (the site of a gender-battle) in Michael Field's 'Fifty Quatrains'.[13] One could argue that the poem's narrator is not gendered and yet Edith Cooper and Katherine Bradley, the women writing under the male pseudonym 'Michael Field', by separating the speaker from the royal house 'full of kings' imply a female perspective.[14] The woman who is observed by the speaker, singing 'fifty quatrains', recalls other female presences, those 'bands of low-voiced women on a happy shore'.[15] The song conveys sensual pleasure to the narrator, another point which favours the argument that this is a woman-focused work, whilst the kings remain silent and unable to act:

Nor dared to seize the marvellous rich pleasure,
Too fearful even to ask in whisperings,
The ramparts being closed, whence she had come.[16]

Unlike the kings, the poem's speaker both celebrates and shares the sensuality of the song, and unlike Johnson's 'low-voiced women' who sing of mourning, Field's single woman conveys the erotic 'low' voices of many women.

In 'Circe' by Augusta Webster, published in Elizabeth Sharp's *Women's Voices* anthology of 1887, the enchantress's voice is equally located as a site of ambiguity, both desiring heterosexual union and maintaining sexual autonomy.[17] Circe, sighting the ship of Ulysses, knows that the men will prove themselves swinish, and that her potion will only reveal animalistic behaviour which already lurks below the surface. Webster's Circe is just one example of the transformation of a demonic female figure by a woman poet. Ellice Hopkins's 'A Vision of Womanhood' (1883) uses the image of the Sphinx but, unlike the later work by Wilde, deploys the Sphinx to convey an outmoded idea of female fatalism.[18] One could regard Hopkins's poem as conventional, as the shattered Sphinx of the East gives way to a European, maternal image:

A wall of fire to guard her round about –
A perfect woman in her weakness rose,
And in her arms the future's child divine.[19]

Yet the poem's complex, near-Nietzschean, imagery prevents such a simple reading. The woman rising 'in her weakness' is weak not due to her sex, which has been defined throughout the poem using images of strength (she creates a wall of fire at the time of her birth), but because of her struggle with the ancient Sphinx who, unlike Wilde's demon, appears to be non-vital and crumbling. A Promethean woman emerges in place of the Sphinx, and this figure is linked to the poem's female narrator. This emergence of a 'new' woman figure, who displaces or re-figures a mythical archetype, also occurs in the poems of Emily Pfeiffer, a poet of Welsh descent.

Pfeiffer's work, particularly her double sonnet 'Peace to the Odalisque', concerns the displacing of an exotic sexual stereotype, the odalisque of Western versions of Eastern myth, whose worth is measured by her fidelity to her master and her 'beauty's transient flower'.[20] The ending of the first sonnet defines the odalisque as 'graceful ephemera', and suggests that she cannot exist within a world which contains working women:

In vain would women's hearts,
In love with sacrifice, withstand the stream,
Of human progress; other spheres, new parts
Await them. God be with them in their quest –
Our brave, sad working-women of the West.[21]

Of course, the poem by no means represents a totally progressive view of the woman's lot; women's work is still here defined by images of sacrifice and philanthropy. Yet, as with Hopkins's Sphinx, the odalisque must be banished to the pages of history books to allow the birth of a new female spirit to take place. Similar to Virginia Woolf's later argument that to write one has to kill Patmore's damaging 'angel in the house', Pfeiffer's working woman must destroy the odalisque in order to work. As the odalisque is a familiar late-nineteenth-century archetype (one only has to consider Andrew Lang's collection of *Tales from the Arabian Nights* to realise how the figure is used as a representation of exotic passivity), it is worth noting that at the beginning of the second sonnet, Pfeiffer banishes the figure to 'live alone in story'.[22] The odalisque, defined only in terms of physical attraction, gives way to a much more ambivalent 'new' woman figure, that of the worker. The 'morning glory' of the odalisque's costume is replaced by the 'dull robes' of the working woman who buys her right to life with 'honest pain'; the passion of mythic romance is thus here dispersed by the 'white light' of charity borne of work.[23] In many of these poems, it appears to be significant that verbal representations of jewel-bright, Pre-Raphaelitic colours are replaced by sober tones associated with work-clothes. The former are traditionally associated either with the adornment and transformation of working-class models, as with Dante Gabriel Rossetti's depictions of Fanny Cornforth and Annie Miller, or with titillating orientalist versions of female sexuality such as those painted by Lawrence Alma-Tadema, Lord Leighton and Albert Moore.

The desire to contain the woman of fantasy, whilst activating a 'new' woman figure to take her place, undoubtedly places Hopkins and Pfeiffer within a female fin-de-siècle tradition. As Elaine Showalter notes, the image of the 'odd' working woman who did not marry is prevalent in much work of the period.[24] Yet, unlike many of the sources from prose works cited by Showalter, the 'odd' women created by Pfeiffer and Hopkins are represented as possessing an already-determined social place, once the mythic, exotic woman has been destroyed. Perhaps locating this type of aesthetic as a kind of feminist Darwinism would be taking the idea too far; however, the concept of exploding ancient images of female sexuality and replacing these with a more practical modern image undoubtedly occurs in many poetic works written by women during the period. The 'odd women' created by Pfeiffer and Hopkins are 'odd' because they suggest a new way of looking at women, both aesthetically and socially. Thus poems which are conventional in form (sonnets, for example) may be regarded as subverting the conventions of that form; Pfeiffer's sonnets, for instance, are not about romantic love but rather seek to explode a romantic myth.

When, in her introduction to *Daughters of Decadence: Women Writers of the Fin de Siècle* (1993), Elaine Showalter comments that: 'women writers needed to rescue female sexuality from the decadents' images of romantically doomed prostitutes or devouring Venus flytraps, and represent female desire as a creative force in artistic imagination as well as in biological reproduction,'[25] she is referring specifically to prose writers. Yet this definition could also stand for many of the women poets outlined here. It is interesting to note that, whilst women short story writers, such as Charlotte Mew and Victoria Cross, have recently been re-established as being as much a part of the world of John Lane's *Yellow Book* as their male contemporaries, the same has yet to happen to women poets. Two anthologies published by Elizabeth Sharp, *Women's Voices* (1887) and *Women Poets* (c.1890), reveal a brief selection of work available for analysis which is breathtaking in scope. Worth study also is a verse drama by Rebecca Sophia Ross, *Ariadne in Naxos* (1882), where the visionary Ariadne prophecies doom, but is not believed by the arrogant Theseus.[26]

Abandoned by Theseus at the play's conclusion, Ariadne speaks the text's longest monologue, defining her own fidelity and the mistake she has made in expecting the same devotion from Theseus. The difference Ross suggests, it seems to me, is one of vocation. Theseus's language defines him in terms of militarism, action, and a quest for personal glory, whilst Ariadne's more poetic language aligns her with the female deities who speak throughout the play. Her penultimate speech urges Artemis to 'light' her 'unto death', thus evading both the unworthy Theseus and the corrupt Dionysus. It is also worth noting that Ariadne was a favourite figure amongst women writers and artists of the period, being depicted in paintings by, amongst others, Evelyn de Morgan.

Just as Ross looks to revise classical mythology, so Violet Fane's volume, *Under Cross and Crescent* (1896), is also worth reclamation.[27] As with Field's female singer in 'Fifty Quatrains', Fane uses images of song to convey 'otherness', and, similar to Mary Elizabeth Coleridge's apparition in the mirror, Fane's 'Siren' could be interpreted as an alternative version of the self.[28] On the surface, this is a conventional version of the Siren as destructive, based as much upon contemporary painting as poetry. Yet what is subversive about the poem is the way in which the Siren reaches the decision to become disruptive, which in itself revises a ballad image of female passivity. As with Arnold's 'The Forsaken Merman' (1849), Fane's Siren is taken with the idea of human love. Unlike the Merman, who becomes involved with a human being who then rejects both him and his children, the Siren soon dismisses the idea as undesirable. What Fane's Siren celebrates is her own difference, both in appearance (human figures in the poem remain shadowy, whilst she is conveyed via a painterly use of colour), and in her decision not to embrace the human concept of love. This solution is reached after the Siren hears the cries of rejected women:

> But oft I hear them moan and sigh,
>   And often weep for woe;
> The summer nights are going by,
>   Yet this is all I know.[29]

The Siren does not, however, wish to lose her lover. She kills him, in the traditional way of luring him into the water by singing a song and then drowning him. In the poem's most chilling moment, the Siren makes her lover's remains into a symbol of her art:

> And he was mine, – my very own.
> I clasp'd him firm and fair....
> (This harp is made of his breast-bone,
> Its strings were once his hair).[30]

This image is taken directly from a Scots-Irish ballad 'The Cruel Sister'.[31] The ballad tells of a lovely young woman who is drowned by a jealous sister, whose lover prefers the young woman's yellow hair to her own. In this work, a harper discovers the body, making a harp from her breast-bone and stringing it from her hair. When played, the instrument's notes speak, condemning the murderous sister. As Elizabeth Gitter indicates, the gifts of 'music and self-expression' are thus transmuted from the sister to her hair.[32] That Fane transfers the fate of the sister to a male figure reveals her desire to re-write mythological tropes.

One cannot help but think that Fane's Siren is better off than Scott's Ariadne, because she hears the cries of the forsaken women before she falls for the concept of romantic love. Just as the song of the strange woman in Field's poem awakes the hearer to her own sensuality, so the cries of women alert the Siren to her possible fate. In re-writing the context of a mythological demon, Fane allows a subversion more pronounced than Hopkins's destruction of the Sphinx. In rejecting romantic love, Fane's Siren settles for art, albeit art of a particularly violent origin, as the harp which is its symbol is created from the bones and hair of her dead lover. Likewise, Field's listener is awoken by a female song which excludes the regal male hearers. Wilde's Sphinx, which the poet uses as a means to project his own fantasies of desire, remains malevolently glowering in a corner of the room for much of the poem, whereas in most of the poetic works by women described, the female figures, whether they be sirens, sphinxes, or working women, take centre stage.

The harp of hair and bone might be an extreme symbol of women's art, but it implies that art can only be achieved through the death of romantic love. Just as Virginia Woolf's writing in the twentieth century negotiates the death of

Patmore's 'angel in the house', so Fane kills the male lover but leaves the symbol of romance denied in the hands of the woman artist. Likewise, the working women outlined by Pfeiffer may lack the glorious dress of the odalisque, but they achieve an autonomy which, for the fantasy figure, remains impossible. In sum, women poets of the 1880s and 1890s use colourful images which are also to be found in decadent and neo-classical works to suggest new possibilities for the female form, effectively re-casting *Teleny*'s medal.

NOTES

1.   Oscar Wilde, 'The Sphinx', *The Complete Works of Oscar Wilde*, London 1977, 833–42.
2.   ibid, 842.
3.   ibid.
4.   'The Harlot's House', ibid, 789.
5.   Alan Sinfield, *The Wilde Century: Effeminacy, Oscar Wilde and the Queer Moment*, London 1994, 4–6.
6.   Ernest Dowson, 'Non sum qualis eram bonae sub regno Cynarae', in R. K. Thornton, ed., *Poetry of the Nineties*, Harmondsworth 1970, 158–9; John Gray, 'Femmes Damnées', ibid, 175–6.
7.   Barnaby Conran, *Absinthe: History in a Bottle*, San Francisco 1988, 25–42.
8.   Bram Dikstra, *Idols of Perversity: Fantasies of Feminine Evil in Fin-de-Siècle Culture*, Oxford 1986; Nina Auerbach, *Woman and the Demon: The Life of a Victorian Myth*, Cambridge 1982; Shearer West, *Fin de Siècle: Art and Society in the Age of Uncertainty*, London 1993.
9.   Oscar Wilde and others, *Teleny: Or the Reverse of the Medal*, London 1986.
10.   Christina Rossetti, 'The World', *Poems*, London 1913, 50.
11.   Mary Elizabeth Coleridge, 'The Other Side of a Mirror', in Jennifer Breen, ed., *Victorian Women Poets 1830–1900, An Anthology*, London 1994, 144.
12.   Mary E. Coleridge, 'The Witch', in Louise Berkinow, ed., *The World Split Open: Women Poets 1552–1950*, London 1979, 138–9.
      The idea of 'letting in' the Witch also applies to many vampire superstitions; see Christopher Frayling, *Vampyres: Lord Byron to Count Dracula*, London 1991.
13.   Michael Field, 'Fifty Quatrains', in Catherine Reilly, ed., *Winged Words: Victorian Women's Poetry and Verse*, London 1994, 56.

14. ibid.
15. ibid.
16. ibid.
17. Augusta Webster, 'Circe', in Elizabeth Sharp, ed., *Women's Voices*, London 1887, 250-7.
18. Ellice Hopkins, 'A Vision of Womanhood', ibid., 360-1.
19. ibid., 361.
20. Emily Pfeiffer, 'Peace to the Odalisque', ibid., 274-5.
21. ibid., 274.
22. Andrew Lang, *Tales from the Arabian Nights*, Hertfordshire 1993; Pfeiffer, op. cit., 275.
23. ibid.
24. Elaine Showalter, *Sexual Anarchy: Gender and Culture at the Fin de Siècle*, London 1992, 19-37.
25. Elaine Showalter, ed., *Daughters of Decadence: Women Writers of the Fin de Siècle*, London 1993, xi.
26. Rebecca Sophia Ross, *Ariadne in Naxos*, London 1882.
27. Violet Fane, *Under Cross and Crescent*, London 1896.
28. ibid., 78-81.
29. ibid., 81.
30. ibid.
31. See Elizabeth G. Gitter, 'The power of women's hair in the Victorian imagination', *PMLA*, 99 (October 1994), 936-54. She lists 'The Cruel Sister' in her article, but does not connect it to Fane's revision.
32. ibid., 939.

11

'For the blood is the life':
the construction of purity in Bram Stoker's *Dracula*

William Hughes

Towards the close of the first volume of *The History of Sexuality*, Michel Foucault initiates a sustained discussion of what he terms 'the blood relation' within society – a mode of cultural organisation whereby 'blood constituted one of the fundamental values', being 'a reality with a symbolic function'. Foucault tempers this analysis through the suggestion that 'we' – the author and the reader – are not implicated squarely within this 'society of sanguinity' but within a subsequent and consequent 'society of "sex"', or rather, a society 'with a sexuality'.[1] This latter assertion has particular implications for the academic criticism of Bram Stoker's *Dracula* at the close of the twentieth century, in that the cultural meanings associated with blood in 1897 have, to a great extent, been eclipsed by post-Freudian readings from the 'society with a sexuality'.

For the nineteenth century, blood, by way of consanguinity, was a potent signifier of relationship. One was related to nation as much as to family by identities vested in blood, as Joseph Chamberlain confirmed in an anti-Home Rule speech in 1886, which proclaimed the Belfast working classes to an English audience as 'your own flesh and blood, of Scottish and English stock'.[2] Ideologies and behavioural standards were similarly encoded within the signifier, so that to depart from accepted practice became, in a sense, to be deficient in, or untrue to, one's 'blood'. This was an accusation, incidentally, levelled against Stoker by one American reviewer of *Dracula*: 'When an Englishman, or, for that matter, anyone of Anglo-Saxon blood, goes into degenerate literature of his own sort, he reveals a horrible kind of degeneracy.'[3] Blood facilitates an identity which is simultaneously cultural and physiological. However, the subsequent critical preoccupation with sexuality in this text – or, more accurately, with sexual relations – has closed off much of this potential signification. In post-Freudian literary criticism, blood has been almost totally appropriated as a synonym for semen. Equated with displaced oral desires, the vampiric act becomes a representation of seduction: to suck blood is to wish to consume another bodily fluid. In consequence, the figure of the vampire, re-coded as the demon-lover or archetypal seducer, has eclipsed the presence and activities of other blood-users in *Dracula*, just as his eroticism has obscured the cultural resonances of their activities.[4]

To acknowledge the presence of this greater cultural context, however, is not necessarily to concede that the preoccupations of the 'society of sanguinity' are replicated without question in *Dracula*. Indeed, it may be argued that the cultural valorisation of blood in *Dracula* is complicated by the novel's participation in a phase of medical discourse characteristic of the closing years of the nineteenth century. These valorisations coexist, although, arguably, the medical discourse with its focus on circulation and infection subsumes its discursive counterparts, realigning their metaphorical energy along its own conceptual structures, forcing their expression through a filter of medical logic. The concept of blood in *Dracula* becomes, in a sense, the 'reality' through which the symbolics of the substance are vocalised. Hence, the symbolics of the text become subject to the central thematic of the loss, transfer, consumption and quality of blood, and – in consequence of the medical discourse's ability to commentate on other areas of fin-de-siècle social life – the relative quality of other substances and phenomena.

The verbal exchange between the lunatic, Renfield, and Mina Harker in the eighteenth chapter of the novel is a significant moment in this discursive realignment. Temporarily lucid, Renfield identifies the focus of his own psychotic disorder:

> I used to fancy that life was a positive and perpetual entity, and that by consuming a multitude of live things, no matter how low in the scale of creation, one might indefinitely prolong life. At times I held the belief so strongly that I actually tried to take human life. The doctor here will bear me out that on one occasion I tried to kill him for the purpose of strengthening my vital powers by the assimilation with my own body of his life through the medium of his own blood – relying, of course, upon the scriptural phrase, 'For the blood is the life.' Though, indeed, the vendor of a certain nostrum has vulgarised the truism to the very point of contempt....[5]

In theological terms, this is a complex passage. The 'life' referred to in Renfield's truncated quotation from the twelfth chapter of Deuteronomy is essentially a sacred or spiritual life: unlike the substance of the body, the blood is made sacred by its association with the continuation of life, and is thus reserved for God, not to be consumed by man.[6] But Renfield's testimony both secularises and literalises the 'scriptural phrase'. For Renfield, organic life and vitality, rather than spirituality, are transmitted through the medium of the bodily fluid; as he later concedes, 'I want no souls. Life is all I want' (268).

Hence, Renfield is not attempting a form of perverted Eucharist, as his ingestion of both flesh and fluid commemorates neither god nor sacrifice. His desire to drink blood is not the expression of a totemic urge to ingest the qualities of the Other, given that he does not attempt to consume the sanguine Absolute, the vessel containing many nutritive fluids, that the vampire represents.[7] Rather, the urge to consume is merely the craving for the physical vitality which may with equal ease be obtained from any of the other creatures – flies, spiders, sparrows – which form Renfield's perverse diet. The eroticism (and, indeed, the sense of blasphemy) associated by critics with the vampire's diet are, notably, not present here. Human blood has simply become another material product in a non-anthropocentric system of value and circulation. Within the logic of Renfield's psychosis, blood is merely an orally-assimilated additive to a system which requires regular sustenance.

Renfield, however, is by his own admission quoting the Bible at second remove. His allusion may thus refer equally to an advertising gimmick frequently employed during the last fifteen years of the nineteenth century by a number of patent medicine manufacturers. The rhetoric associated with one such product, 'Clarke's World-Famed Blood Mixture', which is arguably the 'certain nostrum' to which Renfield alludes, is particularly worthy of note. A characteristic advertisement for the product, placed in *The Times* around three years before Stoker began writing *Dracula*, reads:

> FOR the BLOOD is the LIFE.... Clarke's World-Famed Blood mixture is warranted to cleanse the blood from all impurities from whatever cause arising. For scrofula, scurvy, eczema, skin and blood diseases, and sores of all kinds its effects are marvellous.... Clarke's World-Famed Blood Mixture is entirely free from any poison or metallic impregnation, does not contain any injurious ingredients, and is a good, safe, and useful medicine....[8]

The value of the product, it seems, is vested in its alleged purity. Transferred by whatever method of ingestion into the blood supply, the mixture will itself enhance the purity of the existing matter. The notion of enhanced personal vitality here is not dissimilar to that espoused by the supposedly-insane Renfield. However, the symbolic racial and familial encodings within blood, and its precarious racial nature – which Foucault notes as a consequence of it being 'easily spilled, subject to drying up, too readily mixed, capable of being quickly corrupted' – are here mobilised through a non-sanguine, indeed non-human, fluid.[9] As the advertisement's coda betrays, such 'mixtures' may with equal ease corrupt or poison the system rather than revitalise it. The 'corrupted' individual, the argument follows, may in turn go on to corrupt others.[10]

'Clarke's World-Famed Blood Mixture' is but one medical product participating in a symbolic discourse previously associated with the sanguine fluid. Somewhat more disturbing, by the standards of the late twentieth century, is a preparation marketed towards the end of the nineteenth century under the general name, 'Pure Vaccine Lymph'. A common formulation was the animal by-product 'Dr Warlomont's Calf Vaccine', though a contemporary advertisement discreetly advertises the availability of a related nostrum:

> HUMAN VACCINE, from healthy children only, microscopically examined and source quoted, – Tubes, two-thirds full, 1/8 each.
> Tubes, two-thirds full (same as those mentioned above, but without source), in quantities for export, £5 per 100 Tubes.[11]

Vaccine lymph is the secretion or by-product of a human being actively infected with cowpox. It is gathered by breaking into the mature pustule or vesicle of the donor, by preference 'a child recently vaccinated', and is then subcutaneously injected into the recipient's skin tissue.[12] Though surface bleeding is not essential to ensure a successful administration of vaccine lymph, 'it is requisite that a small quantity of exuded serum from the blood should mingle with the vaccine matter'.[13] Once within the system, the vaccine lymph prototypically functions by 'assisting the natural mechanism of immunity', although its effectiveness may be compromised by the purity or age of the matter administered.[14]

The application of the specific term 'lymph' to this particular body supplement is significant. Lymph, like blood, is a medium by which infection as well as health may be disseminated throughout the system.[15] Derived from blood and naturally filtered by way of the lymph nodes, lymph is closely associated with the sanguine fluid in what the Victorian physician J. M'Gregor-Robertson calls the 'economy' of the human body.[16] Lymph is viewed as a separate secretion from blood yet remains peculiarly intimate to that substance. The application of the term here thus permits Dr Warlomont's preparations to blur the gap between bodily secretions and externally-sourced additives. A guaranteed or accredited source for the substance enhances its value – and presumably affirms its efficacy as a medium of vitality or regeneration. It is advertised, as we can see, with an emphasis on purity and non-adulteration which dissipates its status as a human by-product, and which incorporates it within the same class of commodities as Van Houten's Cocoa – 'perfectly pure' – or Cadbury's Cocoa – 'Absolutely pure, therefore best'.[17] Bodily fluids, and, through them, questions of individual integrity or purity, have here become caught up in the debate centred upon the adulteration of foods, raging from the mid-nineteenth century, and still active in the late twentieth century.

The commodification of bodily fluid in both *Dracula* and the advertising literature of the late nineteenth century appears to signal a conceptual change within the medical discourse's appreciation of the human body, and within the general public's attitude to specific bodily fluids. The commodification of the dead body was legitimised by the 1832 Anatomy Act, where the notion of an 'unclaimed body' transferred the ownership of a cadaver away from the self and into the hands of others, whether the third party be the family or the responsible parish. However, the *living* body – and its component parts – remained at the disposal of the self, except where this ownership was curtailed by minority, insanity or legal captivity. The commodification of the living body, and the sudden availability of its components for transfer between living individuals, would appear, therefore, to be contemporaneous with the development of relatively safe methods of blood transfusion through devices such as the Aveling apparatus in the late 1880s.[18]

Once blood ceases to circulate wholly within a single physiological body, and as soon as it becomes transferable between several such systems, its symbolics are re-energised. The metaphorical coding of a nation as a 'blood'-defined race finds a literal equivalent in the introduction of blood (and other fluids) into both the individual, and, through the medium of the individual, into collective blood streams. Integrity and purity become racial as well as individual concerns. Blood indeed doubles for semen in such rhetoric, although without the erotic connotations imposed by twentieth-century criticism. The act of mixing racial bloods compromises the self. The immigrant, the alien-other, becomes an impregnation, literally an injurious 'foreign body', in the circulation of the national or racial system. Hence, the qualities culturally encoded within blood become even more acutely subject to the same criteria as the real physiological substance: circulation, purity, dilution, corruption, the relative value of anonymity and specificity of source.

These were crucial issues at the close of the nineteenth century. On the one hand, immigration (particularly Jewish immigration into the East End of London) threatened the mythical homogeneity of the indigenous population. On the other, a significant proportion of that population, long subject to empirical study by social reformers, was apparently exhibiting signs, not merely of moral, but also of physiological and mental decline. This culture of impending degeneration, popularised both by the social reporters and the medical writings of Cesare Lombroso, Max Nordau and Edwin Lankester, is the racial – or racist – context of *Dracula*.[19] These fears of disrupted homogeneity, and of debilitation through contact with the alien, map over the complex relationships which link the vampire both to his victims, and to those who oppose him. Furthermore, the homogeneity of the relationships within the latter group becomes itself questionable. Even within the 'homogenous' indigenous race there are, it seems, criteria of acceptability, modes of exclusion.

The relationship between the vampire and his two female victims, Lucy Westenra and Mina Harker, is central here. Traditionally, critics have charted a decline in the moral tenor of Lucy's behaviour as a consequence of her successive meetings with Dracula. As A. N. Wilson puts it, 'the high virtue of Lucy can simply be drained away as her blood is drained away, until she too joins the vampire brood'.[20] An emphasis has further been placed upon Lucy's apparent sexual awakening following her encounter with the vampire (161). Quite clearly, vampirism is signalled here as a condition into which one degenerates through contact, a change which displays both physical and moral consequences that arguably exclude the self from a previous identity in a community.

Mina Harker, however, apparently displays no such degenerative signs when she herself subsequently falls victim to the Count's appetite. It is seemingly only when the vampire forces his own blood *into* her alimentary system – by way of a scene which twentieth-century critics have frequently rendered as a displaced act of *fellatio* – that she progressively displays, in Van Helsing's words, 'the characteristics of the vampire' (287–8, 323).[21] From this point onwards, Mina is no longer admitted to the Council of War ostensibly formed in her defence. She is excluded as Other, her former identity called into question.

The question arises, however, as to why Lucy should so obviously 'degenerate' when her blood has been *extracted* rather than *adulterated*, as is the case with Mina. One answer may be found, again obliquely, in Renfield's last words, following his own fatal encounter with the vampire. Renfield recalls, 'When Mrs Harker came in to see me this afternoon she wasn't the same; it was like tea after the teapot had been watered' (280). The novel makes it clear that Mina's visit to Renfield occurs *prior* to the scene in which she consumes the vampire's blood. Logically, therefore, the vampire has put something *into* Mina's system whilst withdrawing her fluid. This is not the blind, orally-centred sucking of the child or the neurotic, but an incidence of osmosis – an impregnation of one system into another, parallel to and yet masked by the more obvious process of extraction. One becomes a vampire, not through losing blood, but by gaining some other substance whilst blood is being removed. The integrity of Mina's circulation is compromised long before she swallows Dracula's blood – the same is true of Lucy. When Seward speculates on the nature of 'that horrid poison that has got into [Mina's] veins', he is referring to the dilution of her blood through the initial intravenous act, rather than the later oral ingestion which he himself witnesses.

The vampire's intervention into the physiological systems of both women is a complex gesture, in consequence of the multiple cultural meanings associated with blood. Dracula is, as he himself insists, a nobleman, an individual with a clear racial and familial line of descent (28–30). But the Count's indiscriminate ingestion of blood, whether that of Transylvanian peasants, Polish seamen or British heiresses, devalues the 'advertisement' of his body, of his noble line. The vampire's description of Transylvania as 'the whirlpool of European races' thus undermines his later boast that the blood of Attilla the Hun flows in his veins; that blood is well-diluted through contact with lesser men. The body, like the medical bottle with its advertising rhetoric of purity and originality, is merely a vessel for the blood: the claims of either may ring hollow. The action of consuming blurs the boundaries of race and class and devalues the Count. Lacking the West's conventional guarantees of purity of content, the osmotic quality of the Count's blood acts as a catalyst for the degeneration of the blood of both Lucy and Mina, in a literal as well as metaphorical sense. Clearly, though blood functions in its secular sense as a food or a revitalising agent in *Dracula*, its symbolic connotations have not been totally dispersed – they have been mobilised through the medical context.

Dracula absorbs the virility of the West vicariously, as he ingests the blood transfused into Lucy by Van Helsing. But this blood is itself subject to the same valorisation criteria that guarantees human lymph as pure – the acknowledgement of source. Two scenes are especially significant here. The first is Dr Seward's description of the preparations for the first transfusion of blood into Lucy. The physician recalls: 'Van Helsing, turning to me said: – "He [Arthur] is so young and strong and of blood so pure that we need not defibrinate it"' (122). Fibrin is a proteid substance secreted within the blood which facilitates its clotting.[22] Van Helsing is thus asserting not merely the purity and virility of the blood, but also its fluidity, its suitability for circulation rather than stagnation. The explicit reference to fibrin also has a proleptic effect in the novel. The donor is a young nobleman, Arthur Holmwood, the fiancé of the recipient. Thromboplastin, rather than fibrinogen, is deficient in the blood of haemophiliacs – the sufferers of a blood disorder popularly associated with noble blood grown stagnant through inbreeding. Dracula notably makes a deprecating reference to the Habsburgs and Romanoffs in his conversation with Jonathan Harker – an acknowledgement of popular perceptions of 'degeneration' through inbreeding which is highly ironic (29). Hence, Arthur's blood comes not merely from a guaranteed but also from a suitably pure source. The social criteria that underpin the marital match that the donor and recipient plan to make are exactly those that determine the medical act of transfusion.

Lucy's four blood donors are closely associated with Mina and Jonathan Harker throughout the novel, although there appears to be one occasion where they form a functional and symbolic unit beyond the presence of the latter two characters. Renfield, again, is the perversely sane voice who identifies their cultural significance, not merely to himself, but to Lucy too. He addresses the four men in an appeal for his release from the asylum:

"You gentlemen, who by nationality, by heredity, or by the possession of natural gifts, are permitted to hold your respective places in the moving world, I take to witness that I am as sane as at least the majority of men who are in full possession of their liberties" (244).

Nationality and heredity relate immediately to the concepts of racial and familial blood. Within the group, Holmwood is British and noble, Quincey Morris is American, and Van Helsing is Dutch. With the equally British doctor, Seward, all are teutonic professionals, related by race and ability. But Harker, though British and a solicitor, is excluded from the group, both here, and in respect of the donation of blood to Lucy. It may be argued that the blood issue here is that of social class: Harker is not noble born, and is a solicitor only by Articles rather than through possession of a university degree. He is not a 'gentleman' in the sense that the others are. His blood, in cultural terms at least, is somehow therefore 'deficient'. It lacks the solid guarantee of talent, teutonism and ancestry encoded in the independent status of the other men. It is notable that Mina, though attacked by Dracula, is not offered the ingestion of the blood of this *aristos* as an antidote to her contamination. Mina, unlike Lucy, has to work for a living; as an assistant school mistress, she is not of the same independent social standing as her childhood friend (53). Again, the class barrier precludes her being a suitable recipient for their vital fluid, for all the group's public devotion to her person (331). The homogeneity of the *aristos* is thus protected through an exclusivity that markedly resists the sanguine promiscuity exemplified by the vampire.

Dracula is a novel whose fabric is held taut by the tensions of the fin de siècle. The medical discourse of the text, which opens out into further questions of race and heredity, draws frequently on contemporary fears regarding the adulteration of foodstuffs and medicines. Channelled through the physiological qualities of blood, concerns about debilitation, racial and individual decline, invasion from without, and the inadequacy of medicine in the face of epidemics, become fictionalised into a microcosm of a representative community fighting for the greater as well as the individual good. But at the same time, the text betrays the fractured nature of community itself. There are gradations of identity within the threatened social body, which disrupt its seeming homogeneity. Here it is the question of class in the fictional coalition against the vampire, but it could as easily be social and sectarian divisions between Londoners opposing late-nineteenth-century immigration. That which unites may with equal ease be turned in on itself in order to divide. In the final account, *Dracula* demonstrates that racial or cultural homogeneity is at best a façade. For the reader at the Victorian fin de siècle, blood may be seen to embody both a multiplicity of meaning, and the absence of an Absolute signification.

NOTES

1. Michel Foucault, *The History of Sexuality. An Introduction*, London 1984, 147–50, *passim*.
2. Joseph Chamberlain, *Home Rule and the Irish Question. A Collection of Speeches Delivered Between 1881 and 1887*, London 1887, 180. For a fictional example of the intimacy between race and family, see Bram Stoker, *The Mystery of the Sea* [1902], London 1913, 116.
3. 'The Insanity of the Horrible', *San Francisco Wave*, Dec. 9, 1899, 5.
4. See Toni Reed, *Demon Lovers and Their Victims in British Fiction*, Lexington 1988, 17,65.
5. Bram Stoker, ed. A. N. Wilson, *Dracula* [1897], Oxford 1983, 233–4. Further references are to this edition, and are given in the text.
6. Deuteronomy 12:23. Note the reservation of blood for sacrificial offering in Deuteronomy 12:27. See also Sigmund Freud, *Totem and Taboo*, London 1960, 134.
7. Cf. Clive Leatherdale, *Dracula. The Novel and the Legend*, Wellingborough 1985, 179; Richard Astle, 'Dracula as totemic monster: Lacan, Freud, Oedipus and history', *Sub-Stance*, 25 (1980), 98–105; Freud, op. cit., 142.
8. *The Times*, October 4th 1887, 12.
9. Foucault, op. cit., 147.
10. See Edward Foote, *Home Cyclopedia of Popular Medical, Social and Sexual Science*, New York and London 1901, 262–3, 1081–6.
11. H. W. Allingham *et al.*, eds., *The Medical Annual and Practitioners Index*, Bristol 1892, ii.
12. Spencer Thompson and J. C. Steele, *A Dictionary of Domestic Medicine and Household Surgery*, London 1899, 622.

13. ibid., 621–2.
14. Thomas J. Horder, 'Specific Therapy (Bacteriotherapeutics)', in Robert Hutchison and H. Stansfield Collier, eds., *An Index of Treatment by Various Writers*, London 1911, 857.
15. R. V. Pierce, *The People's Common Sense Medical Adviser*, Buffalo 1883, 54–5; David Sinclair, *A Student's Guide to Anatomy*, Oxford 1961, 42.
16. J. M'Gregor-Robertson, *The Household Physician*, London n.d., 203.
17. Allingham *et al.*, op. cit., i, iv; cf. 758, 783.
18. See Laurence Humphrey, *A Manual of Nursing: Medical and Surgical* [1889], London 1900, 239; Harrison Cripps, 'Transfusion', in C. Heath, ed., *Dictionary of Practical Surgery*, London 1886, Vol. 6, 659–60.
19. See Ken Gelder, *Reading the Vampire*, London 1994, 14–5; Peter Keating, ed., *Into Unknown England*, Glasgow 1981, 114; Daniel Pick, '"Terrors of the Night": *Dracula* and 'degeneration' in the late nineteenth century', *Critical Quarterly*, 30 (1984), 71–87.
20. Stoker, op. cit., xviii.
21. For a critical response to the scene, see Victor Sage, *Horror Fiction in the Protestant Tradition*, Basingstoke 1988, 180.
22. M'Gregor-Robertson, op. cit., 215.

12

The importance of being a Freemason: the trials of Oscar Wilde

Marie Mulvey Roberts

All trials are trials for one's life, just as all sentences are sentences of death; and three times have I been tried. The first time I left the box to be arrested, the second time to be led back to the house of detention, the third time to pass into a prison for two years. Society, as we have constituted it, will have no place for me, has none to offer....[1]

Before his three public trials in 1895, Oscar Wilde had already subjected himself, in private, to at least five trials of Masonic initiation. In 1875 he was 'made' a Mason and during the same year advanced rapidly through the second degree of Fellowcraftsman to the third of Master Mason. A year later, Wilde proceeded into the Apollo Rose-Croix Chapter which was the eighteenth degree of the Ancient and Accepted Rite.[2] In 1878 he took the Mark degree in the University Mark Lodge which is a separate Masonic order concerned with the design, loss and rediscovery of the arch in King Solomon's Temple.[3] That a sacrifice lay at the heart of the initiation rites for the third and eighteenth degrees was a tragic prolepsis of Wilde's ritualised ordeals that were to take place at the Old Bailey in 1895.

At the centre of the initiation rite for the degree of Master Mason is the re-enactment of the brutal murder of Hiram Abif, who was the architect of King Solomon's Temple.[4] The neophyte submits symbolically to the fatal blows of three apprentices. His ritual slaying represents the death of the artist who, in this case, had been martyred for his refusal to divulge the secrets of his art. For the first degree of Entered Apprentice, Wilde would have taken a bloodcurdling oath agreeing to Hiramic mutilation and death by disembowelment should he divulge the secrets of Freemasonry.[5]

Wilde's quip about the Freemason's oath is replete with retrospective irony when of 'S[aint] J[ohn] the B[aptist] [who] was the founder of this Order', he said: 'I hope we shall emulate his life but not his death – I mean we ought to keep our heads.'[6] In his second letter from H. M. Prison, Reading, Wilde may be identified more closely with John the Baptist when he says 'I admit I lost my head'.[7] At the time, he had been considering the verdict of the jury who, in more ways than one, had proved to be his Salome. The axe that had fallen in 1895 put an end, not only to Wilde's freedom, but also heralded the social death of the dandy, the demise of decadence and the decline of aestheticism. Wilde, who had declared that 'all trials are trials for one's life', was not alone, since the fin de siècle had been there in the dock with him. What was on trial was the cult of decadence, embodying the sexual and artistic freedom of the individual, and the credo of aestheticism. Wilde died in 1900 but the demise of the 1890s had taken place far earlier, having ended effectively in 1895.

For some, Wilde is the distorted icon of the 1890s, a dandified male aesthete who represents the degeneracy and malaise of Victorianism now worn-out and tottering on its last legs. Revisionists like the liberal social historians Mikuláŝ Teich and Roy Porter, feminists like Elaine Showalter and cultural materialists like Jonathan Dollimore have disrupted the once dominant popular image of the fin de siècle as the fag-end of the century. Recent cultural critics such as Alan Sinfield see dissidence as encoded within aesthetic effeminacy, while the literary critic Regenia Gagnier has rehabilitated the dandy, fag-end and all.[9] The aestheticism and decadence of the dandy has been seen as a powerful symbol of resistance to Victorian utility, the growth of mass consumerism – and the ethics of a commercial society which, in the words of one of Wilde's fictional characters, knew 'the price of everything, and the value of nothing'.[10] Instead of dismissing the dandy as a symptom of cultural degeneration, Gagnier reclaims him as 'the ironic conscience of mass society'.[11] In 27th May 1895, the establishment locked up its conscience and threw away the key when it sentenced Wilde to two years' hard labour for 'gross indecency' with a male person.

Gender ambiguity during the 1890s could be tolerated within specific contexts such as the dandy. Even the privacy of the Freemasons' Lodge opened up a space for transgressive behaviours wherein members could role-play, dress-up, fraternise in an all-male environment, imbibe Masonic aesthetics and even appropriate the absent feminine other. Within this environment, normalised by its hegemonic associations, Wilde could indulge his love of pageantry in ways that were not threatening to the establishment. Even though Freemasonry represents a valorisation of masculinity, it also opens up a means of appropriating areas that have been traditionally associated with the feminine. An example may be found in the posturing taking place within the initiation rites which may be interpreted as a simulation of female submission and giving birth.[12]

Wilde's flamboyant Masonic dress was that of the Apollo University Lodge, Oxford. Members did not wear the conventional evening dress usually worn by Masons at their meetings, but sported instead a slight variation on Court dress that consisted of knee breeches, a tail coat, white tie, and white silk stockings. The disapproval directed at Wilde while he was lecturing in America in this regalia is probably because his attire was considered effeminate. His response was deliberately bemused: 'strange that a pair of silk stockings should so upset a nation.'[13]

The real threat posed by Wilde resided in more than his style of stockings, which could be dismissed as the exhibitionism of a fashionable poseur. Rather it was the point at which his transgressiveness in regard to gender ambivalences, transgressed the boundaries between the public and the private. The affectations of the effeminate homosexual during this period alarmed reactionaries who feared that the traditional image of Victorian manhood was becoming feminised. Even since the 1870s, the aesthete had been regarded in these quarters as 'unmanly' and what was worse, as 'unEnglish'. Ironically, Wilde had proved his masculinity in private by having passed through the Masonic rites of passage. Nonetheless, it was his 'manliness', or apparent lack of it in his private life, that was on trial in the public arena of the libel court.

The trials laid bare Wilde's self-portraits executed through his art, particularly in *The Picture of Dorian Gray* (1890) which exposes the dandy not just as a dangerous representation of himself, but also of the society that he both mocks and caricatures. This was a looking-glass in which the audience could not bear to see its own image; as Wilde pointed out: 'the nineteenth-century dislike of Realism is the rage of Caliban seeing his own face in a glass.'[14] One solution for the reluctant viewer was to smash the mirror held up by Wilde. Such destructiveness was reflected in the verdict of the jury and sentencing by the judge at his trial.

The destruction of the subject that mirrors its destroyers underpins the pillorying of Wilde by the press and public. In *The Picture of Dorian Gray*, the eponymous hero has an inordinate dread of mirrors. When his image is trapped in a looking-glass, he reacts by 'flinging the mirror on the floor' and crushing it 'into silver splinters beneath his heel'.[15] In Wilde's short story 'The Birthday of the Infanta,' (1891) it is not the dwarf, the antithesis of Dorian's narcissism, who destroys the mirror, but the mirror that destroys him.

In addition to comparisons between Wilde's public trials and Masonic rites of initiation, further analogies can be made. These occur in connection with his attraction to the rituals of Catholicism, and the trials of life undertaken by the individual developing towards the maturity and autonomy of adulthood. A recurring trope throughout Wilde's life and work, which ties all these areas together, is the rose, whose mystical properties and nuances of secrecy (*sub rosa*), may be identified with the Masonic degree of the Rose Croix of Heredom into which Wilde was initiated. Within the Rosicrucian tradition, which had some influence on this degree, the iconography of the rose relates also to the feminine and specifically to female sexuality, while the cross represents the male phallus. What was so threatening to the establishment during the 1890s was the way in which, in some quarters, the demarcations between male and female sexuality appeared to be dissolving. As one contemporary commentator claimed: 'in every dandy, it may be said, a woman lies more or less deeply buried.'[16] An unlikely convergence between the masculine and the feminine is signalled by the Masonic rosy cross. For Wilde, the rose and cross was the insignia for his membership of a higher degree, constituted by an all-male brotherhood whose secrecy, as I have argued elsewhere, is posited in a number of ways upon the appropriation of the feminine. In this Rose Croix degree, the central icon of the rosy cross signifies Christ, who is an embodiment of traditional 'feminine' virtues such as self-sacrifice. In 'The Nightingale and the Rose', which is one of two short stories from *A House of Pomegranates* (1891) which will be discussed here, the rose is symbolic of the love motivating Christ's self-immolation.

In both stories the rose is used as a symbol of love, both romantic and divine, and as a bearer of knowledge for the reader. In 'The Birthday of the Infanta', it signifies, along with the symbolism of the mirror, the moments of self-revelation in the trials of life associated with Lacanian individuation. The story concerns a white rose that has been given to a dwarf by a Spanish Infanta. His delusion is that the rose is a token of her love. In fact, the Infanta's appreciation of the dwarf is based solely upon the cruel delight she derives from his physical deformity:

> the funniest part of the whole morning's entertainment, was undoubtedly the dancing of the little Dwarf. When he stumbled into the arena, waddling on his crooked legs and wagging his huge misshapen head from side to side, the children went off into a loud shout of delight, and the Infanta herself laughed so much that the Camerera was obliged to remind her that although there were many precedents in Spain for a King's daughter weeping before her equals, there were none for a Princess of the blood royal making so merry before those who were her inferiors in birth.[17]

Plucked from the forest which he had always inhabited, the dwarf had been taken to the palace as entertainment for the royal family. The Infanta's gift of the rose prompts him to go and declare his love and invite her to live with him in the forest. While he is looking for her in the palace, he catches sight of a hideous and monstrous creature. At first the dwarf is afraid, until he realises, to his horror, that he is looking at a reflection of himself. The image that he sees must have been derived from the portrait of Maribarbola, the dwarf belonging to the Infante Margarita in Diego Velázquez's famous painting of Spanish royalty, 'Las Meninas' (1656).[18] Velázquez's Infanta, like the fictional

141

counterpart in Wilde's story, is also dressed in pink and grey with a halo of golden hair and looks to be about the same age of twelve. The group portrait of Philip IV's family provides us with another narrative frame for Wilde's story since it poses questions, such as, who are the observers? and who are the observed? The artist himself is portrayed with brush and palette in hand painting the scene. In the background is a mirror reflecting the subjects of his canvas, King Philip IV and Queen Mariana, who, at the same time, occupy the space belonging to the observer of the painting.

As Wilde declares in the preface to *The Picture of Dorian Gray*, 'It is the spectator, and not life, that art really mirrors'.[19] In 1892, he exposed the role-playing of the theatre-goers by subversively addressing his audience: 'I congratulate you on the great success of your performance.'[20] In spite of these insights into the way in which art can mirror both the observer and the observed, Wilde's own personal and professional destruction, as prefigured in his art, are brought about by his public and private performances. As Joseph Bristow points out, the trials that led to Wilde's imprisonment uncannily enact a fatalistic narrative structure to be found within his writings.[21]

Comparisons may be made between Wilde's downfall and the destruction of the dwarf in the 'The Birthday of the Infanta'. Mocked by the children, the dwarf's liberty has been taken away by the Spanish royal family, while Wilde's freedom has been removed by the Crown. During this time in prison, he relived the jeers of members of the public when he recollected how he had been transported as a convicted prisoner:

> everything about my tragedy has been hideous, mean, repellent, lacking in style; our very dress makes us grotesque. We are the zanies of sorrow. We are clowns whose hearts are broken. We are specially designed to appeal to the sense of humour. On November 13th, 1895, I was brought down here from London. From two o'clock till half-past two on that day I had to stand on the centre platform of Clapham Junction in convict dress, and handcuffed, for the world to look at.... Of all possible objects I was the most grotesque. When people saw me they laughed. Each train as it came up swelled the audience. Nothing could exceed their amusement. That was, of course, before they knew who I was. As soon as they had been informed they laughed still more. For half an hour I stood in the grey November rain surrounded by a jeering mob.[22]

In 'The Birthday of the Infanta', the dwarf had not realised that the laughter was directed at him since his was a 'complete unconsciousness of his own grotesque appearance' (239). It is not until he is confronted by his own image in the looking-glass that the truth dawns. At the same time, the dwarf fails to accept the reality of its unreality. In being unable to *see through* the mirror as an epistemological void, he is unable to recognise, on an ontological level, that it is a surface where nothing is reflected.[23] This may be interpreted as a failure to pass through the Lacanian looking-glass phase in the formation of human subjectivity, and thereby to be defeated by a trial of life, which results in the death of the subject. Infantilised because of his stunted growth, the dwarf observes himself through the eyes of his mistress as grotesque. The Infanta, whose name is evocative of childhood, has an infantile image of the dwarf's misshapenness as hideous. The ego's desire for integrity would normally militate against what the developing individual in childhood perceives as his or her 'fragmented body', described by Lacan as 'a heterogeneous mannequin, a baroque doll', and 'a trophy of limbs'.[24] In the case of the dwarf, the ego and the integrated self lose the battle for ascendancy and with it the life of the subject. It is not the belief in the mirror image of the ugliness of his fragmented body that kills the dwarf, but, as with Wilde who dies prematurely having been broken by his ordeals, the death-blow is in its reflection of the reality of his shame and humiliation.

When Dorian Gray stabs the portrait of himself, he restores the beauty of his idealised self to the canvas through the mutilation of his own image. Dorian, by destroying the illusion of his own beauty, dies in the reality of his own hideousness brought about by the deformity of sin. The reverse of this takes place in 'The Birthday of the Infanta', for when the Infanta's dwarf sees his reflection in a mirror, he dies at the sight of his own ugliness, wondering:

> why had they not left him in the forest, where there was no mirror to tell him how loathsome he was? Why had his father not killed him, rather than sell him to his shame? The hot tears poured down his cheeks, and he tore the white rose to pieces. The sprawling monster did the same, and scattered the faint petals in the air. It grovelled on the ground, and, when he looked at it, it watched him with a face drawn with pain (246).

By punning on the artist's word 'drawn', Wilde literally draws the observer and the observed together so that they become one. The dismembering of the rose, as the bearer of knowledge, mirrors the fragmentation of self. Because the monster in the looking-glass mirrors the dwarf's own movements with the rose, he realises that this is a reflection of himself:

taking from his breast the beautiful white rose, he turned round, and kissed it. The monster had a rose of its own, petal for petal the same! It kissed it with like kisses, and pressed it to its heart with horrible gestures.

When the truth dawned upon him, he gave a wild cry of despair, and fell sobbing to the ground. So it was he who was misshapen and hunchbacked, foul to look at and grotesque. He himself was the monster, and it was at him that all the children had been laughing, and the little Princess who he had thought loved him she, too, had been merely mocking at his ugliness, and making merry over his twisted limbs (ibid.).

Signalling the onset of horror and then shame, the rose is transformed into a metaphor for the rejection of the love it had once represented. The loss of love, and with it the death of the self, culminates in the destruction of the rose.

The rose is a mirror for the actions of the main characters in Wilde's 'The Nightingale and the Rose' (1891), which concludes with a student throwing under a dust-cart a red rose that has been given to him by a nightingale. The bird had sacrificed herself so that the student could have a red rose to give to his Professor's daughter, who is the object of his unrequited love. Since the only rose in the garden is white, the nightingale impales herself through the heart upon a thorn, in order to dye a white rose red for him. The pouring out of her life's blood for love is evocative of the martyrdom of Christ.

The dwarf in 'The Birthday of the Infanta' is another martyr for love who dies, according to the Chamberlain, because his heart has been broken. On hearing this pronouncement, the Infanta retorts with a curl of her 'dainty rose-leaf lips' (247) that in future she will play only with those who have no hearts. In *De Profundis*, the prison letter Wilde wrote to Lord Alfred Douglas (Bosie) in 1897, he describes prisoners as clowns whose hearts are broken.[25] Later, he was to observe about prison life that: 'the most terrible thing about it is not that it breaks one's heart – hearts are made to be broken – but that it turns one's heart to stone.'[26] In 'The Ballad of Reading Gaol' (1898), Wilde describes how from the mouth and heart of an executed prisoner lying in his grave grows a red and white rose.[27] These symbols of regeneration invoke the sacrifice and innocence of the resurrected Christ.

The dying Christ on the blood-stained cross is represented by the rosy cross, which is the central insignia of the Rose Croix. It was into this higher degree that Wilde was initiated on 27th November 1876 when he was elected to the Apollo Rose-Croix Chapter as a Knight of the Pelican and Eagle, and sovereign Prince Rose Croix of Heredom.[28] As part of his Masonic regalia, Wilde would have possessed a jewelled rose-cross along with a white lambskin apron symbolising the innocence of the lamb-like Christ led to slaughter. Unlike the other degrees into which Wilde had been initiated, the Rose Croix relates specifically to the passion, death and resurrection of Christ. So keen was Wilde upon the ritual that he sponsored four students from his old college Magdalen into the order. Enthusiastically, he adopted the role of conducting candidates during the Perfection (joining) ceremony towards illumination, using the melodramatic rhetoric: 'I come to conduct you from the depths of darkness and the Valley of the Shadow of Death to the Mansions of light.'[29] What is implied here is that those who fail the ritual ordeal, also fail the trial of life, and, like the dwarf and Wilde, who were both humiliated beyond endurance, remain in the Valley of the Shadow of Death. While Wilde survived his ritualised Masonic ordeals, when he proceeded beyond the symbolic, he was destroyed by the establishment's rituals in the form of the judicial and custodial ordeals they set. His failure is as abject as that of the dwarf who is unable to go beyond the Lacanian mirror stage.

It was a very different Wilde masquerading in the rite as the conductor Raphael, who is represented as an angel holding a flaming sword. Although part of the regalia included a sword-belt and sword, the latter was not actually flaming. There is, however, an 1891 version of the Rose Croix ritual worked in England which describes how when a chalice is filled with 'spirits of wine with chloride of strontian' and then ignited, it produces a vivid red-rose flame.[30] It is possible that Wilde's fellow-Masons were able to produce a similar chemical effect. In his poem 'The New Helen', from the collection of poems entitled *Rosa Mystica* (1881), the allusion to a 'red rose of fire' may refer to these pyrotechnics.[31] A synthesis between alchemical symbolism and Christianity is apparent within this degree, and for Wilde, coming from Ireland, it may have been significant that the Irish workings of the Rose Croix gave greater prominence to the symbolism of alchemy than did the English.

Alchemical colour-coding is evident from the initiation rite itself, as when the candidate passes from the Black Room to the Red Room. Here he finds a white altar and white superaltars and red candles and red roses.[32] The alchemists' search for the Philosophers' Stone involves a number of processes including a stage of darkness represented by the liquid *nigredo*. The phase of *nigredo* ends with an appearance on the surface of the liquid of a starry aspect, which is compared to the night sky, that had revealed to kings and shepherds the birth of a child in Bethlehem. The end of the 'second work' is marked by the appearance of Whiteness, *albedo*. It is only one step more before the Red King or Sulphur of the Wise appears out of the womb of his mother and sister, Isis or mercury, *Rosa Alba*, the White Rose.[33]

An alchemical subtext informs the overtly Christian allegory within 'The Nightingale and the Rose', whereby a white rose is transmuted into a red. The philosophy student who discards it not only ignores the nightingale's message that 'Love is wiser than Philosophy',[34] but also fails to realise that he had been within reach of the coveted Philosopher's Stone.

Described as 'the Catholic religion put into a degree',[35] the Rose Croix culminates in a communion rite that has been interpreted controversially as a modern version of the *agape* or pagan love-feast, or even as a parody of the Catholic mass. (Nevertheless, it must be stressed that there is no sacramental dimension to this breaking of bread and drinking of wine ceremony.) Wilde's affinity with Catholicism is affirmed in his declaration: 'I look on all the different religions as colleges in a great university. Roman Catholicism is the greatest and most romantic of them.'[36] It was to this greatest and most romantic religion that he wished to convert, and his desire was shared by Dorian Gray:

> It was rumoured of him once that he was about to join the Roman Catholic communion; and certainly the Roman ritual had always a great attraction for him. The daily sacrifice, more awful really than all the sacrifices of the antique world, stirred him as much by its superb rejection of the evidence of the senses as by the primitive simplicity of its elements and the eternal pathos of the human tragedy that it sought to symbolise.[37]

Opposition to Wilde entering the Church came from his father, who was also a Freemason, and between 1841-2 had been Worshipful Master of the Shakespeare Lodge (No. 143) in Dublin.[38] That his son had sublimated his Catholicism within a Masonic order may not have allayed William Wilde's anti-Catholic concerns. As Oscar confided to his Oxford friend William Walsford Ward (Bouncer): 'I have got rather keen on Masonry lately, and believe in it awfully – in fact would be awfully sorry to have to give it up in case I secede from the Protestant heresy.'[39] What appealed to him most was the ritualised tragedy of the Catholic Mass about which he expressed relief that: 'one cannot but be grateful that the supreme office of the Church should be the playing of the tragedy without the shedding of blood.'[40]

On facing his own judicial trials, the power of ritual to mimic the playing of tragedy without the shedding of blood must have seemed academic. For Wilde, the Old Bailey had turned out to be a Gethsemane wherein he could re-enact a Christian martyrdom. Wilde's identification with the feminised Christ is surely the most blasphemous of loves that dare not speak its name. If this symbolisation lies at the heart of the rose imagery that is scattered throughout his work, one can only concur with him that 'those who read the symbol do so at their peril'.[41]

While Freemasonry served him for a time as the surrogate religion within which he chose to live, 'Catholicism', he insisted 'is the only religion to die in'.[42] On his death-bed on 30th November 1900 at the age of 46, Wilde was received into the Catholic Church and the last sacraments were administered to him. The teleological significance of this was that, in his 'final hour,' he was both baptised and then given extreme unction. The conflation of Masonic rites of passage with the rituals of the Catholic Church, and his trials at the Old Bailey being aligned to Christ's passion, form the ultimate heretical synthesis. While symbolism and ritual had foreshadowed his downfall, they may have unwittingly shielded him from the realities that lie beyond the symbolic.

The trials of Oscar Wilde represent a misalignment of his life and work as acted out against the reality of the fin de siècle. Before his final downfall, he had declared himself to be 'a man who stood in symbolic relations to the art and culture of my age'.[43] Subsequently, the most significant indictment of Wilde came not from the art and culture of his age, nor from the judicial system, the press, the public or even from his immediate contemporaries, but out of the depths of his own prison experience. From here, Wilde took himself beyond victimhood to the realisation that, 'terrible as was what the world did to me, what I did to myself was far more terrible still'.[44]

NOTES

1. Oscar Wilde, *The Works of Oscar Wilde*, ed. G. F. Maine, London 1948, 888.
2. Richard Ellmann, *Oscar Wilde*, London 1988, 39, 65. Since candidates had to be 21 years old, Wilde was given special dispensation so that he could be initiated to the first degree of Entered Apprentice on 23rd February 1875. He entered the second degree on 24th April and the third on 25th May of the same year.
3. ibid.
4. For a detailed history of Freemasonry and its rituals, see Bernard E. Jones, *Freemasons' Guide and Compendium*, London 1950.
5. See Walton Hannah, *Darkness Visible: A Revelation and Interpretation of Freemasonry*, London 1952, 99.
6. Ellmann, op. cit., 39.
7. Wilde, op. cit., 891.
8. See Mikuláŝ Teich and Roy Porter, *Fin de Siècle and its Legacy*, Cambridge 1990; Elaine Showalter, *Sexual Anarchy: Gender and Culture at the Fin de Siècle*, London 1992; Jonathan Dollimore, *Sexual Dissi-*

dence: From Augustine to Wilde, Freud to Foucault, Oxford 1991; Alan Sinfield, *The Wilde Century: Effeminacy, Oscar Wilde and the Queer Moment*, London 1994, and Regenia Gagnier, *Idylls of the Marketplace: Oscar Wilde and the Victorian Public*, Aldershot 1987.

9.   Wilde, op. cit., 48. See Patricia Flanagan Behrendit, *Oscar Wilde: Eros and Aesthetics*, London 1991, 179–82, who argues that through the figure of the dandy Wilde is carrying out a critique of heterosexual society.

10. Regenia Gagnier, ed., *Critical Essays on Oscar Wilde*, New York 1991, 4.

11. See Marie Mulvey Roberts, 'Pleasures engendered by gender: homosociality and the club', in Roy Porter and Marie Mulvey Roberts, eds., *Pleasure During the Eighteenth Century*, London 1996, 48–76, and 'Masonics, metaphor and misogyny: a discourse of marginality?', in Peter Burke and Roy Porter, eds., *Languages and Jargons: Contributions to a Social History of Language*, Cambridge 1995, 133–54.

12. Quoted by Ellmann, op. cit., 157.

13. Wilde, op. cit., 17.

14. ibid., 165.

15. A. Forbes Sieverking, 'Dandyism', *Temple Bar*, 88 (1890), 534.

16. Wilde, op. cit, 239. Further references to this story will be given in the text.

17. See 'Las Meninas', in Michel Foucault, *The Order of Things: An Archaeology of the Human Sciences*, London 1989, 3–16.

18. Wilde, op. cit., 17.

19. Quoted by Joseph Bristow, *Effeminate England: Homoerotic Writing after 1885*, Buckingham 1995, 34.

20. ibid., 22.

21. Wilde, op. cit., 881.

22. See Jacques Lacan, 'The mirror stage as formative of the function of the I as revealed in psychoanalytic experience', in *Écrits: A Selection*, London 1977, 1–7.

23. Malcolm Bowie, *Lacan*, London 1991, 27.

24. Wilde, op. cit., 881.

25. ibid., 866.

26. See ibid., 834.

27. Ellmann, op. cit., 65.

28. ibid.

29. Hannah, op. cit., 206.

30. Wilde, op. cit., 709.

31. *The Ceremony of the Rose Croix of Heredom*, privately printed for the Supreme Council 33, 1984, 19.
32. See Stanislas Klassowski De Rola, *Alchemy: The Secret Art*, London 1973, 11–12, and for connections between the rose, the alchemists' stone and Christianity see C. J. Jung, 'The rose-coloured blood and the rose', in *Alchemical Studies*, in *The Collected Works*, ed. Herbert Read *et al.*, London 1967, 13, 292–97.
33. Wilde, op. cit., 294.
34. A. C. F. Jackson, *Rose Croix: A History of the Ancient and Accepted Rite for England and Wales*, London 1987, 30.
35. See Ellmann, op. cit., 495.
36. Wilde, op. cit., 105.
37. See Ellmann, op. cit., 39.
38. ibid., 65.
39. Wilde, op. cit., 869.
40. ibid., 17.
41. Ellmann, op. cit., 548.
42. Wilde, op. cit., 857.
43. ibid., 856.

13

Ordinary pleasures?: recreational drug use in the literature of the 1880s and 1890s

Julian North

I

We are familiar by now with discussions of this and the last fin de siècle which open with long lists of parallels between the 1890s and the 1990s. Elaine Showalter's *Sexual Anarchy* is perhaps the most thorough-going example of this approach: as she puts it, 'from urban homelessness to imperial decline, from sexual revolution to sexual epidemics, the last decades of the twentieth century seem to be repeating the problems, themes, and metaphors of the *fin de siècle*.'[1] Drugs have sometimes appeared as an item in such catalogues – Waldemar Januszczak notes that we, like the Victorians, have 'a queen who appears to have been on the throne forever ... a disastrous widening of the gulf between rich and poor, a shocking accessibility of drink and drugs'.[2] Terry Eagleton, for whom the current fin de siècle arrived early, in the 1960s, includes 'hallucinatory states' in his series of parallels between that era and the Victorian end of century.[3] Showalter, too, cites 'the drug epidemic' as one of the arguments put forward by 'latter-day Nordaus like Allan Bloom, William Bennett, or John Silber' for what they believe is 'a new American Dusk'.[4]

These kinds of symmetries are at once stimulating and over-neat. Sally Ledger and Scott McCracken caution critics of the fin de siècle against the paralleling urge, and in relation to the issue of the respective drug cultures of the 1890s and 1990s the caution seems judicious.[5] Can we really compare the hugely complex drug scene of late-twentieth-century Western society, with the relatively limited recreational drug use of the Victorian fin de siècle? However, Ledger and McCracken are equally concerned to warn against 'a rigid historicization, a whole-hearted differentiation of the late nineteenth century as a discrete period'. As they argue, both fins de siècles need to be looked at both with detachment and in dialogue with each other.[6]

With this in mind, the following discussion focuses on one area of the current debate surrounding drug use in the late twentieth century, and explores ways in which it might illuminate, and be illuminated in turn, by literary representations of recreational drug use from the 1880s and 1890s.

II

John Auld, Nicholas Dorn and Nigel South argue that the dominant popular and political discourses of the day characterise heroin pushers as 'foreigners and aliens' – 'evil outsiders' who prey on users, who are seen, typically, as socially withdrawn addict-victims.[7] They go on to question these stereotypes, claiming that heroin pushers and users are, in fact, from a variety of backgrounds and, far from being socially withdrawn, are often active participants in an entrepreneurial fringe economy. In short, they are putting forward the view that we must begin to look upon heroin pushers and users not as cultural outsiders, but as insiders: 'both the demand for and supply of plant drugs today has to be situated within British and international political economies and their associated cultures.'[8]

The opposition between the drug user as outsider and insider is one that informs much of the debate on drug use in Britain and America in the 1980s and 1990s. On the one hand, the rhetoric of the War on Drugs draws up the battle lines between the drug user and mainstream society – a House of Commons report of 1985, for instance, refers to the drug problem as 'the most serious peacetime threat to our national well-being'.[9] Even a relatively liberal argument for more understanding of the role of social deprivation in leading to drug addiction asks why heroin use has been allowed 'to invade our cities'.[10] On the other hand, the assumptions underlying such rhetoric have been variously exposed and critiqued. Hartnoll, Daviand and Power, for instance, argue that cannabis and cocaine use in Britain can no longer be identified with a particular social class or 'alternative' culture. Drug use is no longer a socially marginal phenomenon – it is an 'everyday' activity of 'ordinary' people.[11]

One intervention on this debate, by Pat O'Malley and Stephen Mugford, is particularly suggestive in relation to writing about recreational drug use in the Victorian fin de siècle.[12] The authors argue powerfully that the War on Drugs will fail because it has not taken adequate account of the extent to which the demand for drugs, as pleasurable commodities, is integral to modern society. They isolate four main discourses in research and theoretical literature on drugs: the discourses of pathology (the dominant discourse), profit, the state and pleasure. The first three focus, respectively, on 'what is wrong with people (or with the situation in which they find themselves) that leads them to use illicit drugs'; 'the pecuniary motives of drug traffickers'; and 'the question of legislation'. The pleasure discourse is the only one to take the issue of demand seriously, dealing with the pleasure to be derived from drugs, and 'that pleasure as the motive for use'.[13] The War on Drugs, it is argued, draws on the first

151

three discourses at the expense of the fourth, and so persists in constructing the drug user as social alien, rather than paying heed to the fact that 'in modern capitalist societies, there has been a steady growth over the last two centuries in markets for pleasurable commodities and that drugs, linked to this general trend, need to be thought of in this way'.[14] From this perspective, 'drugs *epitomize* modern culture rather than being the aberation that the War on Drugs suggests'.[15]

Indeed, drugs appear to function as a particularly potent form of what the authors, following Colin Campbell, identify as a 'modern hedonism', where the Romantic emphasis on emotional and imaginative self-exploration has contributed to a consumer culture in which one of the principal demands is for experiential novelty – 'the endless emergence of new "wants", the search for new experiences through commodity consumption'.[16] Once more, this confirms the authors in their belief that drug use must be viewed as an ordinary pleasure:

> In such a cultural milieux [sic], we argue, illicit and even dangerous drug taking as a leisure activity appears as an intelligible form of the normatively sanctioned search for the extraordinary – rather than as a bizarre product of pathological minds, social malfunctions, corrupt regimes, or rapacious entrepreneurs.[17]

To what extent may this distinction between the recreational drug user as insider and outsider, ordinary consumer and pathological alien, be applied to the late-Victorian cultural milieu? In comparison to the late-twentieth-century situation, the culture of the 1880s and 1890s was one of acceptance, rather than condemnation, of the drug user. Virginia Berridge and Griffith Edwards have argued that before the 1860s opium was regarded as 'just a commodity like so much tea'.[18] Even after the first restrictions came in, in 1868, the drug and its derivatives were widely available. It was not a climate in which the recreational drug user need fear legal penalties nor, necessarily, social condemnation. Although there is evidence of the beginnings of a drug sub-culture at the period, its limited nature is testimony to the relative liberalism of late-Victorian society towards the drug user.[19]

Nevertheless, Berridge and Edwards have charted the gradual evolution of a 'problem framework' surrounding opium and other drugs in the course of the nineteenth century. What O'Malley and Mugford term the 'pathology discourse' originated in the period from about the 1870s, when addiction began to be defined as a psychological disease.[20] Moreover, in a pattern to be repeated in the present century, this 'infection' was frequently deemed by commentators to be most prevalent within sections of society remote from and potentially threatening to white, middle-class interests – the Chinese and the working-class particularly.[21]

Thus, whilst late-Victorian society was in many respects more accepting of recreational drug use than our own, there were the beginnings, at least, of what has been identified by the late-twentieth-century commentators cited above as the need to dissociate the drug user (and certain kinds of drug users particularly) from mainstream society – a tendency to distance the practice as a pleasure remote from the indulgences of ordinary life. In the following discussion, I want to focus on four fin-de-siècle texts, in order to explore the ways in which this tendency informs literary representations of recreational drug use from the 1880s and 1890s, but is nevertheless interrupted by moments when the practice is acknowledged not as 'theirs' but as 'ours'. At times, as we shall see, the conflicting representations of the drug user as outsider and insider also entail a recognition that the pleasure of drugs is integral to a consumer culture.

III

Dr H. Obersteiner's 'London Opium Dens' (1885), an account of the author's visit to the Chinese opium dens of the East End of London, begins by mapping his journey across the city.[22] As he descends, a self-conscious latter-day Dante, the geographical distance between the Doctor's world and that of the drug user begins to resonate with other, symbolic distances – of race, class, economic circumstance, physical and moral health:

> My path led eastward, away from the spacious scenes where luxury and fashion reign, past the palatial buildings wherein the commerce of a world is centred, onward, through narrower and closer streets, into regions where luxury's foot is rarely set and fashion's face but seldom seen. I was to visit the opium dens of remoter London, and, accompanied by a kindly, courteous guide, to enter those fatal haunts where man in vicious thraldom to an insidious habit, is to be seen perhaps at his weakest and his meanest (188).

The drug user belongs at the edges of the city, not at its heart. The luxuries of central London, maintained by the surrounding commercial district, are of a different order from the luxuries of the opium den.

Obersteiner's positioning of the drug user as social outsider continues when he reaches the den, with remarks on the alienating squalor of the house and the difficulties of communication with the Chinese opium smokers who inhabit it (189). But once communication has been established with one of these smokers, his preconceptions are suddenly overturned. This man was not first introduced to opium in China, he learns, but in London: 'It was not in distant China, in that unhappy land ... that he had acquired the pernicious habit. It was here in *our* midst, here in London...' (190). 'Remoter London' thus reveals itself, after all, as 'here in *our* midst'. However, Obersteiner's shocked acknowledgement that the opium den is a product of his own and not an alien culture is only momentary, and is quickly transmuted into a renewed sense of the remoteness of these people and their vice, with much emphasis on the Oriental inscrutability of these 'heathen' opium smokers (190–1). He ends with an acknowledgement, not of kinship, but of responsibility: 'Has England no duty here? Have those ill-paid servants no claim upon our care?' (192). Dr Obersteiner thus deals with the difficulty of countenancing the drug user as already a cultural insider by representing him as an outcast to be rescued and, only then, brought back into the fold.

In Conan Doyle's 'The Man with the Twisted Lip' (1891) we find Dr Watson confronted with a similar dilemma to that of Obersteiner, but this time the solution proves more problematic.[23] Again, the piece begins with a Doctor's descent into the underworld of the London opium dens, but this time it is to rescue one of his own: Isa Whitney, whose social credentials – 'brother of the late Elias Whitney, D.D.' – are established in the first sentence of the story.[24] Again Watson maps for us the geographical and symbolic remoteness of the den – he must journey by cab to 'the furthest east of the city' – but this time the borders between respectable society and the opium den cannot be so firmly drawn (125).

Whitney has not only been lured into opium-smoking, he has also begun to take on the physical characteristics of the Oriental opium-smoker: 'with yellow, pasty face, drooping lids and pin-point pupils', and as such has become 'an object of mingled horror and pity to his friends and relatives' (124). The white opium user here, as in many other nineteenth-century accounts, raises the spectre of miscegenation.[25] Watson attempts to restore the boundaries which have been transgressed, by rescuing Whitney from the den and sending him back to his wife and to respectability. In the meantime, however, one of the opium-smokers in the den suddenly reveals himself as Holmes in disguise. Watson's attempts at demarcating boundaries between proper and improper pleasures must begin again.

Holmes, like Whitney, is both insider and outsider. He dissociates himself from the den in which he has been found by remarking with disgust the 'incoherent ramblings of these sots' who inhabit it, and identifying the den as 'the vilest murder-trap on the whole river-side' (129). However, he has already suggested a kinship with the opium smokers in joking: 'I suppose, Watson ...

that you imagine that I have added opium-smoking to cocaine injections and all the other little weaknesses on which you have favoured me with your medical views' (ibid.). In inferring that this is not the case, Holmes nevertheless brings to mind his own recreational drug use, a recurring motif in the stories.[26] Indeed, later on Holmes reaches the solution to the mystery in a posture reminiscent of the Oriental opium-smoker, cross-legged on 'a sort of Eastern divan ... an old brier pipe between his lips, his eyes fixed vacantly upon the corner of the ceiling' (142).[27]

Clearly, for Conan Doyle, the drug user as social outsider has more complex resonances than for Obersteiner. What emerges in 'The Man with the Twisted Lip', as in other Holmes stories, is an apparent hierarchy of pleasures to be derived from drugs – on one level, the intellectual and imaginative pleasure of Holmes, the gentleman, who injects morphine and cocaine alone in his private lodgings when he has no cases to stimulate him (the 7% solution a substitute for the more usual solutions of the detective), and, on another level, the sensual pleasure, akin to drunkenness, of the public realm of the opium den, inhabited by Orientals and the criminal underworld. Both orders of pleasure denote the drug user as an outsider, but Holmes's cocaine habit is a relatively acceptable, even glamorous, eccentricity, where the pleasures of the opium den are not. It contributes to his status as the *ennuyé* fin-de-siècle genius, a recognised type. Watson's repeated warnings against Holmes's 'drug mania' only serve to enhance Holmes's mystique.[28] However, this hierarchy is not secure – Whitney and Holmes partake of both orders of pleasure, in the private apartment and in the den, revealing them, in fact, as far from distinct.

Thus both Obersteiner and Conan Doyle position the recreational drug user as an outsider, the object of rescue attempts by respectable society. Yet both also suggest that the pleasure offered by these drugs may have a more problematic place in society, and that borderlines between insider and outsider cannot necessarily be easily drawn. Elsewhere in Victorian fin-de-siècle writing, this possibility is framed in terms which suggest more specifically a continuity between the apparently extraordinary pleasure of drugs and the ordinary pleasures of a consumer culture.

Henry Havelock Ellis's 'Mescal: a new artificial paradise' (1898) describes his own experiences, and those of a few colleagues and friends, under the influence of mescal.[29] Here we have, unlike in the texts cited above, an enthusiastic account of the pleasures of a drug from the perspective of the user. It is an account which veers interestingly between representing recreational drug use as an exclusive pursuit, available only to the few, and as a mass pleasure, akin to other pleasures of ordinary life.

Thus, on the one hand, Ellis nurtures an image of the drug user as a man set apart from the common run. The men who experiment with the drug in Ellis's article are all part of an exclusive, talented minority, whether scientists, painters or poets. Ellis characterises the pleasures of mescal generally as intellectual, but more specifically as aesthetic. After he has taken the drug, his room under gas light becomes like a Monet painting (134); an artist friend, under the influence, has dreams full of images culled from Baudelaire or Beardsley (138); a poet plays the piano and the music comes in waves of colour; ordinary people in the street are transformed into a picture by Albert Moore (139).

On the other hand, Ellis also shows a more liberal attitude towards the prospect of mass recreational drug use than we have hitherto seen. He points out at the beginning of his article that mescal is commonly used by New Mexican Indians during religious ceremonies (130), and he ends his piece by speculating on a more widespread use of mescal in his own country (141). The drug does not seduce the user away from the ordinary world, he argues, and 'is the most democratic of the plants which lead men to an artificial paradise' (141). Ellis draws back from this vision of large-scale consumption at the last minute, but his article also contains comic intuitions of the links between mescal and the more ordinary pleasures of society at large. Painting, poetry and music constitute only some of the experiences under mescal recorded here. The artist also bites into a biscuit under the influence – it streams blue flames and sets fire to his trousers (137). The poet goes out onto the Embankment and experiences intense pleasure gazing at an electric sign advertising Bovril (139). Aesthetic and mundane fuse within the late-nineteenth-century consumer culture. Are the delights of mescal really so far removed from those to be had from biscuits and Bovril?

Ellis hints entertainingly at the possibility that mescal might be viewed as just another pleasurable commodity, but does not develop his perception. A much further-reaching exploration of the possible constructions of the pleasure of drugs – and, indeed, of pleasure in general – is to be found in Oscar Wilde's *The Picture of Dorian Gray* (1890-1).[30] The narrative contains scattered references to recreational drug use: it opens with Lord Henry smoking a 'heavy opium-tainted cigarette' (8), and Dorian Gray later takes up hashish and opium (202ff). If we want to broaden our definition of recreational drug use, we might also note that throughout the novel Lord Henry and Dorian Gray consume cigarettes, coffee, vermouth, wine and champagne. These references are more than merely incidental to the narrative. Recreational drug use forms a crucial part of the lifestyle advocated by Lord Henry and adopted by Dorian Gray, based on self-realisation through a ceaseless search for new spiritual and sensual experiences – the 'new Hedonism', as Lord Henry calls it (30).

From one perspective, this experiment in living, and the drug use that it entails, are self-conscious gestures against the grain of a materialistic bourgeois culture. Lord Henry considers his age 'grossly carnal in its pleasures, and grossly common in its aims', and wages a campaign against such values, both in his own right and through the life of his disciple, Gray (44). Drugs do not merely feature in a literal sense as part of this campaign. They are also present within the narrative in the important structuring metaphor of poisoning. Lord Henry's influence on Dorian is repeatedly referred to as a pleasurable poison.[31] There is a sexual implication here – 'to convey one's temperament into another as though it were a subtle fluid or a strange perfume; there was a real joy in that' (44) – but Lord Henry is also the druggist, seducing Gray into the life of the addict: 'The only way to get rid of a temptation is to yield to it. Resist it, and your soul grows sick with longing for the things it has forbidden to itself' (25). Once addicted, Dorian, in turn, begins to exert his own 'poisonous influences' (133) on others: he causes his fiancée Sybil Vane to commit suicide by swallowing poison (111–12), and subsequently corrupts every friend he makes, some of them ending up as human wrecks in the opium dens he frequents (207–9). As Basil Hallward puts it, 'You have filled them with a madness for pleasure. They have gone down into the depths' (168).

All this suggests Lord Henry and Dorian Gray as the very embodiment of the drug user as invading aggressor, infusing their poison into a culture from which they have deliberately alienated themselves. However, the novel also undercuts this suggestion. The pleasure of drugs is, of course, one amongst many pleasures indulged in by Gray in his pursuit of the 'new Hedonism'. The eleventh chapter of the novel, in imitation of Huysmans, catalogues Gray's indulgences in the form of perfumes, musical instruments, jewels, embroideries, tapestries and so on. These collections, and the sumptuous apartment in which they are contained, label Gray as the insatiable Paterian aesthete, searching after 'experience itself, and not the fruits of experience', but they also label him the archetypal consumer (146). Indeed, Wilde, like Huysmans before him, suggests within his fiction the extent to which the aesthetic lifestyle relies on the very consumer culture it professes to revile. Drugs play an important part in revealing this irony within the narrative.

The key episode here is after Gray has murdered Basil, and is looking for a way of escaping from his guilt. He first of all contemplates taking hashish. Within the hierarchy of drug pleasures already discussed in relation to 'The Man with the Twisted Lip', this is the first, more rarified stage – a private and aesthetic delight, the hashish is hidden away, within a gentleman's apartments, in the secret drawer of 'a large Florentine cabinet, made out of ebony, and inlaid with ivory and blue lapis', and then in 'a small Chinese box of black and gold-dust lacquer' (202–3). However, Gray rejects the hashish and decides instead to venture beyond the confines of his apartment to one of his familiar haunts – the opium den.

Here we have the by now familiar motif of the gentleman's journey across the actual and symbolic gulf which exists between central London and the East End, and from the first to the second stage of the hierarchy of pleasures to be had from drugs. As in the Conan Doyle short story, the opium den, with its associations of drunkenness and the criminal underworld, seems a far cry from the rarified environment of drug use in the private apartment. Indeed, Gray remarks on the 'intense actuality' of the den, which seems to him at that moment to be preferable to 'all the gracious shapes of Art' (206).

However, Gray's distinction collapses. The refrain of the new Hedonism, chanted by Gray as he journeys to the den, is: 'To cure the soul by means of the senses, and the senses by means of the soul' (204). In turning from hashish to opium, he appears to have rejected the soul in favour of the senses, but, as the circularity of the refrain suggests, the two are interdependent. Both drugs are material pleasures, which have been invested with spiritual significance, in the same way as have all Gray's other luxuries, from embroidered dressing gown to onyx bathroom – products of the consumer culture from which he has tried, and failed, to dissociate himself.[32] The juxtaposition of the two episodes – Gray's contemplation of the hashish, followed by his trip to the opium den – is important in revealing the interdependence of the two aspects – spiritual and material – of the new Hedonism. The episodes also, in the context of the novel as a whole, show how the apparent transgressions of the drug user in fact replicate the pursuit of pleasure which is an integral part of the culture of the day. To this extent, the image of the drug user as alien, poisoning society from without, is thrown into question. The self-consciously Decadent drug user participates in, rather than standing in opposition to, the ordinary pleasures of fin-de-siècle culture.

IV

The rhetoric of the late-twentieth-century War on Drugs, and the counter-attacking insistence that recreational drug use plays an integral part in a modern, consumer society, both shed light on the representation of the drug user in the Victorian fin de siècle. The late-nineteenth-century writers I have been looking at tend to cast the drug user as social outsider – whether as alien inhabitant of the opium den, man of genius or subversive aesthete. To this extent, these writers resist the construction of drugs as an ordinary pleasure. Nevertheless, there are moments in each of the texts when the possibility is raised that the apparently outlandish and even pathological pursuit of pleasure through recreational drug use may, after all, be no more than a 'form of the normatively sanctioned search for the extraordinary'.[33]

What emerges from this discussion, however, is something more interesting than an enumeration of symmetries. To re-read these late-Victorian texts, both fictional and non-fictional, in the light of issues that have been debated in the 1980s and 1990s, reveals something about attitudes towards recreational drug use at both periods, but also about the relationship between those periods. It suggests the extent to which what are often assumed to be typically late-twentieth-century anxieties about the drug user as pathological outsider were already at work in late-Victorian culture, at a time when the concept of a drug 'problem' in this country was still in its infancy.

This is not a case of two fin-de-siècle moments with startling affinities, but of continuities between one period and another. The sense of crisis which tends to be precipitated at the ends of centuries doubtless contributed then, as now, to an intensification of anxiety surrounding drug use, but the themes I have been highlighting in the texts under discussion are not exclusively fin-de-siècle themes. All are to be found in writing both before and after the 1880s and 1890s, extending to the present day. The late-twentieth-century debate on recreational drug use discussed in the first part of this essay is a product of a very different world from that in which Obersteiner, Conan Doyle, Ellis and Wilde were writing, but it is also, in part, a legacy of that earlier period.

NOTES

1. Elaine Showalter, *Sexual Anarchy: Gender and Culture at the Fin de Siècle*, London 1992, 1.
2. *The Sunday Times*, 19th February 1995, 'The Culture', 3.
3. Terry Eagleton, 'The flight to the Real', in Sally Ledger and Scott McCracken, eds., *Cultural Politics at the Fin de Siècle*, Cambridge 1995, 11.
4. Showalter, op. cit., 1. Nordau pointed to narcotics and stimulants as one of the causes of fin-de-siècle degeneracy, but felt that opium and hashish were problems of the 'Eastern peoples, who play no part in the intellectual development of the white races'. See Max Nordau, *Degeneration*, (first published in Germany, 1892; first English language edition 1895), Lincoln, Nebraska 1993, 35.

5. Ledger and McCracken, op. cit., 2.

6. ibid., 3, 4.

7. John Auld, Nicholas Dorn and Nigel South, 'Heroin now: bringing it all back home', in Nigel South, ed., *Drugs, Crime and Criminal Justice*, Aldershot 1995, vol. 1, 417.

8. ibid., 417–21.

9. U.K. House of Commons (1985) Fifth Report of the Home Affairs Committee, *Misuse of Hard Drugs* (Interim Report), Session 1984/5, quoted in Gerry Stimson, 'British drug policies in the 1980s', in Tom Heller *et al*, eds., *Drug Use and Misuse: A Reader*, Chichester 1987, 123.

10. Griffith Edwards, 'Addiction: a challenge to society', in Heller *et al*, op. cit., 12.

11. Richard Hartnoll, Emmanuelle Daviand and Robert Power, 'Patterns of drug taking in Britain', ibid., 13, 18.

12. Pat O'Malley and Stephen Mugford, 'The demand for intoxicating commodities: implications for the "War on Drugs"', in South, op. cit., 441–67.

13. ibid., 442–3.

14. ibid., 443.

15. ibid., 445.

16. ibid., 448–9. See Colin Campbell, *The Romantic Ethic and the Spirit of Modern Consumerism*, Oxford 1987.

17. O'Malley and Mugford, op. cit., 449.

18. Virginia Berridge and Griffith Edwards, *Opium and the People: Opiate Use in Nineteenth-Century England*, New Haven 1987, 9.

19. ibid., 122 and 228. See also Virginia Berridge, 'The origins of the English drug "scene" 1890–1930', in South, op. cit., 3–16.

20. See Berridge and Edwards, op. cit., chapter 13.

21. See ibid., chapter 15, and xxviii, 47–8, 97ff, 106 and 189.

22. [Dr H. Obersteiner], 'London opium dens: notes of a visit to the Chinaman's East-End haunts', *Good Words*, 26 (1885), 188–92.

23. Sir Arthur Conan Doyle, 'The Man with the Twisted Lip', *Strand Magazine*, 2 (1891), 623–37.

24. Sir Arthur Conan Doyle, *Sherlock Holmes: The Complete Short Stories*, London 1928 (1971 reprint), 124. Further references are given in the text.

25. For an interesting discussion of this anxiety in Victorian writing about opium, see Barry Milligan, 'Opium smoking and the oriental infection

of British identity', in Sue Vice *et al*, eds., *Beyond the Pleasure Dome: Writing and Addiction from the Romantics*, Sheffield 1994, 93–100.

26. See *The Sign of Four* (1890); 'A Scandal in Bohemia' (1891), 'The Five Orange Pips', 'The Adventures of the Yellow Face' (1893), 'The Adventure of the Missing Three-Quarter' (1904).

27. Though the events in the opium den form only the subplot of the story, the main plot repeats the pattern of an alien vice unmasked as the indulgence of a respectable citizen, when another gentleman, Neville St. Clair, is rescued from the East End, where he has been masquerading as a beggar.

28. See 'The Missing Three-Quarter', *Sherlock Holmes*, 809. For Watson's escalating attempts to get Holmes to give up cocaine, and the medical background to them, see Berridge and Edwards, op. cit., 223–4.

29. Henry Havelock Ellis, 'Mescal: a new artificial paradise', *The Contemporary Review*, 73 (1898), 130–41. Further references to this work are given in the text.

30. Oscar Wilde, *The Picture of Dorian Gray*, Harmondsworth 1981. Further references are to this edition and are given in the text.

31. See, for example, ibid., 44, 89, 105 and 140.

32. See ibid., 204, 106.

33. O'Malley and Mugford, op. cit., 449.

14

Angels of the revolution and saints of the apocalypse: women's science fiction writing in the 1890s and 1990s

Nickianne Moody

I make butterflies – creating ephemeral things make people happy. There's too little pleasure in this nasty dying world. We all need to remember how to play, how to be children together for a while.[1]

The beginning of the 1980s saw a marked change in the publishing and marketing of science fiction. The extrapolative, technological orientation of the genre was gradually edged out of bookshop shelves. As its replacement, science fiction was subsumed by fantasy. These new bestsellers were derided by writers and critics alike as offering little else than the trivial diversion suggested above.

By the mid-1980s, amidst this demise, two particular trends of writing emerged: cyberpunk, and a clearly-signified women's (if not feminist) science fiction. Both evolved their own non-fantasy iconography and sought to be marketed and received outside as well as within the genre. These two distinct and gendered practices of writing appear collectively in two mid-1980s anthologies: Bruce Sterling's *Mirrorshades* (1986), published in Britain by Paladin, and Lefanu and Green's earlier collection, *Despatches from the Frontiers of the Female Mind* (1985), published by the Women's Press.

Nicola Nixon sees cyberpunk fiction arriving to supplant 1960s and 1970s feminist science fiction, in order to act as the new revolutionary imagination. She characterises the earlier feminist writers (Russ, Piercy, Le Guin, Charnas and Gearhart) as providing a critique of their contemporary male science fiction writers, particularly those who proposed female power as the threat to the future.[2] In contrast, the largely dystopian/utopian fiction of women writers in the 1980s posits, according to Joan Gordon, 'dreams of a pastoral world, fuelled by organic structures rather than mechanical ones, inspired by versions of the archetypal great mother'.[3]

Analysis of women writers who appropriated science fiction in the 1970s shows how their fiction renegotiates aspects of feminist philosophical and political thought of the time. Similarly to nineteenth-century women writers, feminists used the utopian form to articulate specific critiques of their contemporary experience, and to visualise an alternative. Writers in the twentieth century have used fiction to put feminist and psychoanalytic theory into popular circulation, the most frequent extrapolations being those which consider the creation of the gendered subject within language and broader social relations. These narratives also discuss the politics and demands of such visualisations. American critics of women's science fiction in the 1980s have been particularly interested in a new move from utopia to dystopia:

> more recent fictions no longer give us images of a radically different future, in which the values and ideals of feminism have been extended to most of the planet, but rather offer depressing images of a brutal re-establishment of capitalist patriarchy.[4]

In the main, such critics refer to Atwood's *The Handmaid's Tale* (1987), Haden-Elgin's *Mother Tongue* (1985), and Murphy's *The City Not Long After* (1991). However, the significant pattern is established by Marge Piercy's *Woman on the Edge of Time* (1980), where, in accordance with Raymond Williams's definition of a political utopia, the future is in our hands and unresolved.[5] The solutions for the dystopian nature of women's contemporary experience are commonly envisaged in women's fiction as separation, or as various forms of anti-technological collectivism. It is seen as very hard work. Very few women writers have considered appropriating the masculine narrative space of the high-tech cyberpunk future.

The title of this essay is drawn in part from George Griffith's novel, *Angel of the Revolution*, serialised in *Pearson's Weekly* during 1893. Griffith has been described as a journalist who crusaded for secularism and socialism.[6] Pearson hoped that the inclusion of a future war story might promote the sales of his magazine, and Griffith wrote *Angel of the Revolution* to the editor's order. Griffith's story is best remembered for its foresight in predicting battle tactics in aerial warfare, radar, sonar and atomic energy. Brian Stableford has acknowledged that the success of Griffith's story confirmed a publishing niche for a series of similar works which played upon the cultural anxieties of the period, and offered a revolutionary response.[7] The 'Angel' of the title has a limited narrative role:

> it is my mournful duty to tell you that she whom anyone of us would willingly shed our blood to serve or save from the slightest evil, our beautiful and beloved Angel of the Revolution as we so fondly call her, Natasha, the daughter of the Master, has, in the performance of her duty to the Cause, fallen into the hands of Russia.[8]

Natasha, having secured the affections of the airship engineer and his decision to join her father's political organisation, completes her role as a victim needing to be rescued. Griffith's sequel considers the opposing side to the Victorian ideology of woman's nature. Originally titled 'The Syren of the Skies', *Olga Romanoff* (1894) pitches the Brotherhood of Freedom against the eponymous anti-heroine. It is similar in tone to Bulwer Lytton's *The Coming Race* (1871) and Walter Besant's *The Revolt of Man* (1882), in which women unleash cosmic destruction.

The subject for discussion in this essay is the role of women as part of such representations of social protest, and in the mechanics of social change. Has women's writing in the 1990s managed to appropriate the non-human, if not angelic, constitution of the fictional revolutionary? Moreover, is popular culture a productive site for feminist intervention? Science fiction has clearly become an important genre for women's writing in the 1980s, and can be seen to debate similar issues to those raised by late-nineteenth-century utopian women's writing.

Identifiable (and obtainable) nineteenth-century scientific romances written by women are few and far between. However, their solutions to 'The Woman Question' have parallels with twentieth-century work. Mary Bradley Lane's *Mizora* (1889) prophesies a time when men have been eliminated. Ilgenfritz and Merchant's recently-republished *Unveiling a Parallel* (1893) creates an anti-heroine who would probably be celebrated in current fiction. This character is a young successful businesswoman with a drink and drug problem, an experienced lover, social leader, and the mother of an illegitimate child whom she has chosen not to rear. Initially, the hero is attracted to her, but turns her down in preference for the 'Angel in the house' he finds in a neighbouring utopia. It would appear that the latter character has not been endowed with masculine 'privileges' in order to critique the 'new woman'; this fictional account exists to explore other cultural anxieties, including the high incidence of venereal disease amongst monogamous middle-class women.

However, there is a concentration of science fiction texts which do debate 'The Woman Question' in early Australian science fiction writing. Both male and female Australian writers in the 1890s evidently saw women as a resource which could be utilised for the good of the nation. Mary Ann Moore-Bentley published *A Woman of Mars; or Australia's Enfranchised Women* in 1901. The angel motif is prominent. Whilst en route to heaven with the soul of a dead earthwoman, an angel makes a stop-over on Mars. This gives the Martian people a chance to learn about conditions of life, work and motherhood on Earth. They are scandalised by what they are told. To rectify matters, a Martian girl is chosen to go to Earth and crusade for the emancipation of women and the overall regeneration of the race.

Moore-Bentley's novel was published in the wake of Sir Julian Vogel's speculative consideration of equality, *Anno Domini 2000; or Women's Destiny* (1889). In the preface, Vogel advises his readers to keep three main propositions in view while they are reading the novel: first, that a recognised dominance of either sex is unnecessary; second, that the materials are to hand for forging the dominions of Great Britain into a powerful and beneficial empire; and thirdly, the question of whether it is not possible to relieve the misery of poverty and oppressive social conditions.

Of all the dilemmas in the novel that face Hilda Fitzherbert, MP for New Zealand, it is the question of succession which most concerns her. Should parliament remove the last remnants of sexual inequality by passing a law which will allow the Emperor to be a woman? Even so, much more consideration is given to the private dilemma of marriage, rather than the public issues raised by the premise. The novel is interesting because 'The Woman Question' is examined in the context of work, work relations and social change. In Vogel's diegesis, foreign labour has been outlawed, requiring all members of the nation to join the workforce. It should also be remembered that Australian women were among the first to achieve the vote, in South Australia in 1894 and federally in 1901.

In North America in the early part of the twentieth century, Charlotte Perkins Gilman explored the detrimental physical and emotional experience of economically-dependent women, both in fiction and non-fiction. She gained an international reputation for *Women and Economics* (1898), but like political utopianists before her such as William Morris and Edward Bellamy, she turned to fiction to maximise the dissemination of her social vision. *Herland*, published in Gilman's monthly magazine *The Forerunner* between 1909 and 1916, also refers to women as angels in its discussion of citizenship:

> try to imagine a devoted and impassioned man trying to set up housekeeping with a lady angel, a real wings-and-harp-and-halo angel, accustomed to fulfilling divine missions all over interstellar space. This angel might love the man with an affection quite beyond his power of return or even of appreciation, but her ideas of service and duty would be on a very different scale from his.... If she was a stray angel in a country of men, he might have had his way with her; but if he was a stray man among angels – ![9]

It is this renegotiation of the private and public sphere, and the duties and expectations in interpersonal and civil relationships, which becomes a new focus for women's science fiction in the 1980s and 1990s. In certain ways, women's writing is in total contrast to the world envisioned by cyberpunk. Cyberpunk's dark future is curiously Victorian, revising as it does eschatological and apocalyptic visions. Its concerns with class division, pollution, the visualisation of the city and youth as iniquitous, its lack of welfare provision, and its overwhelming fear of the street, are all reminiscent of the earlier period. As in the 1880s, one response of recent science fiction is to propose the pastoral and social existence beyond or after the city. Cyberpunk, however, posits a black and/or counter-economy which fights technology with technological expertise.

Cyberpunk has been criticised for being more concerned with the leisure applications of new technology than with the implications of social transition.[10] Representations of leisure and adventure story playgrounds, rather than the work environment, have been seen as failing to transcend the level of diversionary fantasy. William Gibson's female characters have also been criticised, especially by female reviewers,[11] although later writers such as Neal Stephenson in *Snow Crash* (1992), for example, have given a far more complex consideration of women and their work in the future. A significant contribution to this debate has been the recent revision of an earlier influential feminist utopia. Piercy's *Woman on the Edge of Time* proposed a utopia based on tolerance, nurturing, community, economic responsibility and the eradication of gender inequality. Her utopia is set in opposition to a dystopian background of 1970s America. In one chapter, her protagonist accidentally comes across an alternative male-dominated technological ultra-dystopia. M. Keith Booker has stated that Piercy's message is very clear: American society can continue without change and arrive at that dystopia, or change its social practices and work towards the utopia.[12]

If, as Williams has argued, the political utopia requires conscious choice and human agency rather than divine, technological or ecological intervention, then Marge Piercy's *He, She and It* (1991) complies. It is full of human and cyborg entities making those decisions. In this novel, Piercy fundamentally revises her earlier work by re-evaluating the genre, and the synchronic postmodern structure afforded by cyberpunk writing. Just prior to Gibson's publication of *Neuromancer* in 1984, Fredric Jameson declared that we had lost the capacity to think in utopian terms.[13] The disintegration of boundaries between the present and extrapolative accounts now means that it is no longer possible to imagine constructively the future beyond the semblance of a 'futureness'. Piercy proposes a future perfect. She outlines a potentially better future, but her narrative is far more concerned with the experience of the past and the diegetic present. From these perspectives, we can examine the activities of the utopian or revolutionary process. Other women science fiction writers, such as Joan

Slonczewski and Sheri Tepper, have become increasingly concerned with these political and moral processes.

In the acknowledgements to her novel, Piercy mentions a meeting with a reader which led to her revised views. During her residency at the University of Chicago, a student told her that he thought the alternative dystopian universe in *Woman on the Edge of Time* anticipated cyberpunk. The comment prompted Piercy to start reading Gibson, and also led her to read Donna Haraway's critical work, 'A manifesto for cyborgs: science, technology and socialist feminism in the 1980s'.[14] In response, Piercy combines the two sets of characteristics that make up cyberpunk and women's writing in the 1980s. She responds in fiction to Haraway's warning against the romance of nature as a locus of resistance to male white power,[15] and to Haraway's incitement to women and marginalised groups to appropriate technology for themselves.

The narrative of *He, She and It* is structured around the image of the cyborg. Piercy goes back to *Frankenstein*, and to the creation of a Golem in seventeenth-century Prague. Both the twenty-first-century cyborg and the renaissance Golem have been created as weapons by a society that fears physical and economic annihilation. These two narratives – the seventeenth-century Prague ghetto and the future free town of Tikva – are juxtaposed, chapter by chapter. The chapters are personal accounts of the past and the future. Tikva's economic dependence rests on its continued production of high-quality security software. However, this security is threatened by the Multis, the multinational corporations who are sending information pirates and assassins to destroy production. The Golem patrols the gate into the ghetto, but the gate that needs to be patrolled by artificial life in the twenty-first century is the net. It is through this electronic medium that the scientists of Tikva work and sell their products to the devastated outside world.

Piercy's cyborg functions successfully because, although designed by a man, it has been programmed by a woman. In the 1970s, Joanna Russ proposed *The Female Man*, but Piercy's cyborg in the 1990s is the male woman; a perfect weapon as well as 'rational, benign, gentle, infinitely patient and vastly intelligent and strong'.[16] However, Yod the cyborg is not a Pygmalion creation, the perfect man; rather, it is there to form a contrast to the female protagonists. They represent different economic responses to the destruction of the Middle Eastern oil region after the detonation of a nuclear device by terrorists in Jerusalem. The land and the oil were irretrievably lost. Shira, the main protagonist, has left Tikva for the conventionality of corporate life. However, the corporation has the power to rescind custody of her son, and she returns to her grandmother's house in Tikva. In direct contrast to Shira's enclave lifestyle is Nili, who has been brought up in a parthenogenetic society of women in the nuclear desert of Israel.

Shira's first encounter with Nili leaves her unable to decide whether or not she is human. Shira cannot determine Nili's gender, and her experience of Yod leaves her considering the woman as a cyborg and then as a corporate creature: 'The woman smiled at her. She had a way of smiling straight into the eyes, with a little twist of power that reminded Shira of a few men she had met. Dangerous men' (189). Nili is the visitor exploring a strange dystopia. She claims she is the future, because her people have adapted to the new ecological landscape:

> I can walk in the raw without protection, I am tolerant to levels of bombardment that would kill you. We live in the hills – inside them, that is. We are a joint community of the descendants of Israeli and Palestinian women who survived. We each keep our own religion, observe each other's holidays and fast days. We have no men. We learnt to engineer our genes. After birth we undergo additional alteration. We have created ourselves to endure, to survive to hold our lands. Soon we will begin re-building Yerushaleim (198).

Piercy's novel is one of contingency. The visitor Nili has come out of isolation to make alliances and learn about the net, to observe and to trade with the men and women outside her community. She is a mother and a warrior, seemingly impervious to the decadent fantasy world created by her male lover. His values and lifestyle are a continuous reminder of the consumer, corporate cyberpunk world, 'a world of high glamour surrounded by reconstructed females, bodies constantly resculpted by scalpels, implants, gels and the latest range of radiant beauty' (125). He wants to make Nili a media star, but she refuses both the fantasy and the money as irrelevant to her life and her mission. The male becomes the courtesan.

If Nili is the ambassador from Utopia in the tradition of women's writing, she is still not the 'Angel of the Revolution'. Her guide to the complexity of Earth territories, tribes and economies is Shira's mother, who left her daughter with her grandmother to be raised in Tikva. Shira has always imagined her mother, whom she has rarely seen, to be the corporate type, the woman who would put her career before her child. When Riva arrives in Tikva, she is disguised as a kvetching old woman, but she is indeed the hero, the one intimately involved in social change rather than merely survival: 'In his world, only poor women looked like Riva, and there were few enough of those.... But Riva walked in like a general reviewing his best razors, she swaggered, she

168

looked every man and woman straight in the eyes' (305). On meeting her mother, Shira has to come to terms with her relationship with the corporation. She realises that the male dominance she experienced during her time working for the corporation undervalued and undermined her, exploiting her for its own material gain. People are a scarce resource, and fertility even more so. The 'woman question' for patriarchal capitalism in Piercy's account revolves not so much around marriage, but rather around what to do with women who cannot conceive, or who will not conform. Shira's mother is the corporation's enemy because of her very active rather than passive dissent:

> Shira remembered her as a fussy, rather fuzzy woman.... That such a woman can be an information pirate was not credible. A certain amount of industrial espionage was part of the system, multi vs multi but the pirates were total outsiders, renegades, the standard villains in stimmies.... A brief synopsis of the crimes of Riva Shipman appeared on the screen along with a warning about the dangers she posed to the established corporate order (78).

Riva describes herself as liberating information, which prevents a one multi-monopoly, particularly on medical technology. She either sells the data or publishes information on the net so that it is publicly accessible. Her commitment to the circulation of information is dangerous and violent. To do what she does she cannot have a stable home, relationships or family; these are left to her scientist mother. Riva has to be in a position where she can make tough decisions and act upon them. Therefore, she is empowered to act in the dystopia, and to make alliances between the disparate tribes who have a precarious existence with the multis. Riva's sacrifices are the reason that Tikva can survive, but she cannot live there. She is admirable, but difficult to like, a reminder of the narrative impossibility of the socialist hero(ine) in popular fiction.

Towards the novel's conclusion, Riva is described as a saint, rather than an angel: 'Saints are hard to endure, no? A brave woman. A wise woman who pursues just aims regardless of the danger to herself. She sees what must be done and she forces herself to do it' (379). Riva is the interim stage, the means to Nili's future which values personal ties, the social and the communal. As in William Morris's pastoral utopia *News From Nowhere* (1888), the means to realising post-capital communal order are accentuated by their incongruity to that lifestyle. The armed struggle in the penultimate chapter of *News From Nowhere* is a discordant contrast with the results of that conflict: the arcadian utopia.

Angels are messengers who act as intermediaries between the divine and humanity. They instruct, inform or command, but they rarely interact. They have power, and they are visualised as heavenly warriors, but their agency is one of mediation. Like 'The Angel in the House', saints are characterised for virtue and sanctity. Virgins, matrons and widows can be canonised as saints for their suffering and martyrdom. However, in women's contemporary science fiction they can expand their range of activities to include other forms of human heroism, such as evangelism and learning. Their position outside the community, and their non-conformism, is far more evident. Such saints are illustrative of conscious decision-making, not merely obedience to the divine. Decision-making, action, and the means to social change become the object of utopian speculation, rather than the form and content of the society after the effected change.

In women's utopian writing, the move from angel to saint as a motif for social change and social action is significant because of its acknowledgement of concerted communal action. The inclusion of female characters in broader science fiction media can be seen as cosmetic and consensual in many instances. However, women's science fiction has moved beyond nineteenth-century visualisation. It has revised its structure in order to interrogate, as well as identify, political and cultural concerns for women and their families in the twentieth century.

NOTES

1. Marge Piercy, *He, She and It*, New York 1992.
2. Nicola Nixon, 'Cyberpunk: preparing the ground for the revolution or keeping the boys satisfied?', *Science Fiction Studies*, 19 (1992), 219–35.
3. Joan Gordon, 'Yin and Yang duke it out: is cyberpunk feminism's New Age?', in L. McCaffrey, ed., *Storming the Reality Studio*, North Carolina 1991, 199.
4. Peter Fitting, 'The turn from Utopia in recent feminist fiction', in L. Jones and S. Webster Goodwin, *Feminism, Utopia and Narrative*, Tennessee 1980, 142.
5. Raymond Williams, 'Utopia and science fiction', *Science Fiction Studies*, 5:16 (1978), 203–14.
6. Brian Stableford, *Scientific Romance in Britain 1890–1950*, London 1985, 54.
7. ibid.

8.   George Griffith, *Angel of the Revolution*, London 1895, 64.

9.   Charlotte Perkins Gilman, *Herland*, London 1992, 123.

10.   Terry Whalen, 'The future of a commodity: notes towards a critique of cyberpunk and the information age', *Science Fiction Studies*, 19 (1992), 75–89.

11.   Nixon, op. cit.

12.   M. Keith Booker, 'Women on the edge of a genre: the feminist dystopias of Marge Piercy', *Science Fiction Studies*, 21 (1994), 337–50.

13.   Fredric Jameson, 'Progress versus Utopia: or can we imagine the future?', *Science Fiction Studies*, 9:2 (1982), 147–58.

14.   Donna Haraway, 'Manifesto for cyborgs: science, technology and socialist feminism in the 1980s', *Socialist Review*, 80 (1985), 65–108.

15.   Booker, op. cit., 345.

16.   Piercy, op. cit., 365. Further references are given in the text.

15

The vampire at the fin de siècle: postmodern decadence in Anne Rice's *Interview with the Vampire*

Antonio Ballesteros González

The vampire tends to be a representation of fin-de-siècle decadence. The main literary configurator of the myth, Bram Stoker, published *Dracula* in 1897, in the last years of the Victorian Empire and very close to the twentieth century. Manuel Aguirre has conveniently emphasised the Victorian literary background of the vampire: 'As a literary *species* with characteristic attributes and values, the vampire is a Victorian creation. Further, as a haunter of individuals, he belongs (to extend a biological image) in the *population* of 19th-century *Doppelgängers* [sic].'[1]

Vampires have generally been conceived of as figures of 'otherness', of utter alienation. According to Rosemary Jackson, 'they become parasites, feeding off the real and living, condemned to an eternal interstitial existence, *in between* things'.[2] The vampire is thus a liminal being, a marginal figure. *Dracula* is a magnificent instance of the vampire's elusiveness and alien features, for the Count does not enter those parts of the text written in journal style or dictated to the phonograph. The vampire, who has no reflection in the mirror, is not reflected in the documents – the pages and the tapes – created by Van Helsing's allies in order to produce the exorcism of this ultimate 'other'. Dracula, as a figure of folklore and superstition, is rejected from Victorian technology and has apparently no place in the development of a bourgeois and imperial society. In the same way, Lucy, the other character in the novel who completely becomes a vampire, is not allowed to enter the literary world any more, once she has been transformed into a monster. Therefore both Dracula and Lucy, like the other vampires in the book, are outsiders from a textual perspective.

Dracula – like Jekyll and Hyde, Dorian Gray and the Invisible Man – is an epitome of Victorian decadence, here represented by the ancient European aristocrat, the embodiment of evil feudalism who has been overcome by a new order propitiated by the imperial powers of the bourgeoisie. Nevertheless, the novel can also be read, using a grim allegorical interpretation, as the domain of fantasy and creativity being jointly destroyed by folkloric atavistic instruments and by the technological weapons signifying industrial progress. Decadence is a means of facing a world which presents boring and dull 'realities'. The

172

problem is that Victorian decadence was threatened by, and later integrated in, the apparatus of the Establishment, and had to find new metamorphoses and developments in order to safeguard its revolutionary appeal.

We are now living in a fin-de-siècle and millenarian context at the end of the twentieth century, and new 'monsters' substituting – or evolving from – the old seem to menace our peaceful *aurea mediocritas*. However, as Neil Cornwell astutely notes, the old monsters are but metaphors and representations of the new:

> Brian Aldiss ... considers the real subject of *Dracula* to be "that obsession of the fin de siècle, syphilis. *Dracula* is the great Victorian novel about VD, for which vampirism stands in as Stoker's metaphor". Such a view can only appear even more alluring in the age of Aids, a disease with symptoms which seem to bear an uncanny resemblance to the wasting effects resulting from vampirism, at least *à la* Stoker and Le Fanu.[3]

In our age of AIDS and Ebola, the vampire has to claim a new position from an ideological and, subsequently, from a literary point of view. I am going to deal in this essay with one of the most interesting and significant postmodern portrayals of the vampire, that provided by Anne Rice in her tetralogy of the 'Vampire Chronicles': *Interview with the Vampire* (1976), *The Vampire Lestat* (1985), *The Queen of the Damned* (1988) and *The Tale of the Body Thief* (1992). My main concern here – apart from some references to the other novels when required – will be the first book in the series, an even more fashionable work at this moment, due to the successful motion picture bearing the same title, directed by Neil Jordan and featuring Tom Cruise, Brad Pitt and Antonio Banderas. However, the novel and the film are quite different cultural products.

Interview with the Vampire focuses on a new postmodern conception of vampirism, an interpretation which opens up and widens the restricted and limited possibilities of the Victorian vampire as an embodiment of horror and mystery. The term 'postmodern' here has to be explained, for it seems to introduce a suggestion of anachronism: the action of the novel – which is told in flash-back – is mostly centred upon the nineteenth century, although it finishes in the present day. However, Louis, the main character, is always at a loss with respect to his own self, and evolves from his romantic despair to a postmodern attitude of detachment and loss.

In this novel vampires are defined *a contrario*, taking Dracula and other Victorian and post-Victorian vampires as the main parameter of comparison. In one of his first assertions, Louis rejects almost all the folkloric superstitions connected with the literary vampire. The creatures in the 'Vampire Chronicles' are not conventional: they like light and are familiar with technological apparatuses. This is precisely one of the great differences to *Dracula*, where the Count is systematically expelled from the written texts created by his enemies (the journals, diaries, documents, the transcriptions of Seward's phonograph, and so on). Since the Victorian vampire is a creature of folklore and fantasy, he has no direct access to the text, and is defeated because of that.

Louis, on the contrary, as a postmodern vampire, is interviewed by a young man who keeps the former's words in a tape recorder. Thus Rice is offering a direct interaction, where the 'other' tells his life to an addressee in the first person singular, and from the monster's perspective for the first time in vampire literature. Although there are several interruptions in the main narrative, the young man's voice is always subordinated to that of the protagonist, and practically disappears towards the end of the 'document', underlining the young man's fascination with the story he is listening to, a fascination coinciding with the reader's mesmerised reactions while decoding the vampire's words. Louis's desire to communicate integrates the monster into the postmodern world – in spite of the fact that, as Lestat informs the reader in *The Vampire Lestat*, it was traditionally forbidden for a vampire to divulge vampiric secrets. The 'other' takes its place in a new social order, and perhaps the best example of this is Lestat's becoming a rock 'n' roll star and a kind of ironical Robin Hood – a refined murderer of serial killers – in the second volume of the 'Vampire Chronicles'.

Apart from this textual integration, the postmodern vampire offers a contrast to the Victorian vampire in terms of the paraphernalia of superstition. The young man is overwhelmed by Louis's rejection of traditional and conventional views of the vampire:

'I was going to ask, rosaries have crosses on them, don't they?'
'Oh, the rumor about crosses!' the vampire laughed. 'You refer to our being afraid of crosses?'
'Unable to look on them, I thought,' said the boy.
'Nonsense, my friend, sheer nonsense. I can look on anything I like. And I rather like looking on crucifixes in particular.'
'And what about the rumor about keyholes? That you can ... become steam and go through them.'
'I wish I could,' laughed the vampire. 'How positively delightful. I should like to pass through all manner of different keyholes and feel the tickle of their peculiar shapes. No.' He shook his head. 'That is, how would you say today ... bullshit?' ....

'The story about stakes through the heart,' said the boy, his cheeks coloring slightly.

'The same,' said the vampire. 'Bull-shit'.[4]

Moreover, unlike in *Dracula* (for instance, the famous episode of Harker's cutting himself when shaving and the Count's reaction in front of the looking-glass), these vampires can cast a reflection in the mirror. They actually *like* mirrors, for they are extremely narcissistic creatures: indeed, their narcissism is another reminder of their utter decadence. Vampires can cry and make digressions about any 'divine' or human topic, for they are refined beings always willing to acquire knowledge, no matter how aware they are of the inconsistent limitations of human culture.

Louis and Claudia both like reading, whilst Lestat – as the succeeding volumes of the 'Chronicles' will show – prefers writing (Dracula, in contrast, only 'writes' two circumstantial notes to Jonathan Harker throughout the narrative development of the novel). The metafictional parody is increased when, in the second volume of the series, Lestat 'reads' Louis's account of his life in a book entitled – *Interview with the Vampire*. The text establishes a narcissistic relationship with its own self.

These are undoubtedly cultivated vampires, somewhat similar to the male characters in Wilde's *The Picture of Dorian Gray* (1891), perhaps the best example of fin-de-siècle decadence ever created. Armand, the old Parisian vampire, and Lestat to a certain extent, are epitomes of the decadent dandy. According to Ken Gelder, vampirism is 'something akin to a posture or style, a *simulation* of the real'.[5] Vampires are surrounded by luxury and artistic masterpieces, and they can be patient about enjoying everything they want, for time is definitely on their side: they are immortal, on the condition that mankind – their prey, their 'food' – is 'immortal'. Vampires can live 'So long as men can breathe or eyes can see', for their fate is united with that of humanity, its works, its art and its conventions. In a typically decadent fashion, the only thing that can temporarily 'kill' them is boredom.

In *The Vampire Lestat*, Lestat will, significantly, get over his malady, his lethargy, when listening to rock 'n' roll music, and when keeping in contact with postmodern mass culture. This marks out Louis's difference, as a limited and sentimental 'predator', as he is represented in *Interview with the Vampire*. In the latter, the narrator is the embodiment of existential disillusionment, an impression also reflected in his artistic tastes, once he is tired of traditional art.[6] Armand, the old vampire, cannot understand the postmodern world, nor cope with modern and postmodern art. That is why he disappears from the text.

Lestat will understand later the shifting nature of the contemporary world, and will wake up to one of its most attractive symbols, rock music.

The geographic differences between the postmodern and the traditional vampire are also significant. Lestat, Louis and Claudia live in New Orleans, a place of exoticism and decadence, the cosmopolitan epitome of 'otherness'. Like any piece of vampiric literature, Anne Rice's novels are about blood, and New Orleans, a site in the New World rather than the Old, presents a multiplicity and richness of blood mixture where all races, creeds and traditions live – and die – together. Ken Gelder has written perceptively about the meaning of this choice: 'This Southern American city becomes a powerful, occult site for events – a place in the New World which is nevertheless somehow older and more decadent than Europe, simultaneously "primitive" and sophisticated, a "mixture" of all kinds of peoples.'[7] Although the vampire is a clear example of a 'citizen of the world', always travelling and inhabiting old and new territories, Louis will go back to New Orleans at the end of the novel, in a kind of ritualistic circular structure, (although he will soon abandon the place to live in San Francisco, where he is interviewed). At a symbolic level, the city is a metaphor of the mother, a figure which is ironically excluded or mocked at in the book. Here is Louis's significant description of his home town, the perfect place for a vampire to hide and live in perfect anonymity:

> There was no city in America like New Orleans. It was filled not only with the French and Spanish of all classes who had formed in parts its peculiar aristocracy, but later with immigrants of all kinds, the Irish and the German in particular. Then there were not only the black slaves, yet unhomogenised and fantastical in their garb and manners, but the great growing class of free people of colour, those marvellous people of our mixed blood and that of the islands, who produced a magnificent and unique caste of craftsmen, artists, poets, and renowned feminine beauty. Then there were the Indians, who covered the levee on summer days selling herbs and crafted wares. And drifting through all, through this medley of languages and colours, were the people of the port....
>
> This was New Orleans, a magical and magnificent place to live. In which a vampire, richly dressed and gracefully walking through the pools of light of one gas lamp after another might attract no more notice in the evening than hundreds of other exotic creatures – if he attracted any at all... (45–6).

Here, as Dryden said, referring to Chaucer's *Canterbury Tales*, is 'God's plenty'. The reader is dealing with 'colonial vampires', beings possessing a historical and political sense of detachment and objectivity concerning anything human – reversing Terence's most-quoted sentence: *Humanus sum, et nihil humanum a me alienum puto*. Vampires, with their supernatural powers, perceive human events from an objective position.

On the other hand, Rice's emphasis on travelling and decadent tourism provides a fantasy of control, imagining a world without borders, without 'otherness'.[8] Vampires in the 'Chronicles' appear to be characters 'on the road', pursuing a perpetual self-quest which is manifested inwardly in the same way as it is outwardly. Resembling Frankenstein's monster and other Gothic and horror characters, these creatures will be permanently haunted by a quest for origins. They seem to be fulfilling a kind of recurrent initiatory journey. New Orleans is then a good example of integration and occultation, a place which means everything and nothing at the same time. Although Louis will be fascinated by Paris, the 'mother of New Orleans', the Old World represented by Europe will be abandoned in favour of the New World. This is even more evident when one focuses on the events narrated in Part Two, where the 'new' vampire faces and fights the 'old' vampire of Central Europe. Louis and Claudia's feelings, as are the reader's, are disappointed when the mythical vampire (who has nothing to do with the powerful figure of Count Dracula and his 'hideous progeny') appears. For the vampire of Central Europe (Transylvania, Hungary and Bulgaria) is 'a mindless corpse' (212), a creature providing neither referentiality nor semantic values for the New World. The vampiric representative of folklore turns out to be a complete failure, leaving Louis and Claudia with 'no secrets, no truths, only despair' (ibid.).

Furthermore, the episode is probably associated with Louis's former uneasiness in relation to 'procreation' – his reasons very close to those of Victor Frankenstein when he rejects the possibility of creating a female monster – until he decides to 'give birth' to a new vampire: Madeleine, a mock-mother figure for Claudia. The episode, according to Louis, constitutes the end of anything human in him, the vampire discovering at last his 'real' nature. The family, the basic institution of Victorian society defended in *Dracula* with unbeatable bourgeois weapons, is here subverted and transformed into an ironical realm where the prevalent value is desire, although not completely expressed in sexual terms.

The vampires' dissatisfaction seems to culminate in the meeting with their Parisian counterparts, who are commanded by Armand, the oldest vampire in the world. By accepting Armand's company and 'queer' friendship, despite his implication in the events leading to Claudia and Madeleine's death, Louis attempts a symbolic integration or mock-marriage between the Old and the New World. Louis is fascinated by 'history', a concept indicating a kind of 'inferiority complex' for a vampire coming from America and lacking the experience of ancient art and historical events. However, the Parisian vampires turn into another source of disillusionment, for they are not only physically but also intellectually and conceptually 'dead'. They are on the whole 'artificial' beings, in the middle of reality and fiction. Unlike the American vampire, they are not prepared to survive in the new order of postmodernism, and therefore they are destroyed, in an act of poetic justice.

Having proclaimed Satan's and God's death, the only immortal being left in the fictional universe of the book is the vampire. Louis's answers to his existential questions are thus inside the self, and not outside it. It goes without saying that this factor is linked to the ideological dimension of power, as can be seen in the following:

> I'd been astonished to discover those vampires above had made of immortality a club of fads and cheap conformity. And yet through this sadness, this confusion, came the clear realization: Why should it be otherwise? What had I expected? What right had I to be so bitterly disappointed in Lestat that I would let him die! Because he wouldn't show me what I must find in myself? Armand's words, what had they been? *The only power that exists is inside ourselves...* (274).

As Ken Gelder points out, everything, even great art, is transient. But the vampire will always remain.[9]

As in many other literary works dealing with the vampire, one of the metaphoric projections of the monster in Rice's first novel is the vampire's fictional association with plagues, a fin-de-siècle and millenarian phenomenon highly relevant nowadays. This creature of the night is connected with the image of the plague, a disease unknown to science which stands for systematic and mysterious death. The vampire is a lethal killing machine, a being who has substituted God Almighty with his/her mortal kiss, with the 'dark gift' (92). At the same time, for many of these undead, killing is considered 'one of the fine arts', an exciting sensation which nullifies sexual relationships (275). The decadent vampire at the fin de siècle expresses the representation of death, the only really democratic and socially-levelling event in the life of a human being. Equalling the plague, vampires respect no-one and nothing, no matter how rich, powerful and beautiful their victims may be. The symbolic transformation of little Claudia into a vampire by both Louis and Lestat is counterpointed by the ever-present image of the girl's dead mother, a victim of the plague devastating New Orleans. The 'queer' family resulting from the two male vampires' act is converted into a new framework subverting the traditional bourgeois ideal. The plague is the best ally for the vampire, a context where they can exert their deadly powers with the utmost impunity.

Postmodern society, as reflected in *The Vampire Lestat, The Queen of the Damned* and *The Tale of the Body Thief,* reveals its many possibilities for the vampires' survival and successful growth. Lestat fixes his residence in Miami, the perfect place for the vampire to maintain his anonymity, surrounded by many other types of murderers. In fact, vampires are the very epitome of psychopathic behaviour, dandy-like and elegant serial killers.[10] They represent one of the most common psychological disturbances in our fin-de-siècle referential background. However, these novels also contain the technological alienation of the postmodern period, exemplified by the computer files and archives menacing the vampire's elusive existence amongst human beings. Once again, technology threatens the development of fantasy and otherness. Moreover, as in Paul Auster's *New York Trilogy* (or in *Frankenstein,* the seminal source of all postmodern Gothic fiction), the outlines of the plots could be structurally reduced to the act of watching and being watched, pursuing and being pursued. This 'fantasy of control', as Gelder terms it, is not devoid of Foucauldian echoes, of, for instance, the metaphor of the Panopticon.[11] Therefore, the vampire participates in the incarcerating nature of our postmodern society, a model which tries to exclude any representation of 'otherness' and difference.

As a corollary, Anne Rice's 'Vampire Chronicles' depict the vampiric condition as a style or a mask, the vampire standing for the 'mirror of an age' (310). In the fictional universe of these novels, that age corresponds to a fin-de-siècle and decadent period that very much resembles our postmodern world. For the blood is the life, and the vampire – like a paradoxically living myth – will be regenerated once again, haunting our dreams up to the end of human time.

NOTES

1. Manuel Aguirre, *The Closed Space. Horror Literature and Western Symbolism,* Manchester and New York 1990, 135.

2. Rosemary Jackson, *Fantasy: The Literature of Subversion,* London 1981, 118.

3. Neil Cornwell, *The Literary Fantastic. From Gothic to Postmodernism,* London 1990, 111–12.

4. Anne Rice, *Interview with the Vampire,* London 1977, 27. Further references are to this edition and are given in the text.

5. Ken Gelder, *Reading the Vampire,* London 1994, 10.

6.   The Louvre episode is interesting in this respect: see Rice, op. cit., 340.
7.   Gelder, op. cit., 110.
8.   ibid., 123.
9.   ibid., 113.
10.   ibid., 120.
11.   See Michel Foucault, *Discipline and Punish*, Harmondsworth 1977.

16

'Unspeakable rites': constructions of subjectivity in *Heart of Darkness* and *American Psycho*

Tim Middleton

I

Aestheticizing the unacceptable is a common fin-de-siècle pastime.[1]

Eagleton's assertion suggests an interrelation between fin de siècles: an interrelation which this essay examines via a contextualised analysis of Joseph Conrad's *Heart of Darkness* and Bret Easton Ellis's *American Psycho*. By focusing upon two paradigmatic texts from each era, I seek to unpack some of the ways in which fictions can stage a critique of the discursive framework (qua ideologies) upon which they draw. In particular, I will be exploring the ways in which the novels rework dominant notions of the subject. My reading rejects the facile opposition of modernism/postmodernism, and adopts Peter Nicholls's (Lyotardian) notion that the postmodern is 'a mode not an epoch';[2] one in which new ways of seeing are generated 'by putting into question existing paradigms, [and] by inventing new ones'.[3]

Conrad's novella requires no introduction, but Ellis's *American Psycho* is a text which (seemingly) more people heard about than actually read. It was Ellis's third novel, and is concerned with the life of Patrick Bateman, a Wall Street dealer of sorts, with a taste for the good life as sanctioned by the style Bibles of yuppiedom, and with a penchant for picking up 'hardbodies' (as women are described), then using them to gratify his sado-masochistic and cannibalistic desires. Dismissed by some as a merely revolting, the novel is much more a satire of eighties consumer culture than the 'how-to-be-a-serial killer' guidebook which some commentators have suggested it to be. As John Walsh, in one of the few positive reviews of the novel, argued, 'Ellis uses the consumerist surface ... of modern American life to satirise its greed, ignorance, complacency and moral bankruptcy'.[4]

I will be concentrating upon the ways in which the texts explore the construction of subjectivity in specific social and symbolic orders. In addressing the versions of masculinity deployed in each text, it is necessary to suggest the ways in which Kurtz and Bateman are shown to be formed (or deformed) by the discursive formations of their contemporary culture. Masculinity cannot be analysed in the abstract: as Peter Middleton argues, it is 'fluid, unstable, constantly reconstructed and embedded in the symbolic realm'.[5] If subjectivity is an effect of discursive interaction, then masculinities may be read as constructs 'produced in and by different discourses of *representation*'.[6] Approaching masculinity as a discursive construct allows the critic to focus upon textual representations as sites in which competing accounts of masculinity from the wider culture are put into dialogue, and from this perspective, literary representations of gender may be claimed as part and parcel of an era's overall construction of gender.[7] In order to unpack the discourses which contributed to the construction of masculine subjectivity in the two texts under discussion, it is necessary to establish briefly the wider cultural politics within which their representations signify.

II

Many critics have explored the interrelation between the new imperialism of the late nineteenth century, and 'the crisis of identity for men' of that fin de siècle.[8] What happened in the later 1890s is, of course, an intensification of trends evident much earlier:

> during the mid-to-late nineteenth century, heroic masculinity became fused in an especially potent configuration with representations of British imperial identity ... [a] dominant conception of masculinity – the 'true Englishman' – was both required and underpinned by the dominant versions of British national identity.[9]

In the 1890s, empire became both the imaginary and at times the actual space in which heroic masculinity could be acted out. The intersection of the ideals of empire and masculinity is replicated, and thus reinforced, in a host of fictions from the period. Elaine Showalter has suggested that the 'male quest romance' of writers like Haggard and Stevenson offers empire and colonies as sites in which 'men can be freed from the constraints of Victorian morality', and thus as a 'safe arena where late Victorian readers could approach subjects that were ordinarily taboo'.[10] Alongside this view must be placed the fact that, as Patrick Brantlinger notes, 'imperialist ideology ... preserved and nurtured various conservative fantasies, chief among them the mythology of the English gentleman'.[11]

Empire was projected as a mythic or imaginary space within which the era's dominant conceptions of masculinity could be enacted. Empire was both a place where one could be 'a real man' and a place in which the English gentleman was supposed to offer a shining example of 'how to be' to the empire's subject races. The reality frequently fell rather short of these ideals, as the work of historians like Ronald Hyam makes clear.[12] Between the official optimism of imperialist ideology, and the pessimistic accounts of degeneracy theorists, there existed a range of positions concerning masculine subjectivity which are drawn upon in Conrad's *Heart of Darkness*.

As Angela Carter remarked, the 'fin' has come rather early in the present siècle[13] – indeed, Terry Eagleton has recently suggested that it arrived in the 1960s; here, I want to advance a somewhat more narrow claim for the 1980s as our own fin de siècle.[14]

In eighties American cultural politics, the dominant notes were of duplicity and corruption; at the level of government alone we saw bungled foreign and domestic policy on a grand scale. The period began with the electorate still alienated by the run-off from Watergate, and ends with the muddied waters of Irangate. In 1980 the electors turned to the 'grandfatherly' Reagan, who offered values which many found congenial; espousing a free-market Darwinism, he put forward an economic programme based on the notion that existing policy prohibited business growth. The Reagan administration promoted life, liberty and the pursuit of that extra buck as the core motivation for every true-thinking American: making money and conspicuously consuming it became a major goal.

In the popular imagination the eighties have become wedded to excess and double-dealing. The period witnessed the spectacular excess of yuppiedom and the millennial angst of the TV evangelist, and saw the pious corruption of fallen preachers and the born-again fervour of the corporate raider. The image of heroic masculinity of the 1980s is that of the corporate raider sallying forth to build an empire of the senseless, in which the only ideal was Gordon Gekko's notion that 'greed is good'.[15] Eighties America offers a frame of reference which – at the level of beliefs – is at times surprisingly similar to that of the British fin de siècle of the 1890s. In both periods, cultures developed in which 'ideals are mere specious rationalizations of material interests'.[16] For some, the hollow materialism of the eighties is best summed up, not by Reaganomics, but by the phenomenon of Madonna.[17] Her cynically commercial ongoing re-definition of her self catches the spirit of an age in which subjectivity is merely a pose; as Camille Paglia puts it, 'Madonna says we are nothing but masks', and in so doing she is 'the authentic voice of the fin de siècle'.[18]

Given this background of corrupt bungling, fluid subjectivities and cynical exploitation, it might be argued that the depravity which pervades the world of *American Psycho* is not exceptional: it is actually part and parcel of American 'reality' in the period. What happened to the 'American Dream' in the eighties was that its message of striving for success became wedded to a ruthless individualism. *American Psycho* suggests that contemporary American culture can be seen as schizophrenogenic, in that it repeatedly requires the individual to negotiate between 'incompatible and contradictory demands'.[19]

Both *Heart of Darkness* and *American Psycho* rely upon the cultural context of their respective fin de siècles, and offer the reader stereotypes of masculine subjectivities (Kurtz and Bateman) in order to point up the fractures and ruptures in the very codes of representation they draw upon for these stereotypes. Kurtz and Bateman may be read as paradigms of the contradictions of subjectivity in their respective eras. Yet, as I will argue below, the difficulty for the period reader of these novels is that the masculine subjectivities which are at the centre of the texts are 'unspeakable' – both stereotypical and aberrant, incompatible and contradictory. It is the reader's double-bind which provides the key to the ways in which these novels offer a critique of the dominant discourses of their day.

Heart of Darkness works within a largely nineteenth-century episteme, in which identity is an essence – a 'lonely region of stress and strife'.[20] From this perspective, Kurtz's withdrawal into his alienated self – 'he had kicked the earth to pieces ... alone in the wilderness ... [he] had looked within himself and gone mad' - draws upon late-nineteenth-century notions of the opposition between madness and civilisation.[21] However, in my reading, *Heart of Darkness* goes beyond the fin-de-siècle concerns it draws upon. The novella does not simply suggest Africa as a place in which civilisation's writ does not run (the imperial gothic version), nor is it offered as a proving ground for Marlow's masculinity (the Haggardian boy's own version). Rather, it uses the story of Marlow's journey and of Kurtz's 'degeneration' as a vehicle for a critique which encompasses not only the dominant ideologies of imperialism, but also the dominant accounts of subjectivity. In *Heart of Darkness* Conrad undermines the whole edifice of the Victorian rational subject, by suggesting that consciousness is an effect of language.

Marlow's narrative literally presents individual subjects to the reader as an effect of language; it offers, rather than the sustaining illusion of meaning, a tri-partite meditation upon the impossibility of meaning, on the impossibility of narrating that which lies beyond the 'threshold of the visible' (69). It offers, then, a narrativisation of experience, and points up the gaps between the experience and its telling (to the extent that some have argued that the Marlow of Part 1 and that of Part 3 have a radically different perspective).[22] Central to *Heart of Darkness* is Marlow's failure to place Kurtz within extant categories of discourse.[23] The reason why he cannot make sense of Kurtz rests with his socialisation: Marlow is an Englishman, apt to take refuge in established codes of behaviour, bewildered by those who – like Kurtz – do not adhere to them. In *Lord Jim* he notes that 'one *must*' take refuge in 'the sheltering conceptions of light and order' which civilisation offers.[24] Marlow's sturdy Englishness equips him with a world view that is utterly at a loss to make sense of Kurtz's eloquent, depraved and multi-faceted self.

Marlow has no time for 'fine sentiments', or principles, which 'won't do'; just 'the surface truth' and 'his own true stuff' are sufficient. Marlow's code of conduct – his 'deliberate belief' (38) – seems to be associated with the kind of 'singleness of intention' he identifies in Towson's *Inquiry in to Some Points of Seamanship* (39).[25] It is the lack of these qualities which informs the experiencing Marlow's reading of Kurtz. Kurtz's susceptibility to the call of the wilderness stems from his lack of any 'singleness of intention', and is part of his multi-faceted subjectivity – the end of the novella reveals him to have been a myriad of things to a wide range of people. In part, this representation of multiplicity is tied into the novella's concern to reveal subjectivity as contingent upon a specific social order, but arising out of Marlow's perplexed yet probing re-telling of his experiences is a profoundly modern (some might even say postmodern) notion of the subject.[26]

By the end of *Heart of Darkness*, Conrad appears to be offering an almost Nietzschean account of 'the subject as multiplicity', in which the self is disclosed as 'a multiplicity of subjects, whose interaction and struggle is the basis of our thought and our consciousness in general'.[27] Marlow's narration foregrounds the splitting of the subject, contingent upon the entry into the symbolic order of language, by reproducing the disjunction between lived experience and the languages (qua discourse) through which one attempts to communicate that experience. The novella explores the interconnections between social contexts and subjectivity, whilst insisting upon the difficulty of so doing because language cannot access the Real: 'language ... [is] ... always seeking to "rationalise", to "repress" the lived experience, [and thus] reflection will eventually become profoundly divergent from that lived experience.'[28] As Marlow puts it: 'it is impossible to convey the life-sensation of any given epoch of one's existence – that which makes its truth, its meaning – its subtle and penetrating essence. It is impossible' (29–30).

Heart of Darkness explores a world beyond the telegraph cables, and outside representation, in order to offer 'a glimpse of truth', which those readers of *Blackwood's Magazine* expecting an imperial gothic fiction undoubtedly had not asked for. The horror revealed in *Heart of Darkness* is not the marginal experience of a madman, but rather serves as the occasion for 'an unveiling of the abject, an elaboration, a discharge, a hollowing out of [the] abjection', which characterises the other side of the ideals of imperialism.[29] More broadly, the 'horror' which Marlow's narrative rests upon is the late-nineteenth-century anxiety about the dissolution of the subject in a world without God; the 'sheltering conception' of rational subjectivity is replaced by the abject self. We do Conrad a disservice if we read the novella simply in terms of the established discourses of the era of its production, seeing it 'merely' as a text concerned with individual regression, or the failure of civilisation to withstand the shock of the primitive. This is because, as Marlow's interview with the Intended, and his asides to his audience suggest, the truth which Kurtz glimpses cannot be transposed into the period's categories. As Michael Levenson argues: 'it was when Conrad thought past the former possibility, the degradation of a virtuous man ... which reveals the depravity of a social form ... that *Heart of Darkness* ... disclosed another region of subjectivity.'[30]

III

Just as Conrad's *Heart of Darkness* draws extensively upon the codes and discourses of the late-nineteenth-century fin de siècle, so Ellis's *American Psycho* reworks conventions and concepts from eighties American culture. The text is more evidently a critique of the era whose values it reproduces; it is a more playfully literary work. For example, whilst Conrad assumes a readership well-versed in the codes of imperial romance, Ellis's fiction is more profoundly intertextual, actually drawing upon other fictions as well as upon a wealth of detail from the wider culture. As Elizabeth Young has noted, Bateman has already appeared as the older brother of a character in Ellis's second novel, *Rules of Attraction* (1987). Moreover, the firm that Bateman works for is that created by Tom Wolfe in the earlier *Bonfire of the Vanities* (1987). A minor character met with in the opening chapter has the same name (Stash) and profession as a character from Tama Janowitz's *Slaves of New York* (1986). Finally, Bateman has had a violent sexual encounter with Alison Poole, the heroine of Jay McInerney's *Story of My Life* (1988).[31] These intertexts foreground the way in which fictions are central in this text.

The reader of *American Psycho*, like Marlow faced with Kurtz, is initially brought up against the impossibility of reading Bateman in relation to extant categories of discourse. As the narrative unfolds, however, we are forced to make connections between the two aspects of Bateman's 'life' (as Marlow and the reader of *Heart of Darkness* are forced to connect Kurtz's story with all versions of imperialist activity). The latter novel leads us to and then takes us beyond the 'threshold of the invisible' (69), and whilst Ellis's novel is obviously far less circumspect about what lies beyond this threshold than Conrad's text, one should not undermine the shock value of *Heart of Darkness*, particularly for the conservative readers of *Blackwood's*. In the serial version of 1899, aspects of Kurtz's horror were more visible. In a passage Conrad actually added for the serial text but cancelled in the version published in 1902 by Dent, Kurtz says:

> "I have been dead – and damned." … "Let me go – I want more of it."
> "More of what?" [Marlow asks] … "More blood, more heads on stakes, more adoration, rapine, and murder."[33]

Both texts therefore may be claimed to explore abjection, in Kristeva's sense that the abject is 'that which disobeys classification rules peculiar to … [a] given symbolic system'.[34]

The 'symbolic system' underpinning Bateman's world in *American Psycho* is one in which Donald Trump and the *New York Times*' restaurant page seem to be the sole arbiters of value.[35] The novel discloses a world in which identity has been reduced to the clothes you wear, and in which non-conformity of the most minimal kind threatens pariah status – Bateman even wears non-prescription glasses to ensure he fits the identi-kit image of the yuppie. This is a surface-oriented world, in which people 'feel like shit but look great' (106); in which personality is reduced to a pose or a mask – as Bateman comments, 'I've perfected my fake response to a degree where it's so natural sounding that no-one notices' (156-7). With no perspective on events other than Bateman's, we are prompted to question how far his 'revelations' about his hidden life are real, and how far they are fantasies. In a world without values, Bateman's own lack of emotion and belief may well be just another facet of his desire to fit in. The constructed nature of Bateman's reality is constantly on show; the narration frequently adopts terms from film scripts to describe its movement, and so undermines his claim that 'everything outside of this is like some movie I once saw' (345).

Bateman's obsessive attempt to name everything, to classify everything about his world, may be seen as an attempt to ensure that nothing falls outside of its symbolic order:

> I do ninety abdominal crunches, a hundred and fifty push ups, and then I run in place for twenty minutes whilst listening to the new Huey Lewis CD. I take a hot shower and afterwards use a new facial scrub by Caswell-Massey and a body wash by Greune, then a body moisturiser by Lubriderm and a Neutrogena facial cream (76).

The often tedious overload of detail about the everyday lives of the characters is matched by the sickening overload of detail about Bateman's sexual acts and murders. The novel's integration of murder and serial killing with high fashion and conspicuous consumption suggests the interrelation between the symbolic order and what it excludes. The novel forces the reader to link cannibalism and capitalism: this seeming impossibility is fundamental to Bateman's subjectivity. He is thus abject, in Kristeva's sense that all abjection turns around the revelation of the want, 'the inaugural loss that laid the foundations of its own being'.[36] As Elizabeth Young comments:

> his agony consists of the way his interior life keeps leaking into the public arena only to be inauthenticated, so that he has to reinforce his "self", his "identity", in even more extreme and violent ways.... An individual "personality" cannot sustain these contradictions; an individual personality in which Id, Ego and Super-Ego go into melt down is doomed ... to psychosis, schizophrenia.[37]

The novel focuses upon a subject (Bateman), whose desire for what is excluded disrupts the symbolic order on which his subjectivity is predicated: in this, Bateman, like Kurtz, is caught in the schizophrenogenic double-bind of a fractal culture.

The anomalies of Bateman's reality mean that both his story and his status as a speaking subject are continually called into question. In some sequences of the novel, his first-person narration is replaced with a third-person narrative in which he appears as a character (349ff); he is seeing an analyst (334-5); he tells us he has watched chat shows in which Bigfoot is interviewed (381), and in the final section of the novel, he tells us that his cash point machine has 'started speaking' to him, and that a park bench has followed him for six blocks (395). These anomalies do not mean, however, that we can simply dismiss the murder scenes as fantasies: the fact that they are part of his fractured subjectivity is central to the novel's critique of the 'greed is good' culture he represents. Bateman is an identi-kit persona, the only way he is made different is in his imaginary acts of violence. Like *Heart of Darkness*, Bateman's story explores the schizophrenogenic tensions of a de-personalised culture, in which the Darwinian edict of 'adapt or die' has been replaced with an interdiction that if you do not participate according to society's norms – the codes of the Symbolic – then you risk destroying your self: as Bateman puts it 'die or adapt' (345).[38] The characters in these fictions are not the outlaws and exiles which at first they may appear to be, for in having to mediate between inner desires and the constraint of the social, they are engaged in the essentially *familiar* activity of negotiating the anomalies of contemporary culture.

IV

In her 1994 Reith Lecture, 'Boys will be boys: the making of the male', Marina Warner explored the paradoxical notion that the images of the dehumanised self being produced in popular culture – from *Frankenstein* to *Transformers* – work to emphasise the similarities between the monstrous and the everyday.[39] It is the familiarity of the so-called abnormal which makes it so disturbing: Kurtz and Bateman are monstrous, not because they are Other, but rather because they are recognisable types whose monstrousness is contained by the recognisable facets of their culture. These texts reveal the complex interrelation of abjection with the social and symbolic order of a culture at both an individual and collective level.[40] The 'fascination of the abomination' (*Heart of Darkness*, 10) is central to the culture of Kurtz's fin-de-siècle Europe, and to Bateman's Reaganite America. Both texts examine the ways in which these cultures have learned to repress abjection by daring to focus on the unnameable; the unspeakable rites which Kurtz and Bateman indulge in are not to be dismissed as marginal, but rather to be seen as an elaboration of the abjection which characterises the subject in both of these fin de siècles. By 'aestheticizing the unacceptable', these works utilise what Kristeva calls the 'power of horror' to open up their era's 'most intimate and most serious apocalypses'.[41]

The hollow men on display in works like *Heart of Darkness* or *American Psycho* may be read as representations of the wider cultural conditions in which they signify.[42] These texts offer critiques of their era's dominant conceptions of subjectivity, and their concern with the decentered subject might be seen as part of an engagement with what Michael Foucault has identified as *the* 'political, ethical, social, philosophical problem of our day', namely:

> to liberate us both from the state and the type of individualisation which is linked to the state. We have to promote new forms of subjectivity through the refusal of this kind of individuality which has been imposed on us for several centuries.[43]

What links both works (and both fin de siècles) is a sceptical, postmodern stance regarding the meta-narratives of the age, and a related search for 'new presentations' which can encompass the unspeakable (or abject) 'in order to impart a stronger sense of the unrepresentable'. In so doing, they can point up the limitations of extant models of subjectivity, and confirm the need for resistance to imposed models of selfhood.[44]

NOTES

1. Terry Eagleton, 'The flight to the Real', in Sally Ledger and Scott McCracken, eds., *Cultural Politics at the Fin de Siècle*, Cambridge 1995, 16.
2. Peter Nicholls, 'Divergences: modernism, postmodernism, Jameson and Lyotard', *Critical Quarterly*, 33:3 (1991), 4.
3. I quote from Steven Best and Douglas Kellner's helpful exposition of Lyotard, *Postmodern Theory: Critical Interrogations*, London 1991, 166.
4. *The Sunday Times*, 21st April 1991, 'Books', 6.
5. Peter Middleton, *The Inward Gaze: Masculinity and Subjectivity in Modern Culture*, London 1992, 145.
6. Carolyn Born, Ann Cullis and John Mumford, *Laws of Gender: Concerning Some Problems Encountered in Studying Representations of Masculinity*, Birmingham 1985, 1. Cited in Middleton, ibid., 142.
7. Teresa de Laurentis, *Technologies of Gender*, London 1987, 3. Cited in Middleton, ibid., 143.
8. Elaine Showalter, *Sexual Anarchy: Gender and Culture at the Fin de Siècle*, London 1991, 8.
9. Graham Dawson, *Soldier Heroes: British Adventure, Empire and the Imagining of Masculinities*, London 1994, 1–10.
10. Showalter, op. cit., 81–2.
11. Patrick Brantlinger, *Rule of Darkness: British Literature and Imperialism: 1830-1914*, Ithaca 1988, 19–45.
12. Ronald Hyam, *Empire and Sexuality: the British Experience*, Manchester 1990.
13. Cited in Showalter, op. cit., 1.
14. See Eagleton, op. cit., 11.
15. Gekko is the central character in Oliver Stone's film *Wall Street* (1987): the view that the character captured the eighties zeitgeist is supported by the fact that Michael Douglas won the Best Actor Oscar for this role.
16. Eagleton, op. cit., 18.
17. Carmen A. Vidal, 'The death of politics and sex in the eighties show', *New Literary History*, 24:1 (Winter 1993), 173.
18. I quote from Paglia's essays on Madonna in *Sex, Art and American Culture*, Harmondsworth 1993, 'Madonna 1: animality and artifice', 5, and 'Madonna II: Venus of the radio waves', 8.
19. I am paraphrasing Charles Rycroft's account of the 'double bind' which generates schizophrenia. See *A Critical Dictionary of Psychoanalysis*, Harmondsworth 1972, 36.

20. Reprinted in the Penguin Modern Classics edition of *The Nigger of the 'Narcissus'/Typhoon and Other Stories*, Harmondsworth 1965, 11–14.
21. Joseph Conrad, ed. Robert Kimborough, *Heart of Darkness: An Authoritative Text*, New York 1988, 65. Further references are to this edition and are given in the text.
22. See, for example, Michael Levenson's reading in *Modernism and the Fate of Individuality: Character and Novelistic Form from Conrad to Woolf*, Cambridge 1991, 1–77.
23. John Bachelor makes a similar point in his account of the novella: *The Life of Joseph Conrad*, Oxford 1994, 91.
24. Conrad, *Lord Jim*, Harmondsworth 1949, 236.
25. Cf. Batchelor, op. cit.
26. As Michael Levenson has cogently argued, '*Heart of Darkness* does not simply record the unfolding of an action; it unfolds its own mode of understanding action, and by the time it reaches its conclusion it has redrawn its portrait of society, redefined a notion of subjectivity': op. cit., 38.
27. Christopher Butler, *Early Modernism: Literature, Music and Painting in Europe 1900–1916*, Oxford 1994, 92.
28. Anike Lemaire, trans. D. Macey, *Jacques Lacan*, London 1977, 53.
29. Julia Kristeva, trans. S. L. Roudiez, *Powers of Horror: An Essay on Abjection*, New York 1982, 208.
30. Levenson, op. cit., 49.
31. See Elizabeth Young's essay on *American Psycho*, 'The beast in the jungle, the figure in the carpet', in *Shopping in Space: Essays on American "Blank Generation" Fiction*, London, 108.
32. Conrad, *Heart of Darkness*, op. cit., 69.
33. Cited in ibid., 72. It is worth noting that in *American Psycho* Bateman wants to be adored: as he reveals, 'I want you to call me king'. Bret Easton Ellis, *American Psycho*, London 1991, 339.
34. Kristeva, op. cit., 92.
35. Ellis, op. cit., 106. Further references are given in the text.
36. Kristeva, op. cit., 5.
37. Young, op. cit., 118–19.
38. See Baudrillard's essay on 'The Hostage', *Fatal Strategies (Semiotext(e)*, New York 1990, 42.
39. Marina Warner, 'Boys will be boys: the making of the male'. Broadcast on BBC Radio 4, Wednesday 2nd February 1994.
40. See Kristeva, op. cit., 68.
41. Eagleton, op. cit., 16.

42. Kristeva, op. cit., 208.
43. Jean Baudrillard, 'Transaesthetics', in *The Transparency of Evil: Essays on Extreme Phenomena*, London 1993, 16.
44. Michel Foucault, 'The subject and power'. This originally appeared in B. Wallis, ed., *Art after Modernism: Rethinking Representation*, New York 1984, 417–32. I quote from Robert Siegle, *Suburban Ambush: Downtown Writing and the Fiction of Insurgency*, Baltimore 1989, 396.
45. Jean-François Lyotard, 'What is postmodernism?', reprinted in Charles Harrison and Paul Wood, eds., *Art in Theory*, Oxford 1992, 1014.

17

Centuries end:
Oscar Wilde and Quentin Tarantino

Neil Sammells

Regenia Gagnier's introduction to a 1992 collection of reprinted essays (selected to represent state-of-the-art Wilde criticism as it appears in the United States) claims that: 'Wilde means many things to our time. Most important among them, he means – whether in gay activism, social theory, or interpretive margin or latitude – freedom and toleration.'[1] Despite confessing that her favourite among the biographies of Wilde is Rupert Croft-Cooke's *The Unrecorded Life of Oscar Wilde* (1972), which 'loved its data not wisely but too well', she goes on to quote Richard Ellmann approvingly: 'we inherit [Wilde's] struggle to achieve supreme fictions in art, to associate art with social change, to bring together individual and social impulse, to save what is eccentric and singular from being sanitized and standardized, to replace a morality of severity by one of sympathy.'[2] For Gagnier, her collection signals this fin de siècle paying tribute to the last, 'in the hope of freedom and necessity of toleration' (2). In specific terms, Wilde is seen as peculiarly relevant to fin-de-siècle America; Gagnier's introduction summons up his languid spectre as a potential corrective to a number of the ills of contemporary American society. *The Soul of Man Under Socialism* is, she tells us, 'an essay for our time' in the lessons it can teach a U.S. media which 'invariably equate capitalism with democracy and socialism with totalitarianism' (6). The prison-letter *De Profundis* has especial urgency, 'as the United States has taken the lead of all nations in the proportion of its citizens incarcerated, as our number of prisoners has exceeded 1 million, as more and more Americans fall through the safety net, become homeless, and, as homeless, are incarcerated' (17–18). Indeed, Wildean wit is even proposed as a possible antidote to a malady much commented upon 'in the popular press and pedagogical literature': 'Americans' increasing inability to comprehend irony' (15).

Gagnier's collection is, of course, testament to the extraordinary transformation that has taken place in Wilde's critical status in the last ten years: the variety of approaches to his work that she anthologises is offered as representative of 'our collective critical moment' (2). In other words, the totality of critical writing about Wilde is seen as state-of-the-art in every respect. 'Wilde'

– as variously constructed and, indeed, deconstructed – can tell us as much about ourselves as about the Victorians he was long thought of as simply entertaining and teasing. It is, though, an irony of which Gagnier seems unaware that her attempt to claim Wilde for the USA ignores one of the most important current contributions to our understanding of him, and in particular the political implications of his life and writing: the work of Declan Kiberd, Davis Coakley and others to emphasise the importance of his nationality, to restate his Irishness.

In a poignant moment of self-congratulation and self-torment, Wilde, prisoner of Reading Gaol, described himself as 'a man who stood in symbolic relations to the art and culture of the age.'[3] One hundred years since the trials which destroyed him, and turned him ('the best known Queer ever'[4]) into one of the most celebrated and vilified victims of Victorian morality and hypocrisy, his image now appears before us on postcards, coffee mugs, T-shirts, handkerchiefs, ties and, no doubt, other objects I have yet to encounter, let alone collect. Wilde has been repackaged, commodified, relocated among the artefacts of a super-sophisticated culture both intoxicated and repelled by the excitements of consumerism. It is not simply within the discourses and ambit of institutionalised, professional literary and cultural criticism that Wilde has found himself remade. What I want to suggest is that, to understand Wilde, we need to see him as Janus-faced. His aesthetic theories, as outlined in the 1880s and 1890s, look back to Baudelaire, Gautier, Poe, as well as to more recent influences and predecessors such as Whistler and Pater; he also anticipates, to a sometimes astonishing degree, 'the insights of contemporary cultural theory'.[5] In a sense, then, Wilde's double-face is indeed symbolic of his fin de siècle; he looks back into his own century and forward into ours. Second, I want to argue that Wilde's sensibility is as important to our fin de siècle as to his own, and that – without wishing to endorse Gagnier's assumption that Wilde is peculiarly relevant to American culture – he finds an unlikely successor in the Hollywood *wunderkind* Quentin Tarantino, as is demonstrated in the notorious *Reservoir Dogs* (1992), and his comedy of murderous manners *Pulp Fiction* (1994).

Despite the recent attention of queer theorists, cultural materialists, deconstructionists, and so on, the best introduction to Wilde's work remains Susan Sontag's brilliant 1964 essay, 'Notes on Camp'. For Sontag, Wilde embodies the camp sensibility in his conscious reduction (or elevation) of all experience to the level of the aesthetic, and his refusal to observe the binary oppositions between the ethical and the aesthetic, the serious and the trivial, the central and the marginal. She also locates Wilde in a particular historical moment. His career, she claims, exemplifies a transitional phase in the history of dandyism, when the 'old-style dandy' who hated vulgarity is displaced by the connoisseur of Camp: 'the dandy held a perfumed handkerchief to his nostrils and was liable to swoon; the connoisseur of Camp sniffs the stink and prides himself on his strong nerves.'[6] Had Sontag looked more closely at Baudelaire, she may have reassessed her own attempt at historical specificity (Baudelaire cancelled the distinction between High Art and other cultural forms, finding the imagery of advertising as powerful and worthy of note as the 'masterpieces' in the salons he reviewed in the 1850s),[7] but the central point holds good. Wilde refused the distinction between 'high' and 'low' culture: recognising the equivalence of all objects, he was prepared to praise a buttonhole or a tea-cup in much the same terms as he would a painting or a sculpture. Thus, according to Sontag, Wilde displayed a fundamentally 'democratic *esprit*'. She goes on to provide, unwittingly, the cultural link between Wilde and Tarantino: the films of Jean-Luc Godard.

In effect, although Sontag does not herself draw the comparison, Godard takes up where Wilde left off, bringing a discriminating and transforming eye to the artefacts of 'popular culture'. Sontag places Godard in good company here, claiming for him a hypertrophy of appetite for culture which he shares with Joyce, Stravinsky and Picasso.[8] Godard's fondness for American kitsch (his redeployment of gangster-film motifs in *Band à Parte* (1964), for instance, or of comic-strip plotting in *Alphaville* (1965)) parallels Wilde's own taste for popular theatrical forms: in particular, his use of the tired conventions of West End farce in *The Importance of Being Earnest*.[9] Wilde explicitly announced in *The Critic as Artist* that 'all fine imaginative work is self-conscious and deliberate' (1020), and this tactic – the 'canonisation of the junior branch', as Russian Formalists would have it – was also outlined in *The Soul of Man Under Socialism* (1891), when he observed that 'delightful work may be produced under burlesque and farcical conditions, and in work of this kind the artist in England is allowed very great freedom' (1091). Sontag argues that the self-consciousness of Godard's work 'constitutes a formidable meditation on the *possibilities* of cinema'; it is meta-cinema and, I suggest, demonstrates Wilde's central contention in *The Critic as Artist* that criticism is a creative act (another example of the Wildean paradox collapsing binary oppositions). 'I'm still as much of a critic as I ever was during the time of *Cahiers du Cinema*', claimed Godard, referring to his journalism of the late 1950s. 'The only difference is that instead of writing criticism, I now film it.'[10]

Godard's films are, according to Sontag, not so much exercises in style as in *stylisation*. Stylisation 'reflects an ambivalence (affection contradicted by contempt, obsession contradicted by irony) toward the subject matter. This ambivalence is handled by maintaining, through the rhetorical overlay that is stylisation, a special distance form the subject'.[11] This 'special distance from the subject' is, in my view, entirely characteristic of Wilde, determining the way he handles morality and melodrama, politics and passion. Tarantino is a self-confessed admirer of Godard (the name of his production company, A Band Apart is a covert acknowledgement of his debt to the French director), and recognises in his own work a similar ambivalence and rhetorical overlay. Of both *Reservoir Dogs* and *Pulp Fiction* he says: 'I like the idea that I'm taking a genre and reinventing it, like Leone reinvented the whole Western genre.'[12] Such reinvention of genre, equivalent to what Wilde tried to do with Gothic fiction in *The Picture of Dorian Gray*, and with Victorian melodrama and the 'well-made play' in his society comedies, but only fully achieved in *The Importance of Being Earnest*, cannot be fulfilled by a simple, dismissive attitude to the models that are being redeployed. Tarantino wants to 'subvert the Hollywood staples, but with respect, not in a superior or pastichey way'.[13] He draws an instructive parallel between his own work and Stanley Kubrick's *The Shining*: 'I always felt that Kubrick felt he was above the horror genre, above giving the audience a real good scare. Now Godard, I always thought, was at his most engaging when he worked within a genre and ran with it the whole way to the moon. *Breathless* is a good example.'[14] The works of Wilde and Tarantino are camp, not 'campy': they preserve a delicate balance between the arch and the innocent. Wilde's parodic engagement with other texts and other writers shows that he regards artistic originality as being as illusory and disabling as all other forms of authenticity. As Wilde said, 'it is only the unimaginative who ever invents. The true artist is known by the use he makes of what he annexes, and he annexes everything'.[15]

A crucial element of the stylisation in Godard's films is his treatment of violence. The pervasive quality of Godard's films, claims Sontag, is its 'coolness': 'the films have a muted, detached relation to the grotesque and painful as well as to the seriously erotic. People are sometimes tortured and often die in Godard's films – but almost casually.'[16] Indeed, it is this casualness, rather than the explicitness, of the violence in Tarantino's movies which has earned him notoriety: the best example of this being the scene in *Reservoir Dogs* in which Mr Blonde tortures a hostage cop with a razor-blade, gasoline and Stealer's Wheel. At the moment that Mr Blonde slices off his victim's ear, Tarantino pans away to a ceiling-light. The cop doesn't die until Nice Guy Eddie arrives and dispatches him with a revolver: Tarantino denies his audience the relief of a reaction-shot of either witnesses or victim. Such peremptory violence is a feature of *Pulp Fiction* too, as is Tarantino's emphasis on the sheer contingency of urban violence (the accidental, incidental killing and maiming of bystanders adds considerably to the body-count in both *Reservoir Dogs* and *Pulp Fiction*). Tarantino's defence of the violence in his films – which includes his attitude to the larger question of moral 'content' – makes intriguing reading, unconsciously echoing Wilde's own defence of that 'tale spawned from the leprous literature of the French Decadents', *The Picture of Dorian Gray*.[17]

Responding to an attack on *Dorian Gray*, in a letter to the editor of the *St James's Gazette* on 25th June 1890, Wilde declared that he was incapable of understanding how a work of art could be criticised from a moral standpoint: 'the sphere of art and the sphere of ethics are absolutely distinct and separate.'[18] This both echoes the famous art-for-art's sake doctrine of Gautier's preface to *Mademoiselle Maupin* (1836), and anticipates the Paterese of the preface Wilde added to *Dorian Gray* when it was issued in expanded volume-form in 1891 (having first appeared in *Lippincott's Monthly* the previous year): it is here that we find the famous claims that 'All art is quite useless', and that 'There is no such thing as a moral or an immoral book. Books are well written or badly written. That is all' (17). Wilde elaborated his point the next day in another letter to the same magazine, noting that:

Good people, belonging as they do to the normal, and so commonplace, type, are artistically uninteresting. Bad people are, from the point of view of art, fascinating studies. They represent colour, variety and strangeness. Good people exasperate one's reason; bad people stir one's imagination.

This resolutely aesthetic approach also underlies Tarantino's assertion that violence is simply another colour for the artist to work with.[19] Indeed, Tarantino could be described as applying with uncompromising literalness Wilde's dictum about 'bad people' and colour: the gangsters of *Reservoir Dogs* are called Mr Orange, Mr White, Mr Pink, Mr Blonde, Mr Blue and Mr Brown (played by Tarantino himself). Wilde (who subtitles his essay on a serial-killer 'A Study in Green') turns the tables on his attackers with great dexterity: 'the poor public, hearing from an authority so high as your own, that this is a wicked book that should be coerced and suppressed by a Tory government, will no doubt, rush to it and read it.' Tarantino is conscious of the same irony in the UK's refusal to grant his movie a licence for video release: 'I like that. It's done better in cinemas in Britain than anywhere else in the world, so the ban has been kinda cool in one way.'[20]

Wilde continues with an unexpected twist by claiming that readers in search of forbidden thrills will be disappointed: 'But alas! They will find that it is a story with a moral. And the moral is this; All excess, as well as all renunciation, brings its own punishment.' He goes on to explain how the Dorian-Lord Henry-Basil triangle illustrates this, and ends with another apparent *volte face*: 'Is this an artistic error? I fear it is. It is the only error in the book.' Tarantino is as adept at these tactics as Wilde. 'I'm not trying to preach any kind of moral or get any kind of message across,' he claims, 'but for all the wildness that happens in my movies, I think they usually lead to moral conclusions.'[21] In the *Daily Chronicle*, 30th June 1890, Wilde explained that in taking over the Faustian myth he had, from an artistic point of view, probably failed to keep the moral in its secondary place; however:

> this moral is so far artistically and deliberately suppressed that it does not enunciate its law as a general principle, but realises itself purely in the lives of individuals, and so becomes simply a dramatic element in a work of art, and not the object of the work of art itself.

Of course, Wilde is deliberately confusing and exasperating readers and critics in appearing to have it both ways, but the significance of these letters is the way he collapses the distinction between the ethical and the aesthetic. In effect, he aestheticises the 'moral content' of his narrative. In an incisive subversion of accepted categories, Wilde defines the moral content of *Dorian Gray* as an element of its aesthetic design, a 'dramatic element in a work of art'. This refusal of antithesis is behind the loaded phrasing of another letter, this time to the *Scots Observer* (13th August 1890): 'You ask me, Sir, why I should care to have the ethical beauty of my story recognised. I answer, simply because it exists, because the thing is there.' There we have it: *ethical beauty*.

Again, we can trace these Wildean manoeuvres in what Tarantino says about *Reservoir Dogs* and *Pulp Fiction*. The 'morality' of the former is conceived in the same dramatic terms as that of *Dorian Gray*, realising itself in the lives of individuals: 'I find what passes between Mr White and Mr Orange at the end of *Reservoir Dogs* very moving and profound in its morality and its human interaction.'[22] The violent, sacrificial denouement provides a dramatically and aesthetically satisfying conclusion to the movie's '12-gauge pump-action homo-erotic love-story'.[23] In the original screenplay of *Pulp Fiction*, super-cool Jules Winnfield simply blows away Honey Bunny and Pumpkin as they attempt to hold up the coffee-shop; in the movie this ending is replaced by one in which Jules spares them, deciding to give up the gangster-life and walk the Earth like Caine in *Kung Fu*. This allows Tarantino to claim that '*Pulp Fiction* is ultimately a film about forgiveness and mercy, albeit in a hard and brutal world'.[24] (After all, *Pulp Fiction* does feature a motorbike – sorry, *chopper* – called Grace, so how could it be otherwise?) Elsewhere, however, Tarantino admits that his 'moralistic' conclusions are, in reality, shaped by the pressures of genre rather than the abstractions of what Wilde called 'general principle'.

'In some ways,' he says:

> my films go by the old Hays code. You can do anything you want in the first 88 minutes as long as in the last two minutes there's some retribution for what the characters have done. I never set out to do that. I always thought if I wrote a heist film, I'd do one where they all got away. But it didn't quite work out that way.[25]

Tarantino is obliged by the demands of genre and aesthetics to provide a moralistic conclusion, just as Wilde is obliged to visit retributive justice upon Dorian Gray and his dedication to a life of pleasure-seeking.

Tarantino has been accused of applying 'style to sheer slaughter',[26] and in this respect his work may seem a long way from Wilde's drawing rooms, even if the voracious appetite of Tarantino's drug-dealers and killers for junk-food like hamburgers and tacos is recognisably the same as Algy's 'callous' consumption of muffins and cucumber sandwiches. In fact, Wilde's world is one of violent potential, a potential that is distanced, ironised, refracted through the stylistics of wit. His short story 'Lord Arthur Savile's Crime' (1887) is perhaps the best case in point: fin-de-siècle London is one in which international terrorists can be consulted on matters of domestic violence, poisoned bon-bons and dynamite-laden clocks are available at a price, and (as in the fate of Podgers) execution is summary and contingent. Lady Bracknell speaks prophetically of acts of violence in Grosvenor Square and enquires if, the fiction of Algy's double-life having been 'exploded', Bunbury has been the victim of a revolutionary outrage. *The Importance of Being Earnest* must – as Wilde says – 'go like a pistol shot', and not just in terms of pace.[27] A good production should drive towards a climax in which the principals confront each other in an aristocratic stand-off: Lady Bracknell, Algy and Jack hold pistols to each other's heads over the question of marriage. Wilde, of course, was performing Russian Roulette for Lady Bracknell and her ilk, and was soon to hit a loaded chamber.

Tarantino's denouements, his Leone-style stand-offs, are self-consciously and deliberately theatrical. Indeed, the 'stagey' quality of his work is insistent. The long takes and involved dialogue of *Reservoir Dogs* and *Pulp Fiction* are clearly indebted to Godardian, European art-house cinema, but they also have a theatrical dimension: Jules and Vincent, for instance, torment their victims in a discussion of hamburgers that is Pinteresque in its comic menace. *Reservoir Dogs*, with its bleak warehouse setting and 'real-time' action, is a clear attempt to observe the unities of classical drama. More explicitly, some of Tarantino's *dramatis personae* call attention to themselves, and their theatrical existence, in much the same way as Gwendolen in *The Importance of Being Earnest*: 'This suspense is terrible', she announces as Jack crashes around in search of the handbag which bred him, 'I hope it will last' (379). 'Let's get into character', counsels Jules as he and Vincent go to work. The Wolf wants to know the 'principals' names' in *The Bonnie Situation*. He tells Raquel that 'just because you are a character doesn't mean you have a character'.[28] Tarantino's movies thus combine the theatrical with the pervasively meta-cinematic. *Pulp Fiction* does not just refer to the hard-boiled narratives of *Black Mask* writers like Dashiell Hammett, Eric Stanley Gardner and Raymond Chandler, it is a compendium of implicit and explicit references to other movies: *Deliverance, The Untouchables, The Texas Chainsaw Massacre, Superfly T.N.T, The Guns of Navarone*, to name a few. Here Tarantino is clearly following the example of Godard, whose films Sontag describes as 'casually encyclopedic, anthologizing, formally and thematically eclectic, and marked by a rapid turnover of styles and forms'.[29] In this respect, the movies conform to Wilde's anti-naturalistic aesthetic, and his contention in *Pen, Pencil and Poison* that 'in a very ugly and sensible age, the arts borrow not from life but from each other' (1001). Tarantino is as wary as Wilde of the prison-house of realism, preferring self-referentiality to representational authenticity: 'My movies obviously take place now, but they also seem to take place in a never-never world: the clothes don't correspond with the cars, that sort of thing.'[30]

Interviewers and journalists have constantly emphasised Tarantino's borrowings from 'pop' or 'junk' culture: he is, according to *Sight and Sound*, a 'pasticheur and pop-cultural relativist',[31] and to the *Guardian*, a 'Movie Junkie'.[32] Of course, such claims can be turned against him. According to one of Tarantino's most hostile and clumsy critics, James Wood, he suffers from the 'cultural anorexia of our age; an education sheared of anything but popular media-forms'.[33] However, this is not only to perpetuate a dubious distinction between 'high' and 'low' culture – one which, as we have seen, Wilde would not have recognised – it is also to ignore the cultural inclusiveness of Tarantino's work, one hinted at in a remark which collapses cultural distinctions with some aplomb: 'If ever I see Tennessee Williams's play *Orpheus Descending*, I think Elvis would have been the best person to play that part.'[34] The crucial point here, though, is that the inclusiveness of Tarantino's cultural appetite is based on the desire to discriminate rather than simply absorb. He says, for instance, of the 1970s blaxploitation films which influenced him: 'I was going to see all these movies, and they weren't put under any critical light, so you made your own discoveries, you found the diamonds in the dustbin.'[35] Sontag claims of the connoisseur of camp that he sniffs the stink and prides himself on his strong nerves, but in Tarantino's case the image needs revising: like Wilde (and the Baudelairean *flâneur*) he never abandons the dandy's desire to discriminate, to sift the patterns among what others might think of as cultural debris. Central to this discriminatory project is the distinction Tarantino draws between films and movies. Films, claims Clarence Worley in Tarantino's screenplay for *True Romance* (1993), are for people who don't like movies. Films are summed up as Merchant-Ivory claptrap, 'safe, geriatric, coffee-table dogshit'. However, '*Mad Max*, that's a movie. *The Good, the Bad and the Ugly*, that's a movie. *Rio Bravo*, that's a movie. *Rumble Fish*, that's a fuckin' movie'. Clarence's excited exposition elicits the puzzled response: 'What's this guy doin'? Makin' a drug deal or gettin' a job in the New Yorker?'.[36] Movies are stylised, distinguished by a Godardian rhetorical overlay and a Wildean perspective on 'content'. Their use of music is mannered and slick, and has nothing to do with the creation of simple 'period' feel along naturalistic lines; it is closer to the operatic excesses of Morricone's embellishment of Spaghetti Westerns. Tarantino displays all the contempt for Oscar-winning films like *Sophie's Choice, Kramer vs Kramer* and *Gandhi* that Wilde reserves for the moralising Victorian three-volume novel and the respectable contents of Mudie's circulating library in *The Importance of Being Earnest* – a play, of course, about the necessity of being the exact opposite. In *The Soul of Man Under Socialism*, Wilde neatly sums up his attitude to the 'safe, geriatric, coffee-table dogshit' of his age: 'No country produces such badly-written fiction, such tedious common work in the novel form, such silly, vulgar plays as England' (1091).

One of the most telling examples of Tarantino's cultural inclusiveness, and of the rhetorical overlay and stylisation that he shares with Wilde, is his reworking of Biblical motifs and allusions in *Pulp Fiction*. Jules quotes a pastiche of Ezekiel 25:17 before going to work, but in finding grace (not the motorbike) at the end of the movie he struggles to interpret its significance, rather than using it as 'just a cold-blooded thing to say to a motherfucker 'fore you popped a cap in his ass'.[37] The original screenplay has an exchange, cut from the movie, in which Vincent calls Jules 'Pontius Pilate' for not helping to put Marvin out of his misery after he has been shot. When Vincent is asked to squire Mia by Marsellus Wallace while he is away on business in Florida, he finds himself in a situation out of *film noir* and out of the Bible, with Mia Wallace in the role of Potipher's wife and Vincent cast as Joseph (see Genesis 39:7-23). Indeed, the Mia-Vincent relationship also echoes Wilde in that it replays that between Salome and John the Baptist, Wilde having refracted the Biblical Salome through a series of continental artists: Flaubert, Mallarmé, Huysmans, Moreau. When Mia dances alone to Urge Overkill's version of Neil Diamond's 'Girl, You'll Be a Woman Soon' (Tarantino mercifully spares us the original), she is virtually indistinguishable from Wilde's Salome, the predatory adolescent dancing for herself, rather than Herod, in an act of auto-erotic self-definition. Wilde imprisons John the Baptist in a cistern; Vincent Vega acts out his drama of sexual temptation in the toilet: 'so, you're gonna go out there, drink your drink, say "Goodnight, I've had a very lovely evening," go home and jack off. And that's all you're gonna do.'[38] Like Wilde's, Tarantino's handling of the Bible is essentially camp: according to the Sontag definition, ideas are held in a playful way, in an atmosphere of failed seriousness.[39] In a sense, the urge overkill at work in both cases is a deconstructive one; the Bible – the Book of books, the Text of texts – is split apart, and new, provisional, momentarily satisfying patterns assembled from its shards. Wilde's *Salome* was, of course, banned for its presumption.

One hundred years ago Wilde's *Dorian Gray* was, as we have seen, attacked for failing to supply readers with moral co-ordinates. Today Tarantino is condemned in a much the same terms, for being a product of a new decadence and fin-de-siècle uncertainties: James Wood claims, for instance, that: 'sometimes one doesn't have to look very hard for symptoms of the age we live in – they squat like visible toads in our postmodern pond. Quentin Tarantino is one of them.' According to this analysis, Tarantino is a symptom and a victim: 'he represents the final triumph of postmodernism, which is to empty the artwork of all content, thus voiding its capacity to do anything but helplessly *represent* our agonies (rather than contain or comprehend).'[40] True, neither Wilde nor Tarantino offer us the certainties that Wood, and others before him, feel art should embody; instead, their achievements consist in 'the intelligent gratification of consciousness' which, for Sontag, is the 'moral pleasure' inherent in the aesthetic experience.[41]

Comparing our turn of the century with Wilde's, Terry Eagleton concludes that what we are left with is 'something of the culture of the previous *fin de siècle* shorn of its politics'.[42] The 1880s and 1890s were, he argues, a period of extraordinary spiritual *and* material ferment: 'we are speaking of the period of Aubrey Beardsley *and* the Second International; of aestheticism and anarchism; of decadence and the Dock Strike.'[43] Wilde championing socialism, and Yeats veering between theosophy and the Irish Republican Brotherhood are, to Eagleton, symbolic figures marrying experimental aesthetics with revolutionary politics. Today, the capitalist system:

> approaches the millennium, as it did the last, in grave disarray; but the political forces which mustered around the turn of the century to offer an alternative polity to this failed experiment have been temporarily scattered and diffused.[44]

Eagleton thus finds curious agreement with James Wood: our fin de siècle is more concerned with endings than beginnings.

However, Eagleton's critique can be refuted if the relationship between Wilde and Tarantino is properly understood, if we accept that style is politics: shaping our world, the way we represent it, and the way we present ourselves to it. Sontag is surely wrong to conclude that camp is apolitical; its gestures are a refusal of the oppressive, the limiting, the normative, the authentic. It is, as a consequence, liberating, subversive and sustaining. What Wilde refused in his life, no less than his writing, was the limiting and oppressive notion of authenticity. In *Pen, Pencil and Poison* (1891), his study of the dandy, artist, forger and serial killer Thomas Griffiths Wainewright, Wilde notes that 'the permanence of personality is a very subtle metaphysical problem and certainly the English law solves the question in a very rough-and-ready manner' (1006). Given that Wilde was himself maintaining contradictory personalities, Bunburying, in effect, at the time of writing this essay – husband/homosexual, Irishman/Englishman, socialite/criminal, insider/outsider, and so on – it is impossible not to acknowledge the prophetic irony in this statement. Wilde was soon to become subject, in the dock at the Old Bailey, to the roughness and readiness of the English law. Indeed, Alan Sinfield argues that, in effect, Wilde's conviction was a defining moment in modern subjectivity: it *fixed* the homosexual man as twentieth-century western society came to understand him. After Wilde's trials, according to Sinfield, 'the entire, vaguely disconcerting nexus of effeminacy, leisure, idleness, immorality, luxury, insouciance, decadence and aestheticism, which Wilde was perceived, variously, as instancing, was transformed into a brilliantly precise image'.[45] The verdict against Wilde was an attempt to name him as criminal, to authenticate him, to discipline and to punish. Wilde's camp gestures – including his ill-fated performance in the Central Criminal Court – were political gestures too, strategies for disarming an implacable adversary.

Central to Wilde's camp strategies was his 'enculteration' of the natural world by means of an anti-representational aesthetic. The opening paragraphs of *The Picture of Dorian Gray* are perhaps the best example of this. Wilde gives us here an environment that is emphatically *written*: the aestheticisation of the Natural, and the naturalisation of the Cultural, is consistently foregrounded. Lawrence Buell notes of literary representations of the natural world grounded in *mimesis* that:

> environmental facticity in any era might be felt to smack of acquiescence, fatalism, even death. Sooner or later the implacable *thereness* of the external world is found to represent the adversary. No matter how resolutely cheerful

or stoic one's temperament, in some moods or phases nature will metamorphose from possibility into fate, as for the aging Emerson.[46]

Wilde's 'enculteration' of the natural world, his anti-naturalistic theory and practice, is – of course – a conscious disavowal of facticity, and Nature is thus brought into the realm of human action, responsibility and choice.[47] By denying the 'implacable *thereness* of the natural world', Wilde enacts an aesthetic version of his political choices; Wilde the radical socialist affirms an optimistic belief in the possibility of human agency and change. He also prevents nature being annexed simply for human use. This is evident in the ironies of *Pen, Pencil and Poison*, and its series of witty asides at the expense of Wordsworth and his propensity for turning the natural world into a kind of moral gymnasium.

Deprived of an anchorage in a natural world which has the brooding facticity of fate, which is instead fashioned for the human agent and not for the human subject, the individual personality is free-floating, supremely and stylishly indifferent to a hostile normativity. For Wilde, the distance between such aesthetic choices and gestures and material politics was easily traversed. Declan Kiberd's *Inventing Ireland* is instructive here. For him, Wilde does not so much collapse high and low culture into each other, as counterpoint them to specific and political effect. Wilde, he claims, was always concerned to feed back his most subversive ideas to the ruling class, as when he published *The Soul of Man Under Socialism* in the upmarket *Fortnightly Review*:

> in such feedback may be found the essence of that carnivalesque moment towards which each of his plays moves: when the wit and laughter of the low rejuvenate the jaded culture of the high, and when polyphonic voices override the monotones of perfunctory authority.[48]

Indeed, Kiberd goes further, by seeing in Wilde's anti-naturalist aesthetic a specific political application. Wilde the Irish-nationalist republican declines a style which is that of his imperialist masters: 'Wilde refused to write realist accounts of that degraded Ireland he only partly knew, and he took instead Utopia for a theme, knowing that this would present not only an image of revolutionary possibility for Ireland but also a rebuke to contemporary Britain.'[49]

In repelling James Wood's charges of political and moral impotence against *Pulp Fiction* and *Reservoir Dogs*, Antony Easthope says of Tarantino's movies that 'people recognise the world of sympathetic gangsters because it echoes our own – intense local consumerism accompanied by long term anxiety'.[50] It is because Wilde's sensibility lives on at our century's end in the work of Tarantino and others that 'brooding facticity' and material conditions seem capable of refabrication – and we can confront those anxieties with laughter, exhilaration and style.

NOTES

1. Regenia Gagnier, ed., *Critical Essays on Oscar Wilde*, New York 1992, 2. Further references to this work are given in the text.
2. Richard Ellmann, *Oscar Wilde*, London 1987, 553.
3. *The Complete Works of Oscar Wilde*, London 1966, 1020. All further references to Wilde's works are to this edition and are given in the text.
4. Alan Sinfield, 'Wilde and the queer moment', *Irish Studies Review: Oscar Wilde Special Issue*, 11 (1995), 47.
5. Terry Eagleton, *Saint Oscar*, Derry 1989, vii.
6. Susan Sontag, 'Notes on camp', *A Susan Sontag Reader*, Harmondsworth 1983, 117.
7. See, for instance, Baudelaire's comments on fashion plates in his seminal essay on Dandyism, *The Painter of Modern Life* (1863), in P. Charvet, ed. and trans., *Baudelaire: Selected Writings on Art and the Artist*, Cambridge 1972.
8. Sontag, op. cit., 235.
9. Kerry Powell identifies some of the specific plays Wilde was indebted to, both in *The Importance*, and his 'society comedies', but makes the mistake of seeing Wilde as a prisoner of these conventions and formulae, and not as consciously reworking them to deliberate effect. See Kerry Powell, *Wilde and the Theatre of the 1890s*, Cambridge 1990. For a detailed critique of Powell's assumptions, see Sos Eltis, *Revising Wilde: Society and Subversion in the plays of Oscar Wilde*, Oxford 1996.
10. Quoted by Sontag, op. cit., 236.
11. ibid., 141.
12. Quoted by Sean O'Hagan in 'X Offender', *The Times Magazine*, 15th October 1994, 10.
13. ibid., 14.
14. ibid.
15. *Dramatic Review*, 30th May 1885, 278.
16. Sontag, op. cit., 261.
17. Stuart Mason, *Oscar Wilde: Art and Morality*, London 1971, 65.

18. For a full discussion of the critical reception of *Dorian Gray* and Wilde's response to it, see Mason, ibid.
19. O'Hagan, op. cit., 13.
20. ibid.
21. See Graham Fuller, 'Quentin Tarantino: answers first, questions later', *Reservoir Dogs*, London 1994, xv.
22. ibid., xv–xvi.
23. Clancy Sigal, 'Killing jokes?', *The Guardian*, 19th September 1994, 9.
24. O'Hagan, op. cit., 13.
25. Jim McClellan, 'On the run: Tarantino', *The Observer*, 3rd July 1994, 29–30.
26. Stanley Kauffmann, quoted by R. Guilliat, 'QT', *The Sunday Times*, 3rd October 1993, 32.
27. Quoted by Richard Ellmann in *Oscar Wilde*, London 1987, 399.
28. Quentin Tarantino, *Pulp Fiction*, London 1994, 22, 152, 170.
29. Sontag, op. cit., 236.
30. Quoted by Andrew Pulver, 'The movie junkie', *The Guardian*, 19th September 1994, 9.
31. Manohla Dargis, 'Pulp instinct', *Sight and Sound*, 4:5 (1994), 6–9.
32. Pulver, op. cit.
33. James Wood, 'You're sayin' a foot massage don't mean nothin', and I'm sayin' it does', *The Guardian* Supplement, 19th November 1994, 31.
34. Quoted in 'Rock 'n' Reel', *The Guardian*, 14th April 1995, 9.
35. 'Quentin Tarantino on *Pulp Fiction*', *Sight and Sound*, 4:5 (1994), 10.
36. Quentin Tarantino, *True Romance*, London 1995, 116–17.
37. Tarantino, *Pulp Fiction*, 186–7.
38. ibid., 69.
39. Sontag, op. cit., 115–16.
40. Wood, op. cit., 31.
41. Sontag, op. cit., 145.
42. Terry Eagleton, 'The flight to the Real', in Sally Ledger and Scott McCracken, eds., *Cultural Politics at the Fin de Siècle*, Cambridge 1995, 11.
43. ibid., 12.
44. ibid., 11.
45. Alan Sinfield, *The Wilde Century; Effeminacy, Oscar Wilde and the Queer Moment*, London 1994, 3. For a critique of Sinfield's argument, see Scott Wilson's review in *Irish Studies Review: Oscar Wilde Special Issue*, 11 (1995), 49–53.

46. Lawrence Buell, *The Environmental Imagination*, Cambridge, Mass. 1995, 111.

47. For a fuller discussion of a possible eco-critical reading of Wilde, see my 'Wilde nature' in Richard Kerridge and Neil Sammells, eds., *Writing and the Environment*, London, forthcoming, 1997.

48. Declan Kiberd, *Inventing Ireland*, London 1995, 45–6.

49. ibid., 50.

50. Antony Easthope, *The Guardian*, 23rd November 1994, 10.

Notes on Contributors

Antonio Ballesteros González has taught English and American literature at the Complutense, CEU and Autómoma Universities in Madrid, and is currently Associate Professor of English Literature at the Universiy of Castilla-La Mancha, Ciudad Real, Spain. He is the author of *Narciso: mito y dualidad conceptual en la literaturia inglesa victoriana* (Madrid, forthcoming). He has published widely on Gothic and Horror literature, Wilde, Sterne, Joyce, Beckett and English Renaissance literature.

Bridget Bennett is a lecturer in the Department of English and Comparative Literary Studies at the University of Warwick. She has just completed an edition of short fiction by American and British women at the turn of the century, *Ripples of Dissent: Women's Stories of Marriage from the 1890s* (1996). Her forthcoming work includes a book on Harold Frederic called *The Damnation of Harold Frederic*, and a jointly-edited collection of essays on the relations between literature and journalism.

Tracey Hill teaches in the School of English at Bath Spa University College. She is co-editor (with William Hughes) of *Contemporary Writing and National Identity* (Bath 1996), and is the author of a number of articles on early modern cultural history. Her research interests include: Anthony Munday, theatre history, New Historicism, and late-sixteenth-century political pamphlets.

William Hughes is a lecturer in English at Bath Spa University College. He is currently working on a biography of Bram Stoker, and several articles on the connections between Gothic fiction and medicine. He is co-editor of *Contemporary Writing and National Identity* (Bath 1996) and editor of *The Monk*, published by the International Gothic Association.

Denis Judd teaches History at the University of North London. Among his publications are *Balfour and the British Empire, The Victorian Empire, The British Raj, The Crimean War*, and with Peter Slinn, *The Evolution of the*

208

Modern Commonwealth. His analysis of British imperialism, *Empire: the British Imperial Experience from 1765 to the Present*, was published in 1996 and became the main choice for a major book club. He has written a number of other historical studies and biographies, as well as stories for children and two novels. He is editor of a series of concise histories, *The Traveller's Histories*.

Sally Ledger is a lecturer in English at Birkbeck College, University of London. She is the author of *The New Woman: Fiction and Feminism at the Fin de Siècle* (Manchester 1997) and co-editor of *Cultural Politics at the Fin de Siècle* (Cambridge University Press 1995) and *Political Gender: Texts and Contexts* (Harvester Wheatsheaf 1994).

Tim Middleton is a senior lecturer in Literary and Cultural Studies at the University College of Ripon and York St John. He is co-convenor of the University College's MA in Contemporary Literary Studies and Head of the English Studies programme. He is co-editor of *Writing Englishness* (Routledge 1995), and is currently completing work on an introductory text-book, *Studying Culture* (forthcoming, Blackwell 1998) and developing a web-site for teaching contemporary American literature.

Nickianne Moody is a senior lecturer in Media and Cultural Studies at Liverpool John Moores University. Her areas of research include: empirical methodology for cultural studies, representations of plague in popular fiction, cyberpunk, and chemical generation fiction. She is the editor of the newsletter for the Association for Research in Popular Fictions, and of the forthcoming journal, *Popular Fictions*. She has published on Poldark, women's science fiction writing, Lovejoy and heritage tourism, multi-media narrative and story-telling, and representations of disability in contemporary science fiction.

Marie Mulvey Roberts is a senior lecturer in Literary Studies at the University of the West of England, Bristol, and is the author of *British Poets and Secret Societies* (1986), and *Gothic Immortals: The Fiction of the Brotherhood of the Rosy Cross* (1990). She has co-edited *Literature and Medicine During the Eighteenth Century* (1993), *Secret Texts: The Literature of Secret Societies* (1995), *Sources, Perspectives and Controversies in the History of British Feminism* (1993–5), and *Pleasure in the Eighteenth Century*. Besides being General Editor of three series, she also co-edits the journal *Women's Writing*.

Peter Nicholls is Professor of English and American Literature at the University of Sussex. He is author of *Ezra Pound: Politics, Economics and*

Writing, Modernisms: A Literary Guide, and of numerous articles and essays on twentieth-century literature and theory. He is currently writing a book about contemporary American poetry.

Julian North lectures in English at De Montfort University. She has published on De Quincey and nineteenth-century drug literature. Her book *De Quincey Reviewed*, due out in 1996, is an assessment of De Quincey's critical reputation from the 1820s to the present day.

Michael Paris has taught at Middlesex University and for the Open University, and is currently teaching at the University of Central Lancashire. His main area of research is popular culture and warfare. His most recent publications include: *Winged Warfare: The Literature and Theory of Air Power in Britain* (Manchester 1992) and *From the Wright Brothers to 'Top Gun': Aviation, Nationalism and Popular Cinema* (Manchester 1995). He is now working on a study of popular militarism in Victorian Britain.

Terence Rodgers is Assistant Dean of Humanities and a member of the School of History at Bath Spa University College. A political and cultural historian, he now teaches and writes mainly in the field of postcolonial studies. He is currently working on a major reappraisal of Rider Haggard.

Neil Sammells is Dean of Humanities at Bath Spa University College. He is the author of a book on Tom Stoppard (London 1988), and co-editor of three collections of essays: *Irish Writing: Exile and Subversion* (London 1991), *Writing and Censorship in Britain* (London 1992), and *Writing and America* (London 1996). He is General Editor of Longman's interdisciplinary *Crosscurrents* series, and co-editor of *Irish Studies Review*.

Deborah Tyler-Bennett is a poet and lecturer. She has published critical work on Djuna Barnes, the Victorian anthologist Mrs Elizabeth Sharp, and suffrage and poetry. Her book on Edith Sitwell, *Edith Sitwell: The Forgotten Modernist*, was published in 1996. She has published poems in *Writing Women, Sheffield Thursday, Golden Section, Working Titles, Indelible Ink, Poets '94* and *Feminist Review*. She recently completed a novel, *The Victim*, for which she is in search of a publisher.

Tim Youngs teaches English at the Nottingham Trent University. He is the author of *Travellers in Africa: British Travelogues 1850–1900* (Manchester

1994), editor of *Writing and Race* (London, forthcoming, 1997), and founder-editor of the journal *Studies in Travel Writing*.

Sue Zlosnik is Head of the Department of English at Liverpool Hope University College, and has research interests in nineteenth and twentieth-century literature. Together with Avril Horner she wrote *Landscapes of Desire: Metaphors in Modern Women's Fiction* (Harvester Wheatsheaf 1990). They are currently working on *Daphne du Maurier: Writing, Identity and the Gothic Imagination*, to be published by Macmillan in 1997.

Index